NIGHT AND DAY
BOMBER OFFENSIVE

NIGHT AND DAY
BOMBER OFFENSIVE

ALLIED AIRMEN IN WORLD WAR II EUROPE

PHILIP KAPLAN AND JACK CURRIE

Pen & Sword
AVIATION

First published in Great Britain in 2006
By Pen and Sword Aviation
An imprint of Pen and Sword Books Ltd
47 Church Street
Barnsley
South Yorkshire
S70 2AS

For
Margaret and
Kate

ISBN 1 84415 451 3
ISBN 978 1 84415 451 7

A CIP record for this book is available from the British
Library.

Typeset by Philip Kaplan
Printed and bound by Singapore
By Kyodo Printing Co. (Singapore) Pte Ltd

Pen and Sword Books Ltd incorporates the imprints of
Pen and Sword Aviation, Pen and Sword Maritime, Pen
and Sword Military, Wharncliffe Local History, Pen and
Sword Select, Pen and Sword Military Classics and Leo
Cooper.

For a complete list of Pen and Sword titles please contact
Pen and Sword Books Limited
47 Church Street, Barnsley, South Yorkshire, S70 2AS,
England
E-mail: enquiries@pen-and-sword.co.uk
Website: www.pen-and-sword.co.uk

Grateful acknowledgment is made to the following for the use of
extracts from their previously published material. Efforts have been
made to trace the copyright owners of material used in this book.
The authors apologize to any copyright owners we were unable to
contact during this clearance process.
Ambrose, Stephen E., *Wild Blue*, Simon & Schuster, 2001.
Armstrong, Roger W., *USA The Hard Way*, Quail House, 1991.
Caidin, Martin, *Flying Forts*, Meredith Press, 1968.
Campbell, James, *The Bombing of Nuremberg*, Doubleday, 1974.
Charlwood, Don, *Journey Into Night*, Angus & Robertson.
Cheshire, Leonard, *Bomber Pilot*, Hutchinson & Co., 1943.
Comer, John, *Combat Crew*, Sphere Books, 1988.
Cooper, Alan, *The Men Who Breached The Dams*, Airlife, 1993.
Crisp, N.J., *Yesterday's Gone*, Penguin Books, 1983.
Currier, Donald R., *50 Mission Crush*, Pocket Books, 1992.
Deighton, Len, *Bomber*, Harper & Row, 1970.
Dunmore, Spencer, *Final Approach*, Peter Davies Ltd., 1976.
Dunmore, Spencer, *Bomb Run*, Pan Books, 1971.
Fletcher, Eugene, *Fletcher's Gang*, Univ. of Washington Press, 1988.
Frankland, Noble, *The Bombing Offensive Against Germany*, Faber
and Faber, 1965.
Freeman, Roger A., *The Mighty Eighth*, Macdonald and Co., 1970.
Galland, Adolf, *The First and The Last*, Henry Holt and Co., 1954.
Gibson, Guy, *Enemy Coast Ahead*, Pan Books, 1946.
Godfrey, John T., *The Look of Eagles*, Random House, 1958.
Harvey, J. Douglas, *Boys, Bombs and Brussels Sprouts*, McClelland
and Stewart, 1981.
Hastings, Max, *Bomber Command*, Michael Joseph, 1979.
Hawkins, Ian, *The Münster Raid*, Tab Books, 1984.
Hersey, John, *The War Lover*, Alfred A. Knopf, 1959.
Horwitz, Julius, *Can I Get There By Candlelight*, Atheneum, 1963.
Hutton, Bud, and Rooney, Andy, *Air Gunner*, Farrar & Rinehart, 1944.
Koger, Fred, *Countdown!*, Algonquin Books of Chapel Hill, 1990.
Lay, Jr., Beirne, and Bartlett, Sy, *12 O'Clock High!*, Ballantine Books,
1948.
LeMay, Curtis E., and Kantor, MacKinlay, *Mission With LeMay*,
Doubleday, 1965.
Mayhew, Margaret, *The Crew*, Corgi Books, 1997.
McCrary, John R., and Scherman, David E., *First of the Many*, Simon
& Schuster, 1944.
Middlebrook, Martin, *The Battle of Hamburg*, Charles Scribner's Sons,
1981.
Merrill, Sandra D., *Donald's Story*, Tebidine Publishing, 1996.
Morrison, Wilbur H., *Fortress Without A Roof*, St Martin's Press,
1982.
Murrow, Edward R., *This Is London* broadcast, December 4, 1943.
Nalty, Bernard, and Berger, Carl, *The Men Who Bombed The Reich*,
E.P. Dutton, 1978.
Newhouse, James Keith, unpublished Second World War diary.
Overy, R.J., *The Air War 1939-1945*, Stein and Day, 1981.
Peaslee, Budd J., *Heritage of Valor*, J.B. Lippincott Co., 1964.
Stiles, Bert, *Serenade To The Big Bird*, W.W. Norton & Co., 1952.
United States War Department, *Instructions For American Servicemen
in Britain 1942*, 1942.

CONTENTS

PREFACE

There is something evocative about a wartime airfield; strangely, the more derelict the site the more evocative it is. Time and nature may have rusted the ironwork, rotted the timber, cracked the glass and concrete, and overwhelmed all but the most substantial structures; nettles, scrub and brambles may flourish everywhere, but a certain aura lingers on.

Beside the roadway, near what was once the entrance, there may be a column or a cross carved out of stone, and possibly a plaque inscribed with unit numbers, names and mottoes. That memorial was probably erected by the veterans of a group or squadron in honour of their comrades who never saw VE-Day, nor enjoyed the peace for which they gave their lives.

If you leave the memorial and force a way through the undergrowth, you may find a dilapidated Maycrete or Nissen hut where once somebody lived—someone whose squadron is remembered on the plaque; now, that wartime billet is a store for farm machinery. Walk out across the grass onto what was once the airfield, and you may feel the solid remnants of a mile-long concrete runway underneath your feet.

Relax, look around, and absorb the atmosphere. Listen for a moment—could that be the sound of distant aero engines, or is it merely the moaning of the wind? Is someone towing a bomb trolley back there on the taxiway, or is it just another of the farmer's tractors? Look back through the mist (there often is a mist), and there stands the control tower, square-built and solid, always the structure most likely to survive. Behind it, through the trees—trees so much higher than they were in wartime— there may be another building, tall, with double doors, where they used to house the fire truck when the field was operational.

Half a century ago, it cost a million man-hours and two million pounds (just under five million dollars) to construct a base like this; now what is there to show for all the expenditure of treasure, toil and time? Where are the hangars, the workshops and the armoury? Where are the squadron offices, the operations block and crew rooms? Where are the cinema, the Red Cross Club, the NAAFI? What happened to the sick bay and the guard room, the instrument and radar huts? Is there now no sign of the huts where they packed the parachutes, serviced the machine-guns, ran the teleprinters—no sign of the bomb dump and the motor pool? No wonder that a veteran, taking one last look, is not entirely sure of where it was he ate his meals or hit the sack, or where they used to brief him for his bombing missions.

In 1944, there were about four hundred buildings here, of one sort or another. Ten or twenty years ago, you might have found some sign of them. Not now. They have simply vanished— gone like the warplanes and the men who flew them, gone like the ground crews who toiled by day and night to keep them flying.

And those famous aircraft—the USAAF's fabled Flying Fortresses and faithful Liberators, the low-flying Marauders and the Bostons, the well-remembered "little friends", Lightnings, Thunderbolts and the splendid long-range Mustangs, with the RAF's early Whitleys, Wellingtons and Stirlings, the mighty Lancasters and Halifaxes, the versatile Mosquitoes, sleek Spitfires and sturdy Hurricanes—all but a precious few of them have also gone.

As for the airfields of the 1940s, the only ones extant and operational are the permanent

We don't need the expensive heavy bomber; it demands an excessive amount of material by comparison with the two-engined dive-bomber.
–Ernst Udet, First World War German fighter ace and consultant to the German Air Force in 1940

6

RAF stations which still have a role to play in Britain's air defences, but the men and women who served there in wartime would hardly recognise them now: their buildings and facilities have been updated to meet the requirements of a modern air force.

There was nothing planned or deliberate about the disappearance of the wartime bases which most veterans, USAAF and RAF, got to know so well: the majority of Britishers, in fact, would have preferred that they stayed where they were, and local communities have often organised petitions for their preservation. But the authorities, seldom moved by sentiment, have simply let nature or the market forces take their course. Britain, after all, is a densely populated island: farmland is valuable, and housing space is more so.

It has to be accepted that old buildings show their age—so do the veterans, and so would their aircraft if they had survived. It is only natural and fitting that they should: the ageing process is part of life. There is something slightly phoney about a sixty year-old control tower newly decorated, in pristine state throughout, with reconstructed mission boards, radios and telephones, and with dummies dressed in uniform propped up at the windows or seated at the desks. A Nissen hut restored, with stoves, beds and lockers, is equally suspect. Restorations of this sort, often with the best of motives, have been painstakingly undertaken by various societies, in the name of "aviation heritage", "air museum" or some such cause. But to see them is to be reminded of henna-tinted hair upon an aged head, or of lavish make-up on a withered face. It is when they stand gaunt and empty on the edge of cornfields, with doors and windows broken and ivy on the walls, that the buildings look more truthful—more the way they should.

This is not to say that they should be allowed to disappear—to be entirely lost—for once something is really lost it cannot be recovered, and soon will be forgotten. No one wants to make a fetish of nostalgia—indeed, to feel nostalgic about windswept fields of mud and freezing Nissen huts might seem a little crazy—but those same fields and huts bore witness to the greatest battles in the story of air warfare, and to the fortitude and courage of the men who fought them. In the end it must be left to the farmers and estate managers—to their good sense and feeling for history—to retain a few of the wartime buildings that stand upon their land. Not to cosset them, not to fence them in, neither to misuse them nor allow them to be vandalized, but just to let them stand there, to take their chances with the wind and weather until, in God's good time, long after those who knew them have gone to their last rest, they crumble quietly into dust.

"The warrior provides for his grandfather and his grandson at the cost, if necessary, of his life. But his sacrifice only makes sense within a time-span of at least three generations. There can be no genuine soldier or army unless there is a past to hand on to the future after the war is over."
– Rosenstock-Huessy

"The war's a long time ago, but every Remembrance Day, you think, well, we wouldn't be here now if it hadn't been for them. The young ones need to be told that."
– Richard Stamp, Lincolnshire farmer

I fled the earth, and naked, climbed the weather, reached a second ground far from the stars: And there we wept, I and a ghostly other . . .
–Dylan Thomas

Let us then be up and doing, With a heart for any fate; Still achieving, still pursuing, Learn to labour and to wait.
–Henry Wadsworth Longfellow

WELCOME TO BRITAIN

The road from commercial artist in Chicago to combat pilot in England is a devious one, full of mental hazards, doubts, frustrations and downright hard labour. When my wife and I parted it was with the understanding that our letters were to be complete enough so that our separation would not leave a void which would make us feel like strangers if and when we were able to live together again. With this in mind, we tried to write to each other every evening as though we were chatting across the supper table. Naturally, this dropped all barriers. Statements were made without thought of a record being kept. Imagination at times ran wild, and assertions were put down that in retrospect were based on half-truths or wholly false ideas.

This is a flow-of-consciousness log. With this in mind, the reader will have to be tolerant. Things that are in black and white here were written in despair, in the heights of enthusiastic accomplishment, and, often, the realm of Never-Never Land.

So much has been written about war adventures. Somewhere I've read that adventure has two faces: one showing the excitement, the other

Much of the world was at war in 1942, including the United States of America. Many young American servicemen and women were about to be shipped to Britain to participate in the conflict and the U.S. War Department issued a little pamphlet to help prepare them for wartime life there. It was called *Instructions for American Servicemen in Britain 1942*. The pamphlet was of considerable interest to many in England at the time of its publication due to its direct, candid view of the British as they were seen by others. A London Times editorial of 14 July 1942 argued that it should be widely read by Britons, comparing it to the efforts of Emerson, Hawthorne, and Irving to explain Britain to the Americans. "None of their august expositions has the spotlight directness of this revelation of plain common horse sense understanding of evident truths."

YOU are going to Great Britain as part of an Allied offensive—to meet Hitler and beat him on his own ground. For the time being you will be Britain's guest. The purpose of this guide is to start getting you acquainted with the British, their country, and their ways.

America and Britain are allies. Hitler knows that they are both powerful countries, tough and resourceful. He knows that they, with the other United Nations, mean his crushing defeat in the end. So it is only common sense to understand that the first and major duty Hitler has given his propaganda chiefs is to separate Britain and America and spread distrust between them. If he can do that, his chance of winning *might* return.

NO TIME TO FIGHT OLD WARS If you come from an Irish-American family, you may think of the English as persecutors of the Irish, or you many think of them as enemy Redcoats who fought against us in the American Revolution and the War of 1812. But there is no time today to fight old wars over again or bring up old grievances. We don't worry about which side our grandfathers fought on in the Civil War, because it doesn't mean anything now.

We can defeat Hitler's propaganda with a weapon of our own. Plain, common horse sense; understanding of evident truths. The most evident truth of all is that in their major ways of life the British and American people are much alike. They speak the same language. They both believe in representative government, in freedom of worship, in freedom of speech. But each country has minor national characteristics which differ. It is by causing misunderstanding over these minor differences that Hitler hopes to make his propaganda effective.

BRITISH RESERVED, NOT UNFRIENDLY You defeat enemy propaganda not by denying that these differences exist, but by admitting them openly and then trying to understand them. For instance: The British are often more reserved in conduct than we. On a small crowded island where forty-five million people live, each man learns to guard his privacy carefully—and is equally careful not to invade another man's privacy.

So if Britons sit in trains or busses without striking up conversation with you, it doesn't mean they are being haughty and unfriendly. Probably they are paying more attention to you than you think. But they don't speak to you because they don't want to appear intrusive or rude. Another difference. The British have phrases and colloquialisms of their own that may sound funny to you. You can make just as many boners in their eyes. It isn't a good idea, for instance, to say "bloody" in mixed company in Britain—it is one of their worst swear words.

To say "I look like a bum" is offensive to their ears, for to the British this means that you look like your own backside. It isn't important–just a tip if you are trying to shine in polite society. Near the end of this guide you will find more of these differences of speech.

British money is in pounds, shillings, and pence. (This also is explained more fully later on.) The British are used to this system and they like it, and all your arguments that the American decimal system is better won't convince them. They won't be pleased to hear you call it "funny money", either. They sweat hard to get it (wages are much lower in Britain than America) and they won't think you smart or funny for mocking it.

DON'T BE A SHOW OFF The British dislike bragging and showing off. American wages and American soldier's pay are the highest in the world. When pay day comes it would be sound practice to learn to spend your money according to British standards. They consider you highly paid. They won't think any better of you for throwing money around; they are more likely to feel that you haven't learned the common-sense virtues of thrift. The British "Tommy" is apt to be specially touchy about the difference between his wages and yours. Keep this in mind. Use common sense and don't rub him the wrong way.

You will find many things in Britain physically different from similar things in America. But there are also important similarities–our common speech, our common law, and our ideals of religious freedom were all brought from Britain when the Pilgrims landed at Plymouth Rock. Our ideas about political liberties are also British and parts of our own Bill of Rights were borrowed from the great chapters of British liberty.

Remember that in America you like people to conduct themselves as we do, and to respect the same things. Try to do the same for the British and respect the things they treasure.

THE BRITISH ARE TOUGH Don't be misled by the British tendency to be soft-spoken and polite. If they need to be, they can be plenty tough. The English language didn't spread across the oceans and over the mountains and jungles and swamps of the world because these people were pantywaists. Sixty thousand British civilians–men, women and children–have died under bombs, and yet the morale of the British is unbreakable and high. A nation doesn't come through that, if it doesn't have plain, common guts. The British are tough, strong people, and good allies. You won't be able to tell the British much about "taking it." They are not particularly interested in taking it any more. They are far more interested in getting together in solid friendship with us, so that we can all start dishing it out to Hitler.

THE COUNTRY You will find out right away that England is a small country, smaller than North Carolina or Iowa. The whole of Great Britain–that is England and Scotland and Wales together–is hardly bigger than Minnesota. England's largest river, the Thames (pronounced "Tems") is not even as big as the Mississippi when it leaves Minnesota. No part of England is more than one hundred miles from the Sea.

If you are from Boston or Seattle the weather may remind you of home. If you are from Arizona or North Dakota you will find it a little hard to get used to. At first you will probably not like the almost continual rains and mists and the absence of snow and crisp cold. Actually, the city of London has less rain for the whole

showing men darning socks. This log has something to do with the darning– not so much with the actual plying of the needle, but with the thoughts in a man's head as he does his work.
–Keith Newhouse

Sunday, 23 August 1942, Nashville, Tennessee
Nobody knew where we were headed until we stopped in Louisville. It rained all night and most of today. This is a brand new camp built in 'good' clay soil–soft, gooey gumbo in varying depths. Some of the boys have been out to the toilets. No water running in the urinals and the showers not working either. We have been given a mess kit and a blanket.

Saturday, 29 August 1942
We turned in our mess kits tonight because some china finally arrived for the mess hall. Also, the fixtures are in for hot showers; no hot water, of course, but what the hell, a guy can't have everything in the Air Force.

below: A German propaganda leaflet intended to cause American soldiers and airmen to give up the fight.

year than many places in the United States, but the rain falls in frequent drizzles. Most people get used to the English climate eventually.

If you have a chance to travel about you will agree that no area of the same size in the United States has such a variety of scenery. At one end of the English channel there is coast like that of Maine. At the other end are the great white chalk cliffs of Dover. The lands of South England and the Thames Valley are like farm or grazing lands of the eastern United States, while the lake country in the north of England and the highlands of Scotland are like the White Mountains of New Hampshire. In the east, where England bulges out toward Holland, the land is almost Dutch in appearance, low, flat, and marshy. The great wild moors of Yorkshire in the north and Devon in the southwest will remind you of the Badlands of Dakota and Montana.

AGE INSTEAD OF SIZE On furlough you will probably go to the cities, where you will meet the Briton's pride in age and tradition. You will find that the British care little about size, not having the "biggest" of many things as we do. For instance, London has no skyscrapers. Not because English architects couldn't design one, but because London is built on swampy ground, not on a rock like New York and skyscrapers need something solid to rest their foundations on. In London they will point out to you buildings like Westminster Abbey, where England's kings and greatest men are buried, and St. Paul's Cathedral with its famous dome, and the Tower of London, which was built almost a thousand years ago. All of these buildings have played an important part in England's history. They mean just as much to the British as Mount Vernon or Lincoln's birthplace do to us.

The largest English cities are all located in the lowlands near the various seacoasts. In the southeast, on the Thames, is London—which is the combined New York, Washington, and Chicago not only of England but of the far-flung British Empire. Greater London's population of twelve million people is the size of

Is your life worth 1.000 bucks ?

No !

It's not worth 10 cents since you have left « God's own country » and come to Europe, to get killed in battle.

Honestly now !

Do you know why you are fighting us ? — Formerly, you were glad enough to take a trip to Europe on our big boats, and we were good friends until Roosevelt, Churchill and Stalin drove us into war.

You've got to die for F. D. R.

Don't you realize it's only for Roosevelt's re-election.

You've got to die for Churchill.

So that the English plutocrats, who own half the world, may haul in more money.

You've got to die for Stalin.

So that Bolshevist murderers should light the brand of revolution in your own land.

THINK OF THE TEARS OF THOSE YOU LEFT AT HOME.

So long as you keep on fighting, you have nothing but death to look forward to.

Come over to us, you will be treated well and in a friendly manner !

Come to us and you will certainly some day embrace your loved ones again and live your young life as you are entitled to do.

Greater New York City and all its suburbs with the nearby New Jersey cities thrown in. It is also more than a quarter of the total population of the British Isles. The great "midland" manufacturing cities of Birmingham, Sheffield, and Coventry (sometimes called "the Detroit of Britain") are located in the central part of England. Nearby on the west coast are the textile and shipping centers of Manchester and Liverpool. Further north, in Scotland, is the world's leading shipbuilding center of Glasgow. On the east side of Scotland is the historic Scottish capital, Edinburgh, scene of the tales of Scott and Robert Louis Stevenson which many of you read in school. In southwest England at the broad mouth of the Severn is the great port of Bristol.

REMEMBER THERE'S A WAR ON Britain may look a little shop-worn and grimy to you. The British people are anxious to have you know that you are not seeing their country at its best. There's been a war on since 1939. The houses haven't been painted because factories are not making paint–they're making planes. The famous English gardens and parks are either unkempt because there are no men to take care of them, or they are being used to grow needed vegetables. British taxicabs look antique because Britain makes tanks for herself and Russia and hasn't time to make new cars. British trains are cold because power is needed for industry, not for heating. There are no luxury dining cars on trains because total war effort has no place for such frills. The trains are unwashed and grimy because men and women are needed for more important work than car-washing. The British people are anxious for you to know that in normal times Britain looks much prettier, cleaner, neater.

BRITAIN–THE CRADLE OF DEMOCRACY

Although you'll read in the papers about "lords" and "sirs", England is still one of the great democracies and the cradle of many American liberties. Personal rule by the King has been dead in England for nearly a thousand years. Today the King reigns, but does not govern. The British people have great affection for their monarch but they have stripped him of practically all political power. It is well to remember this in your comings and goings about England. Be careful not to criticize the King. The British feel about that the way you would feel if anyone spoke against our country or our flag. Today's King and Queen stuck with the people through the blitzes and had their home bombed just like anyone else, and the people are proud of them.

Today the old power of the King has been shifted to Parliament, the Prime Minister, and his Cabinet. The British Parliament has been called the mother of parliaments, because almost all the representative bodies in the world have been copied from it. It is made up of two houses, the House of Commons and the House of Lords. The House of Commons is the most powerful and is elected by all adult men and women in the country, much like our Congress. Today the House of Lords can do little more than add its approval to laws passed by the House of Commons. Many of the "titles" held in the lords (such as "baron" and "duke" and "earl") have been passed from father to son for hundreds of years. Others are granted in reward for outstanding achievement, much as American colleges and universities give honorary degrees to famous men and women. These customs may seem strange and old-fashioned but they give the British the same feeling of security and comfort that many of us get

Thursday, 3 September 1942
Things happen fast around here. A whistle was blown, and a list was read of all pilots that have been classified. Another list of some navigators was posted. I was on neither. I didn't finish my tests until three days after these guys, so I don't know where I am. These boys will be sent out very soon. The barracks is jumping with rumours and gripes. Fellows who listed navigator as their last choice are navigators. Lugs very short on brain power are pilots. Some of them aren't even good physical specimens. Everyone is trying to figure out how they were classified and no one can even suggest a formula. Whatever I get will amaze me. I'm feeling kind of low tonight, but with no real justification for it. I feel like I'll wind up a yard bird yet.

Thursday, 10 September 1942
A gang of us went to the YMCA in Nashville for a cadet dance. There were four guys for every girl so no one got more than a turn or two. I gave up early and shot pool.

Monday, 14 September 1942

Meals are a terror. A lower classman sits in a stiff brace with his stomach touching the table, his head back, his eyes on one point on the table, and the end of his backbone on the edge of the chair. The sadistic upper classmen see to it that this position is not relaxed. If anything is to be passed, the man wanting the article has to say: 'Sir, does anyone wish the bread? Please pass the bread, sir.'

The only answers a new cadet can give are: 'Yes, sir', 'No, sir', and 'No excuse, sir'. Once again, I'll try to explain 'gigs' without going off on a tangent. Seven gigs constitute a 'tour'. A tour means a 50-minute march with a rifle on shoulder and a cartridge belt. Thirty-five tours during the lower class period will automatically bust a boy out of the cadets. This happens only in cases where a fellow is a chronic dummy or has a bad temper. The average cadet receives about seven tours during his lower class period.

The days are very hot but it cools off quite well at night. The worst of the heat is now over and it will gradually get cooler. I am definitely in the Southeast Air Corps now and will do all my training somewhere east of the Mississippi and south of the Mason-Dixon line.

from the familiar ritual of a church service.

The important thing to remember is that within this apparently old-fashioned framework the British enjoy a practical, working twentieth century democracy which is in some ways even more flexible and sensitive to the will of the people than our own.

THE PEOPLE–THEIR CUSTOMS AND MANNERS

The best way to get on in Britain is very much the same as the best way to get on in America. The same sort of courtesy and decency and friendliness that go over big in America will go over big in Britain. The British have seen a good many Americans and they like Americans. They will like your frankness as long as it is friendly. They will expect you to be generous. They are not given to back-slapping and they are shy about showing their affections. But once they get to like you they make the best friends in the world.

In "getting along" the first important thing to remember is that the British are like the Americans in many ways–but not in *all* ways. You will quickly discover differences that seem confusing and even wrong. Like driving on the left side of the road, and having money based on an "impossible" accounting system, and drinking warm beer. But once you get used to things like that, you will realize that they belong to England just as baseball and jazz and coca-cola belong to us.

THE BRITISH LIKE SPORTS
The British of all classes are enthusiastic about sports, both as amateurs and as spectators of professional sports. They love to shoot, they love to play games, they ride horses and bet on horse races, they fish. (But be careful where you hunt or fish. Fishing and hunting rights are often pri-

vate property.) The great "spectator" sports are football in the autumn and winter and cricket in the spring and summer. See a "match" in either of these sports whenever you get a chance. You will get a kick out of it–if only for the differences from American sports.

Cricket will strike you as slow compared with American baseball, but it isn't easy to play well. You will probably get more fun out of "village cricket" which corresponds to sandlot baseball than you would out of the big three-day professional matches. The big professional matches are often nothing but a private contest between the bowler (who corresponds to our pitcher) and the batsman (batter) and you have to know the fine points of the game to understand what is going on.

Football in Britain takes two forms. They play soccer, which is known in America; and they also play "rugger", which is a rougher game and closer to American football, but is played without the padded suits and headguards we use. Rugger requires fifteen on a side, uses a ball slightly bigger than our football, and allows a lateral but not forward passing. The English do not handle the ball as cleanly as we do, but they are far more expert with their feet. As in all English games, no substitutes are allowed. If a man is injured, his side continues with fourteen players and so on.

You will find that English crowds at football or cricket matches are more orderly and polite to the players than American crowds. If a fielder misses a catch at cricket, the crowd will probably take a sympathetic attitude. They will shout "good try" even if it looks to you like a bad fumble. In America the crowd would probably shout "take him out". This contrast should be remembered. It means that you must be careful in the excitement of an English game not to shout out remarks which everyone in America would understand, but which the British might think insulting.

In general more people play games in Britain than in America and they play the game even if they are not good at it. You can always find people who play no better than you and are glad to play with you. They are good sportsmen and are quick to recognize good sportsmanship wherever they meet it.

INDOOR AMUSEMENTS The British have theaters and movies (which they call "cinemas") as we do. But the great place of recreation is the "pub." A pub, or public house, is what we could call a bar or tavern. The usual drink is beer, which is not an imitation of German beer as our beer is, but ale. (But they usually call it beer, or "bitter.") Not much whiskey is now being drunk. War-time taxes have shot the price of a bottle up to about $4.50. The British are beer-drinkers–and can hold it. The beer is now below peacetime strength, but can still make a man's tongue wag at both ends.

You will be welcome in the British pubs as long as you remember one thing. The pub is "the poor man's club," the neighborhood or village gathering place, where the men have come to see their friends, not strangers. If you want to join a darts game, let them ask you first (as they probably will). And if you are beaten it is the custom to stand aside and let someone else play.

The British make much of Sunday. All the shops are closed, most of the restaurants are closed, and in the small towns there is not much to do. You had better follow the example of the British and try to spend Sunday afternoon in the country.

British churches, particularly the little village churches, are often very beautiful inside and out. Most of them are always open and if you feel like it, do not hesitate to walk in. But do not walk around if a service is going on.

You will naturally be interested in getting to know your opposite number, the British soldier, the "Tommy" you have heard and read about. You can understand that two actions on your part will slow up the friendship–swiping his girl, and not appreciating what his army has been up against. Yes, and rubbing it in that you are better paid than he is.

Children the world over are easy to get along with. British children are much like our own. The British have reserved much of the food that gets through solely for their children. To the British children you as an American will be "something special." For they have been fed at their schools and impressed with the fact that the food they ate was sent to them by Uncle Sam. You don't have to tell the British about lend-lease food. They know about it and appreciate it.

KEEP OUT OF ARGUMENTS You can rub a Britisher the wrong way by telling him "we came over and won the last one." Each nation did its share. But Britain remembers that nearly a million of her best manhood died in the last war. America lost 60,000 in action.

Such arguments and the war debts along with them are dead issues. Nazi propaganda now is pounding away day and night asking the British people why they should fight "to save Uncle Shylock and his silver dollar." Don't play into Hitler's hands by mentioning war debts.

Neither do the British need to be told that their armies lost the first couple of rounds in the present war. We've lost a couple, ourselves, so do not start off by being critical of them and saying what the Yanks are going to do. Use your head before you sound off, and remember

Thursday, 15 October 1942
Yesterday orders came through to make us upperclassmen. What a relieved feeling, not to have someone constantly on one's neck! I've been made a cadet corporal.

Tuesday, 20 October 1942
Open Post merely means they change the cadet area from the field to the town. Montgomery is too small to absorb all the thousands, so every-where are innumerable cadets milling around, trying to find a good time. It was disappoint-ing, but just what one should have expected if he had stopped to think. We had a few drinks at the Cadet Club, which was jammed. We had to be back by ten. This get-ting back was a task in itself. Everyone waited as long as they dared, then scrambled. The bus I was on became so crowded that twenty of us had to get out so it could make a hill. The driver tried three times and finally had to ask us to push.

Thursday, 19 November 1942

We had the high pressure chamber yesterday. I came through O.K. There will be another longer test later to see if I can qualify for heavy bombardment. Seventeen of us entered the chamber at one time. There was a test run up to 5,000 feet to let the boys find out how their ears worked. Everyone felt fine as we started. Two men volunteered to be guinea pigs, that is, not to use oxygen up to certain heights. We all went to 10,000 feet before we donned masks. There was a slight exhilaration, our fingernails turned blue and lips tinged purple, but with the light-headedness we felt wonderful. We were advised to chew gum to help us with the swallowing necessary to equalize the pressure in our inner ears. At 10,000 feet, all but the experimenters put on masks. Almost immediately we returned to normal.

The ascent began again until we reached 18,000 feet. Then we observed the guinea pigs. They looked quite natural, but on the dials indicating their heart beats and the hydrogen action in their blood, we knew things were happening. One of the boys began to faint, so was immediately administered oxygen. His revival was rapid, being normal in about two minutes. The other fellow was given a simple arithmetical problem to work. He was to subtract 7 from 100 until he got to 0. He deliberated for a time until he said 93.

how long the British alone held Hitler off without any help from anyone.

In the pubs you will hear a lot of Britons openly criticizing their government and the conduct of the war. That isn't an occasion for you to put in your two-cents worth. It's their business, not yours. You sometimes criticize members of your own family–but just let an outsider start doing the same, and you know how you feel! The Briton is just as outspoken and independent as we are. But don't get him wrong. He is also the most law-abiding citizen in the world, because the British system of justice is just about the best there is. There are fewer murders, robberies, and burglaries in the whole of Great Britain in a year than in a single large American city.

Once again, look, listen, and learn before you start telling the British how much better we do things. They will be interested to hear about life in America and you have a great chance to overcome the picture many of them have gotten from the movies of an America made up of wild Indians and gangsters. When you find differences between British and American ways of doing things, there is usually a good reason for them.

British railways have dinky freight cars (which they call "goods wagons") not because they don't know any better. Small cars allow quicker handling of freight at the thousands and thousands of small stations.

British automobiles are little and low-powered. That's because all the gasoline has to be imported over thousands of miles of ocean.

British taxicabs have comic-looking front wheel structures. Watch them turn around in a 12-foot street and you'll understand why.

The British don't know how to make a good cup of coffee. You don't know how to make a good cup of tea. It's an even swap.

The British are leisurely–but not really slow. Their crack trains hold world speed records. A British ship held the trans-Atlantic record. A British car and a British driver set world's speed records in America.

Do not be offended if Britishers do not pay as full respects to national or regimental colors as Americans do. The British do not treat the flag as such an important symbol as we do. But they pay more frequent respect to their national anthem. In peace or war "God Save the King" (to the same tune of our "America") is played at the conclusion of all public gatherings such as theater performances. The British consider it bad form not to stand at attention, even if it means missing the last bus. If you are in a hurry, leave before the national anthem is played. That's considered alright.

On the whole, British people–whether English, Scottish, or Welsh–are open and honest. If you are on furlough and puzzled about directions, money, or customs, most people will be anxious to help you as long as you speak first and without bluster. The best authority on all problems is the nearest "bobby" (policeman) in his steel helmet. British police are proud of being able to answer almost any question under the sun. They're not in a hurry and they'll take plenty of time to talk to you.

The British will welcome you as friends and allies. But remember that crossing the ocean doesn't automatically make you a hero. There are housewives in aprons and youngsters in knee pants in Britain who have lived through more high explosives in air raids than many soldiers saw in first class barrages in the last war.

BRITAIN AT WAR At home in America you were in a country at war. Since your ship left port, however, you have been in a *war zone*. You will find that all Britain is a war zone and has been since September 1939. All this has meant great changes in the British way of life.

Every light in England is blacked out every night and all night. Every highway signpost has come down and barrage balloons have gone up. Grazing land is now ploughed for wheat and flower beds turned into vegetable gardens. Britain's peacetime army of a couple of hundred thousand has been expanded to over two million men. Everything from the biggest factory to the smallest workshop is turning out something for the war, so that Britain can supply arms for herself, for Libya, India, Russia, and every front. Hundreds of thousands of women have gone to work in factories or joined the many military auxiliary forces. Old-time social distinctions are being forgotten as the sons of factory workers rise to be officers in the forces and the daughters of noblemen get jobs in munitions factories.

But more important than this is the effect of the war itself. The British have been bombed, night after night and month after month. Thousands of them have lost their houses, their possessions, their families. Gasoline, clothes, and railroad travel are hard to come by and incomes are cut by taxes to an extent we Americans have not even approached. One of the things the English always had enough of in the past was soap. Now it is so scarce that girls working in the factories often cannot get the grease off their hands or out of their hair. And food is more strictly rationed than anything else.

THE BRITISH CAME THROUGH For many months the people of Britain have been doing without things which Americans take for granted. But you will find that shortages, discomforts, blackouts, and bombings have not made the British depressed. They have a new cheerfulness and a new determination born out of hard times and tough luck. After going through what they have been through it's only human nature that they should be more than ever determined to win.

You are coming to Britain from a country where your home is still safe, food is still plentiful, and lights are still burning. So it is doubly important for you to remember that the British soldiers and civilians have been living under a tremendous strain. It is always impolite to criticize your hosts. It is militarily stupid to insult your allies. So stop and think before you sound off about lukewarm beer, or cold boiled potatoes, or the way English cigarettes taste.

If British civilians look dowdy and badly dressed, it is not because they do not like good clothes or know how to wear them. All clothing is rationed and the British know that they help war production by wearing an old suit or dress until it cannot be patched any longer. Old clothes are "good form."

One thing to be careful about—if you are invited

Then he fumbled around, mentioning 87, 84, and gave up. He was then to write his name and serial number twice. He scrawled it out the first time, started the second time, and lost contact with the paper. When he couldn't find his way back to the pad and started to slump, the instructor quickly slapped the mask to him. He was normal in a few minutes.

At this time we were told to watch a condom that was suspended from the ceiling, filled with water. This was to represent our intestines. As we went up to 28,000 feet, the thing expanded. We loosened our belts, and belched both directions to compensate for the pressure.

The easier part of the test was over. The ascent is always simple. We stayed 'up there' long enough to look at the various instruments and see

the expansion of the rubber—it was about four times as large as on the ground. Then the descent began at about 3,000 feet a minute. Every time we felt pressure on the eardrums, we yawned, swallowed, or held our noses, closed our mouths and blew. At about 23,000 feet one fellow ran into trouble. His ears wouldn't clear. The descent stopped and we went back to 25,000 feet to relieve the pressure. Off came his mask, the instructor sprayed his nose and throat with ephedrine to clear the canals. On with the mask, the patient blew his nose and down we came. This guy will have a re-check; the rest of us go on.

Sunday, 22 November 1942, Ocala, Florida Now to paradise. Ocala is a beautiful little southern town with wide streets, clean appearance, friendly people who especially like 'their' cadets, and a tangy, fresh atmosphere. We were greeted by smiles everywhere as we marched in to get coffee and cakes.

The mess is out of this world. Today we had a meal that was offered with apologies. There were cold cuts, lettuce and tomatoes, macaroni and cheese served on one plate, not thrown at you army style, but put on a platter in Palmer House style. Then a cup of celery soup—delicious! Brown bread, a choice of iced tea, coffee, milk, chocolate, and a dish of ice cream. We could have seconds if we wished, but have to pay a nickel

into a British home and the host exhorts you to "eat up, there's plenty on the table." Go easy. It may be the family's rations for a whole week spread out to show their hospitality.

WASTE MEANS LIVES It is always said that Americans throw more food into their garbage cans than any other country eats. It is true. We have always been a "producer" nation. Most British food is imported even in peacetimes, and for the last two years the British have been taught not to waste the things that their ships bring in from abroad. British seamen die getting those convoys through. The British have been taught this so thoroughly that they now know that gasoline and food represent the lives of merchant sailors. And when you burn gasoline needlessly, it will seem to them as if you are wasting the blood of those seamen—when you destroy or waste food you have wasted the life of another sailor.

BRITISH WOMEN AT WAR A British woman officer or non-commissioned officer can—and often does—give orders to a man private. The men obey smartly and know it is no shame. For British women have proven themselves in this way. They have stuck to their posts near burning ammunition dumps, delivered messages afoot after their motorcycles have been blasted from under them. They have pulled aviators from burning planes. They have died at the gun posts and as they fell another girl has stepped directly into the position and "carried on." There is not a single record in this war of any British woman in uniformed service quitting her post or failing in her duty under fire.

Now you understand why British soldiers respect the women in uniform. They have won the right to the utmost respect. When you see a

girl in khaki or air-force blue with a bit of ribbon on her tunic—remember she didn't get it for knitting more socks than anyone else in Ipswich.

ENGLISH VERSUS AMERICAN LANGUAGE Almost before you meet the people you will hear them speaking "English." At first you may not understand what they are talking about and they may not understand what you say. The accent will be different from what you are used to, and many of the words will be strange, or apparently wrongly used. But you will get used to it. Remember that back in Washington stenographers from the South are having a hard time to understand dictation given by business executives from New England and the other way around.

In England the "upper crust" speak pretty much alike. You will hear the news broadcaster for the BBC (British Broadcasting Corporation). He is a good example, because he has been trained to talk with the "cultured" accent. He will drop the letter "r" (as people do in some sections of our own country) and will say "hyah" instead of "here." He will use the broad a pronouncing all the a's in "banana" like the a in "father." However funny you may think this is, you will be able to understand people who talk this way and they will be able to understand you. And you will soon get over thinking it is funny.

You will have more difficulty with some of the local dialects. It may comfort you to know that a farmer or villager from Cornwall very often can't understand a farmer or villager in Yorkshire or Lancashire. But you will learn—and they will learn—to understand you.

SOME HINTS ON BRITISH WORDS British slang is something you will have to pick up for yourself. But even apart from slang, there are many words which have different meanings from the way we use them and many common objects have different names. For instance, instead of railroads, automobiles, and radios, the British will talk about railways, motorcars, and wireless sets. A railroad tie is a sleeper. A freight car is a goods wagon. A man who works on the roadbed is a navvy. A streetcar is a tram. Automobile lingo is just as different. A light truck is a lorry. The top of a car is the hood. What we call the hood (of the engine) is a bonnet. The fenders are wings. A wrench is a spanner. Gas is petrol–if there is any.

Your first furlough may find you in some small difficulties because of language difference. You will have to ask for sock suspenders to get garters and for braces instead of suspenders–if you need any. If you are standing in line to buy (book) a railroad ticket or a seat at the movies (cinema) you will be queuing (pronounced "cueing") up before the booking office. If you want a beer quickly, you had better ask for the nearest pub. You will get your drugs at a chemist's and your tobacco at a tobacconist, hardware at an ironmonger's. If you are asked to visit somebody's apartment, he or she will call it a flat.

A unit of money which you will sometimes see advertised in the better stores is the guinea (pronounced "ginny", with the "g" hard as in "go"). It is worth 21 shillings or one pound plus one shilling. There is no actual coin or bill of this value in use. It is merely a quotation of price.

WEIGHTS AND MEASURES The measures of length and weight are almost the same as those used in America. The British have inches, feet, yards, pints, quarts, gallons, and so forth. You should remember, however, that the English (or "Imperial") gallon contains about one-fifth more liquid than the American gallon.

SOME IMPORTANT DOS AND DON'TS

Be friendly–but don't intrude anywhere it seems you are not wanted.

You will find the British money system easier than you think. A little study beforehand on shipboard will make it still easier.

You are higher paid than the British "Tommy." Don't rub it in. Play fair with him. He can be a pal in need.

Don't show off or brag or bluster– "swank" as the British say. If somebody looks in your direction and says, "He's chucking his weight about," you can be pretty sure you're off base. That's the time to pull in your ears.

If you are invited to eat with a family, don't eat too much. Otherwise you may eat up their weekly rations.

Don't make fun of British speech or accents. You sound just as funny to them but they will be too polite to show it.

Avoid comments on the British government or politics.

Don't try to tell the British that America won the last war or make wise-cracks about the war debts or about British defeats in this war.

NEVER criticize the King or Queen.

Don't criticize the food, beer, or cigarettes to the British. Remember they have been at war since 1939.

Use common sense on all occasions. By your conduct you have great power to bring about a better understanding between the two countries after the war is over. You will soon find yourself among a kindly, quiet, hard-working people who have been living under a strain such as few people in the world have ever known. In your dealings with them, let this be your slogan: It is always impolite to criticize your hosts; it is militarily stupid to criticize your allies.

for any extra beverage. The mess hall is finished in knotty pine with wrought iron lighting fixtures. The meal is served cafeteria style and there are only eight men to a table. It's like a club. The PX is adjacent to the dining room, so we get jukebox music with our meal. We can leave the table when we're through eating and smoke in the PX or go to our barracks.

Now, back from supper, I'm convinced I want to stay in primary for the duration! Exquisite veal roast, delicious brown gravy, browned potatoes, string beans, cottage cheese and apricot salad, milk and golden crusted chocolate whipped cream pie. What have I done to deserve such a break?

Wednesday, 25 November 1942
I am now a pilot with one hour and 20 minutes time. About all I can say about flying is that I like it–and it makes me hungry.

below: Lt. James Keith Newhouse in May 1943.

THIS ENGLAND

In the lives of airmen who flew bomber tours from England a strange anomoly constantly recurred. On a Monday evening a group of USAAF fliers could be playing darts or dominoes in the village pub; on Tuesday morning, the same men might be battling through the fighters to drop 500-pounders on the Ruhr. At midnight on Wednesday, a crew of RAF men would be weaving through the searchlights four miles above Berlin; they could be watching a movie in London's Leicester Square on Thursday afternoon. The strangeness lay in the eccentric pattern, in the sudden switch from the commonplace to the cataclysmic, from the comfort to the cold, in the close juxtaposition of friendliness and fearfulness.

For the Americans, of course, a lot of things were strange: the shortages and rationing, the blackout, the funny accents of the English and their even odder customs. Strangest of all, and most alarming, was the realization that a lot of men were dying in the bomber war—that the guys who shared your Nissen hut, or your table in the mess hall, might not be there tomorrow. Nor, of course, might you.

Nearly half a million men and women came across the Atlantic from America to fly or to maintain warplanes of the Eighth and Ninth US Army Air Forces, and to provide their technical, logistic and administrative back-up. A similar number came to serve in RAF Bomber Command from the many lands around the world which owed allegiance to the British Crown. Canada, for example, not only supplied an entire group of fourteen bomber squadrons but contributed many air and ground crews to the other bomber groups. These men, too, were far away from all they recognized as home and, although many thought of Britain as their mother country, she was really just as strange to a New Zealander or a Rhodesian as to a Minnesotan or a Virginian (and as they were to the British in their turn).

This unfamiliarity with the people and their milieu meant that a period of leave was a new experience; it could be enjoyable and interesting, it could be expensive and troublesome, it could be a bit of everything or something in between. There were men who, having tried it once or twice, decided that the crowded, smoke-filled trains, the over-priced alcohol and unexciting food were just not for them, and decided to spend their leaves around the camp. The majority, however, always optimistic and aching for a change of scene, continued to take their chances and the next transport to town.

Some towns, however, in the bomber counties, weren't always as welcoming as they might have been. Australian airmen, whose native poetry was known for its vigour if not for its subtlety, liked to chant a dirge of which one verse ran as follows:

below: In the town of Thetford on VE Day, May 8th 1945; far right: The High street in Lavenham, Suffolk, during the Second World War.

This bloody town's a bloody cuss,
No bloody pubs, no bloody bus;
Nobody cares for bloody us,
Oh, bloody, bloody, bloody.

When RAF men went on leave, most had homes to go to: single men were in the great majority and they could stay with parents or with relatives, while the married minority hurried to their wives. Both married men and bachelors would often take an overseas crew member with them. Many airmen from the Empire, the Dominions and the Commonwealth still had kin in Britain who were glad to welcome them for as long as they could stay—a welcome by no means diminished by the parcels of rare foodstuffs provided by their guests. Others, including most Americans, had to find their own accommodation—no home cooking, no seat by the fire, no hot water bottle in the bed. A room in a hotel or a hostel might be perfectly acceptable for a 48-hour pass, but for a whole week it

might not be a lot of fun—unless you were by nature self-sufficient or could find yourself a soul-mate with whom to pass the time.

An evening out was different—it was a chance to get away from the base for a few hours without the hassle of a train ride and hotel accommodation. The crew would make their way into the local village or the nearest town in whatever kind of transportation they could find; after a drink or two they might stay together or go their separate ways. Some might go to the movies, some to the dance hall, and some might make a tour of all the pubs. They would sometimes meet up later, to catch the last bus back to base or to share a taxi, and sometimes they might not. In the air they were a unity, whether officers or noncoms, and they shared a common purpose; on the ground, as individuals, each man had the option of doing his own thing.

For an evening out, armourer Sam Burchell and his buddies of the 448th Bomb Group at

Friday, 27 November 1942
There are so many planes in the air at one time that there are some very rigid traffic regulations that have to be learned at once. Then, just learning the routine of starting a plane and checking the few instruments in a primary trainer is a job. This, followed by the elementary lesson of taxiing out to the flight line and parking correctly. Every movement on the ground or in the air has to be checked to see that there is clearance for your next move.

The instructor is always on hand, but we are supposed to know what we are doing, because some day he won't be around. You surely get to know he is there. 'Look at your left wing,'–corrected. 'Now look at your nose,' it was too high–corrected. 'Hey, where's your wing?' The Goddamn thing is down again. 'I thought I told you to level off at 1,500 feet.' The altimeter says anywhere from 1,600 to 2,000 feet. 'Now don't forget your throttle!' The things a man does wrong seem endless. 'Use pressure. Don't jerk that stick . . . pressure, never jam the rudder–now why aren't you lined up with the section line?' Do you call that a 90 degree turn? Now, establish a *normal* glide. No, the nose is too low. Don't drop that wing! Now you're off the section line. There, that's pretty good. Now hold it. No, no, no, don't jiggle the stick. Hold it! Now, clear

your motor.' (this is done by a goose with the throttle, which has been cut back for the power-off glide. When the motor comes back on, the prop torque causes a turn to the left which is corrected by right rudder.) 'Whoa, easy with that rudder. Just pressure and not too much.' The instructor is the essence of patience. We try him to the utmost. But it isn't our fault. There is just too much to learn at first. I don't know why I say 'at first.' The job in basic is no less a job. We will just do our best and see how we come out.

Saturday, 5 December 1942
This flying is really something. I had a perfectly rotten day yesterday. I started off by taxiing poorly, so we practiced that a bit at the far end of the field. When we finally took off, I did some very poor climbing turns. Then we landed at our auxiliary field, and in preparation for the landing, I lost the wind direction. As a matter of fact, losing wind direction is one of my worst bugaboos. Back at the main field for another landing, I didn't crab into the wind enough, so I lost my pattern and came in rather badly. I was trying too hard. I had done a lot of reading about flying and some hangar flying before I went up, and was all keyed up for a good trip. I'll have to get some of this 'the hell with it' attitude before I get better.

Seething often took the bus to Norwich. "There were a couple of dance halls," Sam remembered, "where girls would come unescorted, more or less, and pick up soldiers or sailors or whoever was around. Then maybe once every six weeks we would get a weekend to go to London, which wasn't that far away, although in wartime conditions it could be a seven or eight hour train ride. There was one rooming house near the British Museum we used to go to all the time. We'd call up and they'd have a room for us, and give us breakfast and all that. We'd bring girls, a lot of times British Women's Army Corps girls—it was really very pleasant."

For the personnel of the six Lancaster squadrons based in northern Lincolnshire below the Humber estuary, the town of Scunthorpe was the main attraction for an evening off the camp. The streets were narrow, the roof-tops were grimy and the pubs were unremarkable, but the natives were friendly and the beer was good—as was to be expected in a town where steel was made. Of Scunthorpe's hostelries, one stood high in aircrew estimation: "The Oswald was capacious, and had a central floor space which could be used for dancing or, on occasion, for an impromptu form of vaudeville, provided by the more gifted, and sometimes the less sober, members of the clientele. All were given audience, and adequate performances of stand-up comedy, conjuring tricks or song were generously applauded; others, less skilful, were liable to be greeted by a volley of suggestions, most of which were ribald and few of which were kind.

There were few private automobiles on the roads of Churchill's Britain, and even fewer on air force bomber bases. At Waddington, flight engineer Jack Clift was one of the small number to own a form of transportation. "I had a

motor bike, and when you were on ops you could get a petrol ration. It was only an hour's journey to Wakefield, where my Mum and Dad lived. If you weren't on the war-list by lunch time you could get away, and you were free until next morning. The only snag was, when we started doing daylights, that there might be an early one, and then you'd need to be there. The arrangement for that was that one of the crew would ring me at home, and I'd get back early morning."

That operational allowance was specifically provided for travelling home on leave, not to facilitate living off the base, as Clift was to discover. "I got back to camp one morning and looked round the airfield. There were no aircraft on the dispersals. They'd gone off on ops. I found my crew in the mess. They hadn't been able to let me know, because there had been a security clamp-down—all the phones were off, and no one could leave the station. They could have taken a spare bod as engineer, but they'd refused to fly without me. I had to see the Flight Commander. He said they'd been an aircraft short on the trip, and it wouldn't do at all. 'From now on, you be back on camp by eleven o'clock,' he said, 'and you've got to see the CO.' The CO said it was a serious offence, and I wouldn't get any promotion while I was at Waddo, or get a commission at the end of the tour. And I didn't."

"The best things in life are free," Bing Crosby sang. A non-commissioned British bomber crewman, whose daily wage was less than fifteen shillings, might appreciate the tune but have doubts about the sentiment. Certainly, the birds sang and the flowers bloomed for everyone cost-free, but to enjoy the high life and the bright lights you needed money in your pocket. According to the adage, money can't

15

and enjoyed myself, I guess.

My crew got their first mission in today, with another group of crews. (split up amongst 3 crews to get some battle experience) They just returned and are a bit excited — Had a rough trip into Bremen (a long ride) and the planes were quite badly shot up, Tyhech has a scratch on his shin where a 50 calibre grazed him — Germans don't have that size ammo so you know who almost got him — Ah well — see you later —

Incidentally we are on an alert now so I guess we go tomorrow

left: A page from the 1943-44 diary of First Lieutenant Raymond Wild, pilot of a B-17 'Flying Fortress' bomber based at Podington in Northamptonshire, England. Lt. Wild gave the name *Mizpah* to all eight of the B-17s he and his crew flew during their thirty-mission tour of duty. From the Hebrew, Mizpah means "God keep watch between thee and me."

Tuesday, 8 December 1942
We had to report to the flight line this morning, of course, and stay there until noon. This naturally left plenty of time for a bull session. Our parachute rigger came in for quite a panning, because he is such a screwball. He drinks like a fish, to which I can testify, after spending my first Saturday night in town with him. His professional career as a jumper gave him over 300 jumps. But what I'm leading up to is the name for him around here: Rigger Mortis.

Friday, 18 December 1942
I feel no lasting joy over my solo. It was like this. Thursday morning, in spite of all the brooding of the other boys, and the atmosphere of calamity pervading the hangars, I was really on. Peyton and I flew over to Kendrick, the auxiliary field, and he let me show him how hot I was. I knew where the ground was, as he put it. After four landings, he stepped out and I flew it in for three more. The first two were right on the three points. I sort of crow-hopped the third, but did a good job of corrections, so I can now wear my goggles on the helmet instead of around my neck. I didn't get the lift from soloing that I thought I would. Funny thing, but I knew I could do it. Nine hours and four minutes was my dual time before the big event. Peyton climbed

buy you happiness. "Maybe not," said Sergeant Joe Soap, "but at least it helps you to be miserable in comfort."

A Lancaster pilot wrote: "In my crew, we were always broke half-way through the week—all except for the wireless operator. He was better at managing his finances than we were. We used him as a banker, and we were usually overdrawn. He took it jolly well, never read us a lecture, but simply advanced ten shillings here, a pound there, without any fuss., When pay-day came around, the procedure was 'so much for the wireless op, and whatever's left for me."

It was not uncommon for a British airman to travel home on leave with no more in his pocket than a free pass for the train ride and food coupons for the week. For any kind of entertainment he depended on his folks and local generosity. The fact that his American contemporaries had a lot more spending money seldom aroused a feeling of resentment—those Yanks, after all, had no homes to go to and had to pay their way. As Jack Clift put it: "We weren't well paid like the Americans. They were really rolling in it—they had money to burn. It's not

THIS TABLET WAS ERECTED BY THE PEOPLE OF WINCANTON IN HONOUR OF UNITED STATES AIRMEN WHO LOST THEIR LIVES WHEN THEIR FLYING FORTRESS, "OLD FAITHFUL", CRASHED IN FLAMES AT SNAG FARM, NEAR THIS SPOT, WHEN RETURNING DISABLED FROM AN OPERATIONAL SORTIE OVER TOULOUSE, FRANCE, ON 25TH JUNE, 1944.

2ND. LT. PETER MIKONIS, MARGATE CITY, NEW JERSEY
2ND. LT. FRANK E. PEPPER, JNR. BERKELEY, CALIFORNIA.
2ND. LT. JOSEPH B. SULLIVAN, BELMONT, MASSACHUSETTS
2ND. LT. WILL H. STEVENS, SMITHFIELD, NORTH CAROLINA.
SGT. ROY C. ANDERSON, SACRAMENTO, CALIFORNIA.
SGT. DOUGLAS K. DEURMYER, TOPEKA, KANSAS.
SGT. RALPH STEIN, SAVANNAH, GEORGIA.
SGT. RICHARD A. MEHLBERG, MILWAUKEE, WISCONSIN.
SGT. DEAN A. McDOWELL, OMAHA, NEBRASKA.

back in and congratulated me. I felt wonderful, especially back at the field when the boys kept coming up to find out if I had forgotten to put my goggles back around the neck or if it had really happened.

far left: The yoke ornament from a B-17 bomber; center left: A rusted fuel filler cap from a B-17; above: A plaque commemorating the crew of a B-17: This tablet was erected by the people of Wincanton in honour of United States airmen who lost their lives when their Flying Fortress "Old Faithful" crashed in flames at Snag Park near this spot, when returning disabled from an operational sortie over Toulouse, France on 25th June 1944. left: A Nissen hut at Rougham near Bury St Edmunds, Suffolk, wartime home of the 94th Bomb Group.

Wednesday, 23 December 1942
My personal flying is not going well. I'll soon be up for a twenty-hour check. Flying is a peculiar thing. I've seemingly been going bad, but tomorrow may start a good spell. That's where the luck comes in. If I'm hot when I come up for the check ride, I'll do fine. If I'm off, it may be nip and tuck. I was more sure that I could fly that infernal machine the day I soloed than I am right now.

Sunday, 27 December 1942
It seems all Army barbers are men who couldn't earn money in civilian commerce. We have one who went to barber's college. He is the first I've heard of, and he is a barber college wash-out! All others who have scalped me learned what little they know by hard experience. That is, hard on the victims. A man leaves a GI barber chair looking like he's spent the afternoon with the Sioux.

 On the other hand, so each approach is made with the firm resolve, 'He won't get me this time.' 'Just trim it' should prevent a shaving above the ears–and it does. The genius waves his buzzing wand around the vicinity of your head, and then, 'That's all. 35 cents, please.' And you've been trimmed, to the tune of 35 cents, but your hair doesn't know it. When it finally grows bushy over your ears,
you come back for a hair cut and you're back in

that we didn't want them to have it, it's just that we'd have liked to have as much as them."

Most Americans and men from the Dominions made London their primary target when they took off from base on a forty-eight hour pass. The capital might not be looking its best, with windows boarded up, areas of rubble, debris and bomb-scarred buildings, people sleeping in the subways, few theatres open and queues at all the food stores, but all great cities have a magic of their own, and old London town still had its share of that. The off-duty airmen, stepping off the train in King's Cross station and waving down a taxi in the Euston Road, recognized the magic, and meant to enjoy it in what little time they had. They might have selected their aiming point en route—the Piccadilly Hotel, the Regent Palace, Shepherd's Market, Soho Square, the Windmill or Rainbow Corner—or they might just tell the driver to take them some place where they could get a decent steak.

The first thing that struck Keith Newhouse when he arrived in England to join the 467th Bomb Group in the spring of 1944, was the stringency of the official blackout: "We drove through two towns," he noted in his diary, without a single light to be seen. Searchlights played the sky, and ack-ack thundered. Jerry was paying a visit and was being well received."

A jazz fan and pipe-smoker, Newhouse took the train to London on a shopping expedition as soon as he was able. "We arrived about noon. I bought five records and tried to buy a pipe from Dunhills. The shop had suffered a direct hit one time, and was now quite modernized, but one had to arrive at 8 a.m. The queue numbered about fifty every morning, and you hoped that the twelve to twenty-four briars would last until they got to you. Vital

labour being needed elsewhere was the reason. So, until a seven-day leave, I didn't get a pipe." Shortages in England, Newhouse soon discovered, extended to the most basic materials: "Even paper is rationed, so that going to the toilet calls for a search for most any material."

The average Londoner and many of his countrymen, of what might be called the middle class, tended to behave (at least in public) with a measure of reserve. It was not uncommon, on a bus or train ride, for him to share no more communication with his fellow passengers than the first suspicious glance, and to restrict his conversation with anyone outside his immediate circle of acquaintance to "Good morning" and "Good night". Such behaviour patterns did not commend themselves to people unfamiliar with the arcane disciplines of English social life. For them, it was not a criminal offence to be cheerful and outgoing, even occasionally boisterous and loud. They were young, they were friendly, they wanted a good time and were prepared to pay for it. As radio operator Roger Armstrong said: "We were in a holiday mood. It was great to realize that for two days you didn't have to worry about that corporal shining a light in your face at three or four a.m., repeating times for breakfast, briefing and stations."

"Tell me, Mr Ponsonby, do you like the Americans?"
"Not particularly, Sir Geoffrey, but without them it might be difficult to bring the war to a satisfactory conclusion within the forseeable future".

"England was always many things but never only one thing . . . the trains running fast along the tracks, the roofless houses and the bombed rubble on the station platform, and the sunlight beyond the glassless depot roof with the barrage balloons silver-grey and motionless in the windless afternoon. It was that, and for the first time the fields of London rooftops rushing past blurred in the rain beyond the carriage window, and me excited and happy, and Waterloo Station, and the Bond Street whores in their coloured slacks standing in doorways out of the rain, holding their bright parasols and leashed lap-dogs. It was not Westminster Abbey, nor Parliament, nor the Tower of London, nor all the places I had been taught to see. It was all people's faces and Leicester Square and tube stations and taxis and pubs up in Chelsea, and finally tired and ready for the country. And in the country a great stone house in a valley in Buckinghamshire, and an old woman who wore hats and dresses like Queen

Mary and asked polite questions about America, in a long drawing room with the French windows open and May sunlight on the terrace. It was that, and on the table a picture of her son, long dead, among the lost forgotten dead of Flanders."
- from *One Of Our Bombers Is Missing*, by Dan Brennan

the vicious circle. I think the words 'clip joint' originated in an Army barber shop.

far left: The young Princess Elizabeth meeting the crew of the B-17G *Rose of York*; left: Film star Lt. Clark Gable, during his stint with the bomber crews of the Eighth Air Force. Gable joined up after the tragic death of his wife, actress Carole Lombard, who was killed in an air crash. He flew several missions and participated in the making of the training film, *Combat America*.

right: An early morning briefing session on a heavy bomber station of the U.S. Eighth Air Force in 1944; on the following spread: A crew member signs for his wallet after a mission to Leipzig, Germany in 1944.

On the permanent British bomber bases, including those occupied by the USAAF, mission briefings were often conducted in a massive steel and concrete "C-type" hangar, in a room built for the purpose, spacious and well heated. The "J-type" hangars on the wartime-built bases had no such facilities, and the flying crews were briefed in Nissen or Romney huts, 96 feet long and 35 feet wide, with entrance doors at one end and, at the other, a platform with a large-scale map of Europe on the wall behind it. Rows of chairs and trestle tables were divided by a central aisle. The doors were guarded and the windows closed and curtained when a briefing was in progress, which probably accounted for the fact that, ten minutes through the session, the fog of tobacco smoke sometimes made the atmosphere resemble that of Pittsburgh, Pennsylvania, or Sheffield in South Yorkshire, with every mill and foundry at full blast.

There was a certain type of officer for whom the requirement to deliver a briefing was an ordeal. In the bar, the crew room or the flight office, he could hold his own with anyone in snappy repartee, but stand him on a dais, as the focal point of many eyes, and all confidence deserted him. Staring at the notes that he held in trembling fingers, he tended to mumble and stumble through the words. There were others, less inhibited, who discovered in themselves a flair for public speaking, if not to say of histrionics, and enjoyed being the center of attention for a while. The majority, however, neither feared the occasion nor enjoyed it; they simply followed the counsel of their seniors: stand up, speak up and sit down. There was always the chance that a nervous weather man would provide some light relief by putting his slides into the lantern upside down, but basically briefings

THE GEN

Friday, 1 January 1943
I got that twenty-hour check yesterday. I gave the boy the worst possible ride. Didn't do a thing right. I still don't believe I could have planned a worse ride. When we landed he asked me what the trouble was. I couldn't attempt a rational answer. We talked for a while and he said he would give me a three-hour extension. After further conversation, I told him about my recent change of instructors, etc. He told me I'd get five more hours and then a final check ride with him. Most important is my own attitude. For the past several hours I've been slipping. I seem to have lost the feel for the ship that I had. If I regain this touch, I'll be all right, I know. Because of this, I seem to have developed a fear of flying. This is the real source of my trouble, but whether I'll get straightened out in five more hours remains to be seen. My new instructor is quite capable of doing the job, I think, but then I now have 28 hours. He'll have to undo a lot which will put me behind. Just how far may decide the outcome.
  My new instructor is very good, and with five hour work maybe I can pull through. If not, why it is water over the dam, and I do know how to fly. The experience has been good, and while I'll feel there has been a lot of time wasted, the gov-

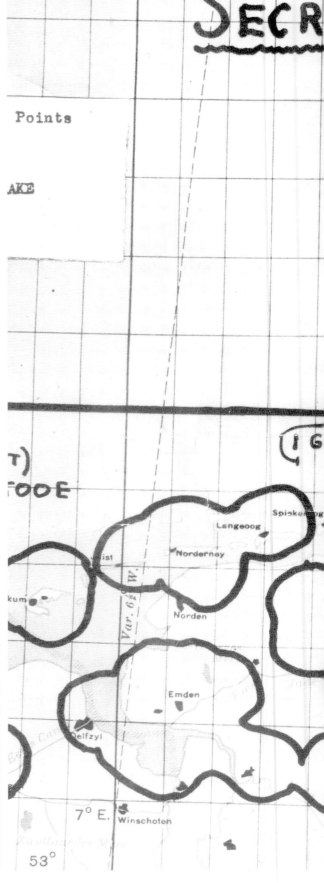

ernment is footing the bill and maybe I'll get a crack at something else. Here is the preamble of THE BLUEBIRD WASHOUT AND CULTURAL SOCIETY. Being of sound body and uncoordinated mind, possessing poor judgement, with adeptness for ineptitude, with a facility for dangerous flying while moving in a block of air, being allergic to simple patterns, with that zest for freedom at all times, with a remarkable disregard for any instructions, unmindful of the disposition of other aircraft in other blocks of air, inclined toward such perverse aerial activities as are deemed inconsistent to local operations, being dangerous to ourselves and those about us, we hereby band together for the purpose of mutual self-destruction.

right: A briefing map of flak locations

were devoid of fun.

One way or another, the essential information was imparted and, before the CO pronounced his valediction, the operations officer or navigation leader would call for a time hack: "Okay, men, let's all check our watches on my mark. In twenty seconds time, it will be exactly . . . " Strangely, a briefing rarely ended in the recommended academic style with "Any questions?" The implication may have been that bright young airmen were expected to hoist the data in first time.

"At Grafton Underwood," said pilot Lawrence Drew of the 384th Bomb Group, "there was a raised platform in the briefing room with a large map of Germany behind it, and they would have a roll-up shade covering it. We all assembled in there and we didn't know where the mission was. There'd be a lot of tension at that time. Of course, we would all be hoping for a milk run, a short mission, one we'd be back from in four or five hours. Then rather dramatically, they would pull up the shade, and you'd see the red ribbon on the map showing our flight path into the target and

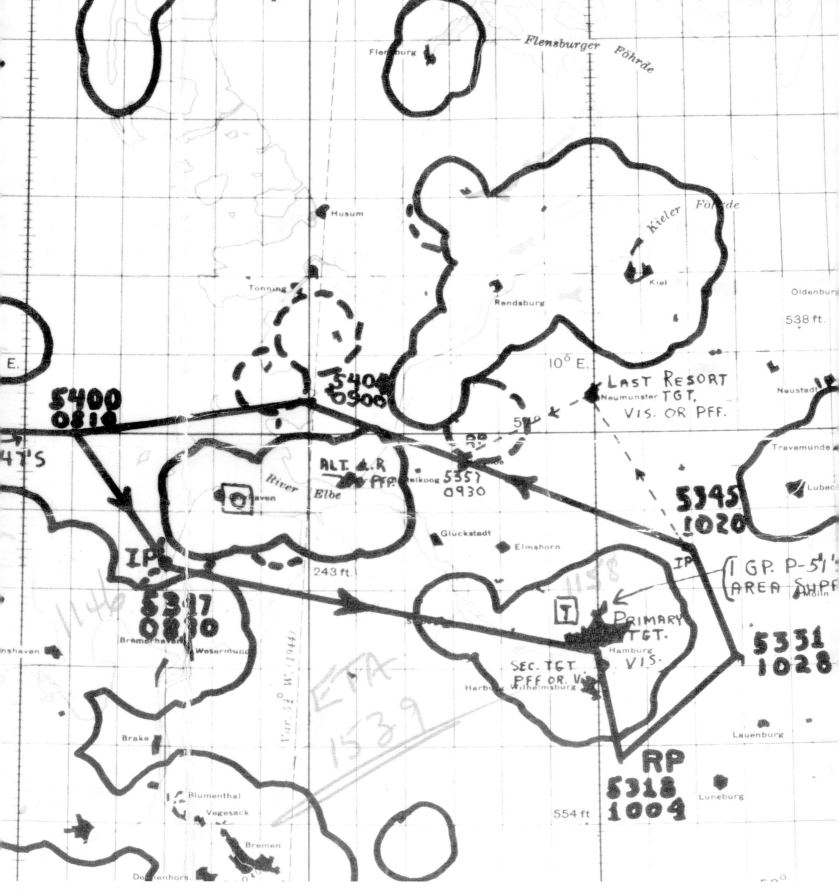

Flensburger Föhrde

Flensburg

Kieler Föhrde

Oldenbur

Husum

538 ft.

Tönning

Kiel

Rendsburg

10° E.

LAST RESORT TGT.

Neumünster VIS. OR PFF.

Neustadt

5400
0900

5400
0818

4TS

5345
1020

Travemunde

ALT. & R.
PFF.

5357
0930

Lubec

River
Elbe

Glückstadt

Elmshorn

IP

IP

(GP. P-51's
AREA SUPP

243 ft.

5317
0840

T

PRIMARY
TGT.

5331
1028

shaven

Bremerhaven

Wesermund

ETA
1539

Hamburg
VIS.

SEC. TGT
PFF OR. V

Harburg Wilhelmsburg

Brake

Lauenburg

RP
5318
1004

Luneburg

Blumenthal

Vegesack

554 ft

Bremen

Dechenhors.

29

Now I have about 44 hours. There's talk of combining my 40- and 60-hour checks into one. This would be all right with me because if I should wash I'd get that many more hours in. I know now I can fly. I like it so much I have a let-down feeling, figuratively and literally, when I get back on the ground. I'm asking for the bigger jobs, twin engine at least, but I'm sure hoping at this point they'll let me fly.

I'm scheduled for a dual ride with my instructor, Olds. I honestly think I can feel the flying in this ship. I know up until my 20-hour check with the toughie, Wolfe, I was flying mechanically. I've improved enormously since then. A great deal is due to Olds' teaching, but, too, something has gotten into me. I don't think I'm a hot pilot, but certain sensations and my reactions tell me I'll be good if I can stay in.

My landings were shaky for a while, even on my last check, but during the shooting of those stages, the same confidence that came to me for my solo has come back, and I'm three-pointing them all. It is a wonderful feeling. It is simply: Have you the feel of the ship or not? Right now, I have. Let's hope I don't lose it.

back. We generally had three targets. If we couldn't hit the primary on account of weather, the mission leader would go on to the secondary, or the tertiary. If we couldn't hit any of them, we had what they called targets of opportunity."

On April 9th 1944, a force of five hundred and forty Eighth Air Force bombers was assigned to carry out a series of simultaneous attacks on aircraft construction plants in east and north Germany. The target for the 384th, with the 1st Bomb Division, was an aircraft factory in Marienburg. The Group Commnander, Colonel Dale O. Smith, who was to lead the wing himself, commenced the briefing with these words: "Today our target is the FW-190 assembly plant. If we clobber it there won't be so many enemy fighters after us in the future. So I know you won't miss. But

it's no milk run. It's one of the longest missions we've ever had. We'll be at maximum weight and we'll climb out slowly to conserve fuel. Tanks will be topped up at twenty-seven hundred gallons after engine warm-up. Keep your mixtures lean and your RPM low. We'll have just enough fuel to get home."

The red ribbon on the map stretched over the North Sea and the Jutland peninsula, east across the Baltic, then southeast on a dogleg to the distant target. Ignoring the chorus of whistles, groans and catcalls with which the assembled flight crews greeted the display, the operations officer took the stage and described the wing formations, assembly routes and rendezvous; the intelligence officer gave warning of expected flak and fighter opposition, and showed the latest recce photos of the aiming point; the armament officer announced that each aircraft would carry twelve 500-pound general purpose bombs. The bombing altitude would be 15,000 feet. Communications followed, and finally the latest weather information.

It is good to note that, after twelve hours in the air, all but one of the 384th's B-17s returned safely from Marienburg, that nine days later the group received a Presidential Unit Citation—a distinction in which every Joe, every sad sack, every ground pounder, as well as every flier, could feel he had a share. Strangely, the RAF had no equivalent award.

Ball turret gunner John Hurd of the 401st Bomb Group is another flier who remembered the tension before the target was revealed: "If it was known to be a tough one, there would be some nervousness, and grumbling would be heard. An officer would give us the weather, temperature and cloud cover to expect, and another would tell us what altitude to fly and what to expect from fighter defenses and flak along the route. The Group Chaplain would give a prayer, and the Commanding Officer would give a short talk and tell us to give them hell."

RAF wireless operator Reg Payne recalled a briefing for No. 50 Squadron at Skellingthorpe in Lincolnshire: "They went through the start-up and take-off times, the order of taking off and the details of the turning points on the route, A, B, C, D and so on. The PFF would put coloured markers down on the turning points to try to keep us together. We were split up into waves, and each wave had a different time and height to fly over the target. There was something in the briefing for each crew member. We wireless ops were told which normal and emergency WT channels to use, which stations to use if we wanted a fix, what time to listen out for the Group broadcasts, and what the bomber codes were. We used to carry two codes, and

they would change at maybe midnight or one o'clock. We had to send all our messages in the current code, then if you asked for a bearing they would know you were a friendly aircraft, and they would give your latitude and longitude, and whether it was a first, second or third class bearing, which meant how accurate it was."

At some RAF briefings it was the practice to display a map showing the tracks of squadron aircraft as they crossed the enemy coast outbound on the preceding mission, followed by a second map revealing the position at the coastline coming back. Judged for accuracy of navigation, the latter frequently tended to compare unfavorably with the former. The operations officer or navigation leader having drawn attention to the wanderers and stragglers, would often see it as his duty to deliver a homily on the virtues of maintaining a concentrated stream.

far left: A warning tag from a Norden bombsight, the type used in the B-17 and B-24 heavy bombers of the U.S. Eighth Air Force in World War Two; below: B-17s of the U.S. 385th Bomb Group on a food drop mission in aid of the people of Rotterdam in spring 1945.

Monday, 25 January 1943

It's curious to look back now and think of how darned low I was at times. Basic will probably be the same thing over again. I've found everyone went through a similar period sometime between 20 and 40 hours. Funny thing how some darned good men were washed, and how some stinkers are still flying. There is no way of telling who will make it and who won't. Some Harvard graduates are through in six hours. Fellows too lazy to yawn are Hot Pilots. Some guys are just plumb lucky, and others do it on ability, cool and capable. Some boys cut out cigarettes and drinking to improve their flying and other guys drink and smoke anything that comes their way. What makes a pilot is still an unanswered question. My final grades are somewhere between 90 and 95. I'm in the upper third of the class academically. Olds put me in for twin-engine, medium bombardment. This was my second choice, as I'd prefer four-engine, heavy bombardment, but either would be O.K.

right: Royal Air Force heavy bomber crews are briefed for a raid on a German target.

During the course of a Lancaster squadron briefing, the green scrambler telephone at the CO's elbow would sometimes emit a muted ring. The briefing would continue but no one would be listening: they would be watching the CO and observing his reactions, seeing him nod his head and scribble on his notepad. At the next break in the briefing, he would rise and announce: "The Stirlings and Wellingtons won't be with you tonight. Carry on, Wing Commander."

There would be a murmur from the seated ranks: "Lucky bastards", "That means a scrub?" Five minutes later, another quiet ring. "The Halifaxes are stood down, too", the CO would announce, "you'll have the target to yourselves, chaps." Everybody understood the purport of the message: it had been decided at High Wycombe that, in the target area, the cloud tops were so high that only the Lancasters could climb into the clear; even for an area attack, with no thought of precision, the bomb-aimers had to see the PFF's sky markers, and any aircraft that couldn't reach the necessary altitude might as well stay home. The USAAF commanders often faced the same problem on the daylight missions: the B-24s couldn't reach the altitude that the B-17s could scale. Sometimes, they sent the Liberators anyway, for the sake of their fire power on the out-bound route, and have the division leader either bring them home or attack another target if the cloud tops were too high.

Once the briefing was over, you were committed to the task, and however much you dreaded it, in some ways you were glad. The mission was important, it had clearly been well planned, you had faith in your crew and in the aircraft, and you were ready—as ready as you

right: A wing access panel from a damaged 8AF bomber; centre: A hardstand tie-down on a disused former American air base in the English midlands; below: A warweary B-17G on its hardstand; far right: 8AF bomber crewmen listen intently in their mission briefing.

Wednesday, 27 January 1943
In town at Eddie's Lunch. There were twelve Lionel Hampton, Duke Ellington, Count Basie, Erskine Hawkins, Jimmy Lunceford disks in a beat-up juke box. We supplied most of the nickels and got a big bang observing the effect of a nickel's worth of jive. There weren't any zoot-suiters there, but everyone wore pegs, long-pointed shoes, oxfords so run down that the walking surfaces had slipped over to the side of the shoe. The pants were ankle-tight, with full drape, narrow belts that told the chest measurement rather than the waist. A couple of guys used ties to hold up their drapes. Most of them wore gaudy polo shirts of the conventional T-design. And the head coverings—let's not say 'hats.'! The crowns, supporting six to ten inches of brim, were in blues, greens, buffs, pearl greys, with a dash of colour in the band running from sunset orange to kelly green. Then there were caps built along the lines of circular, over-stuffed cushions. The smaller the head, the larger its adornment—or was is only relative?

Such wonderful, loose-jointed rhythm, free and easy motion, soft shuffling, effortless shrugs of the whole body, every so often a throaty, panting 'Hey'. No stomping and banging like we've seen at the Club DeLisa or the Terrace. Just flowing motion, quiet ecstasy—Let the band make the noise. Of course, we had to

ever would be—to do what was required of you. You had stiffened the sinews and summoned up the blood. It would be one more mission on the record, and one less to contemplate before the RAF "screened" you or the USAAF sent you home.

It was time to check your pockets, to ensure there were no documents or letters, no rail or bus tickets that could identify your squadron or your base if you had to bail out and were captured by the enemy. Then collect the flying rations, gather up the kit and ride out to the bomber, load the guns, check the radio and oxygen, kick the tyres, run the engines and settle in the seat. Sometimes, what followed was total anti-climax: a red flare from the tower, and a message "Mission cancelled, transport for the crew is on its way". The instant reaction might be one of relief—another day, another

night, in which to live your life—but you knew in your heart that the mission wasn't really cancelled: it was just postponed. All the stomach-wrenching tension, all the hours of preparation—which for many was the worst part of the mission—would come again tomorrow, or the next day, or the next.

This time, let us say, the weather was all right—at least it wasn't bad enough to jeopardize the mission. You got the bomber airborne, climbed to the rendezvous with all the other planes, and reached the coastal crossing point more or less on time. The skies of Europe were, as usual, unfriendly, but you made it to the target with everybody else—well, nearly everybody. The bomb run—as usual—seemed to take for ever, but at last you closed the doors and turned for home. The flak and the fighters didn't seem to want to let you go: you kept

going, anyway—well, most of you kept going.

How good it was to see the coast of England, or perhaps the shelf of cloud that told you it was there, or just to hear the navigator saying that it was. You took your turn in the let-down to the field, heard the squeal of rubber on the tarmac, received a welcome from the ground crew, felt your feet on *terra firma*, and tasted that first magic cigarette.

Soon there would be a meal—how long was it since you ate—seven hours, eight, nine? Soon there would be a bed, not much of a bed, maybe, but somewhere you could sleep. Soon, but not just yet. First, you had to be debriefed.

For compiling their reports to headquarters at "Pinetree" or "The Hole" at High Wycombe, the interrogators had to elicit the story of the mission: was the primary target bombed, if not—why not, and what did you bomb instead?

How strong were the defences, how active were the fighters, was your aircraft attacked, where and by how many, and what were the results? Casualties? Damage? Did you witness other combats, did you see any 'chutes go down, and where? Any unusual sightings . . .

The return of RAF bombers to their bases might be spread over half an hour or more, and progess through debriefing could be timed accordingly. The crews seldom had to wait long before they took their places at the interrogator's tables. Every attempt was made to speed the process, and a "hot news" table was set up for reports of matters which might need urgent action: of aircraft seen to be in trouble, of ditchings or forced landings, and of enemy ships' positions.

Lawrence Drew recalled the scene at Grafton Underwood. "There were tables—kind of like barbeque tables—with seats on either side, and an intelligence officer took down the information on the mission from the crews, for somebody, somewhere, to put it all together. They would give you coffee and donuts, and serve a little shot of booze. It was always a good grade of booze, better than you could get at the club, and they served it straight. There was always someone who would drink yours if you didn't want it. And you ate while you talked. We were always half-starved, because from breakfast at maybe one o'clock you didn't have anything to eat, only candy. So the coffee and donuts disappeared and it didn't dull our appetites at all. We'd still go to the mess hall."

"Debriefing at Waddington usually took about twenty minutes. But if the crew was tired and fed up, they would sometimes clam up and say 'nothing to report', to get it over quickly."
- Jack Clift, flight engineer, 463 Squadron

leave before the evening had begun; maybe they do get loud as the excitement lasts.

We stayed awake long enough to hear the 'momentous' news at ten o'clock. It was the meeting at Casablanca. The fanfare implied that a second front had been started or that Rommel had capitulated, to my way of thinking.

Some groups later carried two five-thousand pound "Disney" bombs mounted on external racks. These armor- piercing bombs were designed to penetrate the roofs of the submarine and E-boat pens. Those who dropped them soon learned, as one pilot said, that their ballistics were "about as consistent as a fart in a windstorm." Another pilot said that flying a B-17 with these monstrosities under the wings was like trying to tap-dance on a billiard ball resting on an ice cube. Such tactics were quickly discontinued because even these large bombs could not penetrate the submarine pens. –from *Fortress Without a Roof* by Wilbur H. Morrison

left: The time hack, when all watches are synchronized just before these airmen leave their briefing for the crew room where they will dress for the day's mission.

Engine run-up with
a high-visibility jeep
on the hardstand.

"In the European theatre," wrote the authors of *Target Germany*, "the heavy bomber base covers several hundred acres of farmland. The core of each base is the airdrome, criss-crossed by 150 foot-wide concrete runways. A perimeter track . . . skirts the inner border, and concrete dispersal points on which the bombers are parked between missions dot the fringes of the area. Scattered around the airdrome are "sites" on which the personnel are housed. On the edges of the field are placed the administrative buildings, the shops, and one or two large hangars for heavy repair work. Dovetailling into the irregular outline of the area are the neighbouring farms."

To a casual observer, that irregular layout, with the living and working sites widely separated, perimeter fences going in all directions, with a bomb store to the south, oil tanks to the north, and hangars east and west, might appear to be the product of a random exercise by an eccentric architect. This was not, in fact, the case: the buildings were scattered and, whenever possible, hidden among trees, as a defensive measure against enemy attack, in the same way as the bombers were camouflaged and dispersed around the field. As to the perimeter, its delineation was to some extent dictated by the shape of the meadows and plantations that were there before the war began—indeed, that had been there longer than anyone could tell.

The Air Forces had a way—a simple but effective way—of ensuring that an airman, on first arriving at a base, got to know his way around within a day or two. When he first reported at headquarters, he was given an "arrival chit"— an official piece of paper which bore the designation of every section and departmental office. He was required to visit each of these in turn, and to obtain a signature from someone there who either noted his arrival and took documentary action, or told him "There's no one here right now, you'll have to come back tomorrow."

By the time he had discovered the location of the clothing and barrack stores, the sick bay and the barber shop, the battle HQ, the Post Exchange or NAAFI, the pay accounts office, the library, the chaplain's office and the squadron orderly room, the safety equipment and parachute sections, the mail office, the fire station and the MT yard—by then the new arrival had walked five miles and his tour of exploration had only just begun. He had yet to find the laundry, the tailor's shop, the armoury, the gymnasium, the fuel store, the signals room, the flight publications office . . . if he could only find the mess hall and somewhere to sleep, he could really say he knew his way around.

The new arrival would by now have got accustomed to standing in a queue—a pattern of behavior which the British public had adopted when wartime shortages began (and seem to have accepted ever since). He would queue to use the wash room when he got up in the morning, he would queue for breakfast in the mess hall and for all his other meals, for his "cuppa and a wad" when the ladies of the YMCA, Red Cross or Salvation Army brought their mobile canteen to his work place, for his pay, his laundry, his haircut, his leave pass and the liberty bus. Once he was established on the base, with his name, rank and number on every list and roster, he would be assigned to all sorts of fatigues, and to extra duties such as crash crew, duty crew, fire picket, gate guard and funeral party. At least, for those, he didn't have to queue.

The servicemen and women, RAF or USAAF, who served on the hastily-constructed wartime bases (Ludford Magna was reputed to have been built in thirty days), sometimes took a perverse,

Tuesday, 16 February 1943
I flew two hours and fifteen minutes today. Half the time in a solo ship and the rest in the rear cockpit 'under the hood' taking my first flight on instruments. What an ordeal! 'Needle, ball, air speed, altitude.' 'Needle, ball, air speed, altitude.' 'Needle, ball, glance over the air speed, watch altitude,' came as a steady monotone from Cohen (my new civilian instructor) in the front. Once in a while an explosion, 'For Christ's sake, when I say line up the needle, I mean line it up. Absolute center. Don't fall asleep; make a correction!! Now, watch your altitude. ALTITUDE. Use your head. Don't watch any one instrument. Needle, ball, air speed, altitude. Use the rudder. Rudder for needle, stick for ball, elevators for air speed. LEAVE THAT THROTTLE ALONE. ELEVATORS for air speed. Needle, ball, air speed, altitude.'

I'm busy like a beaver. My eyes just spin around those instruments. I get anxious to do it right. Comes the answer to that situation: 'Don't tense up. Just your finger tips on the stick. RELAX. Get in the center of the seat. Slump down like a

sardonic pride in the hostile nature of their environment and their stark style of living. They tended to regard those of their comrades who were based on permanent stations as feather-bedding softies. "Those guys at Bassingbourn (or Debden or Coningsby or Scampton)," they would say, trudging through the quagmirre, shivering and sniffling, while another passing truck doused them in dirty water, ". . . those guys don't know they're in a war zone."

In passing it is noteworthy that the *de luxe* bases are no more well-remembered than the other sort. Cliff Chatten was based at Coningsby for most of his tour as a pathfinder pilot with 97 Squadron—a Lancaster unit which sometimes found itself in No. 8 Group and at other times in No. 5, according to which group commander was currently in favor with the C. in C. "I lived there for seven months," said Chatten, "but when I went back a year or two ago, I didn't know it at all. It was as though I'd never seen the place before."

"Some men had bicycles at Seething," said Sam Burchell, "that they had bought in town or in one of the villages. Otherwise it was just walking. When we went into Norwich, on a day's leave, it would be in army trucks. They had an hourly schedule and took us to a drop-off point, close by the cathedral, and picked us up later. But on the base it was mostly walking."

"If you had a bicycle you were lucky," remembered Larry Bird, "and I was lucky. It had no fenders or anything, but it was a bicycle and I rode it everywhere. When the war was over, I gave it to an old man who worked there at the base. He was as happy as if I'd given him a Rolls-Royce."

At Abbots Ripton, crew chief Ira Eakin's buddy wasn't quite so lucky. "I can't imagine a kid," said Ira, "growing up in the depression

sack of flour. Don't get tense! Relax! Needle, ball, air speed, watch the altitude. No, no, NO! Don't stare at the altitude. If it's wrong, correct, but don't become fascinated by it. Needle, ball, air speed, altitude, in that order. Divide your attention. All right now, relax. Get in the center of the seat. Don't try to feel the flight. Just correct by instruments. Needle, ball, etc etc.

'O.K.', says Cohen, 'now try a turn to the right. Lead with rudder. LEAD with the rudder. Just pressure. Let's try again. As soon as the needle is at the near edge of the indicator, neutralize the stick. That's it. Don't release the pressure. Ball on the top side now. Now roll it out. Center the needle. Hey, where's your altitude? What about the air speed? Needle, ball, air speed, altitude. All right, I'll take over.' And, by golly, an hour's gone by. We're over the airport, and he lands the damn thing. This is going to continue for twenty hours.

left: RAF air crew pedalling around the perimeter track of their Cambridgeshire bomber station.

Wednesday, 10 March 1943
This afternoon I passed some spot stages. A piece of canvas is put on the ground and we had to hit it five out of eight times. I undershot the field and then put five in. This, with an almost 90 degree crosswind was pretty good flying. If I can lick this instrument bugaboo, maybe I will be a flyer.

Saturday, 13 March 1943
Once again I've set down–this time because of weather. I'm sitting comfortably in the cock-pit, with the canopy let-ting only a drop of rain in once in a while, on the edge of the runway of the auxiliary field. About eight of us are here. The control ship says we'll stay here until it blows over. It looks like soup and no openings.

We are scheduled for all day at the flight line tomorrow. We surely are a bunch of tired boys. Everyone has some com-plaint: leg aches, back aches, ears feel numb from radio and engine noise, and just a general 'lay me down to rest' feeling.

There are 70 hours in basic and 70 more in advanced, and then a transition period, before I touch a bomber. Two hundred hours as a cadet.

and never learning to ride a bicycle. Anyway, he'd never ridden one before. After a while, he got so he could kind of wobble along on the thing. They had these huge trees there, and going down the road he hit one of them head on. It broke his arm and his collar bone. He was in a plaster cast for weeks."

In the winter of 1943-44, RAF Melbourne in North Yorkshire consisted of three runways, a taxiway, two hangars, a scattering of concrete hardstands and two hundred huts. All the rest was mud. "Be sure to walk on the duckboards," new arrivals were advised, "or we might never find you." Non-commissioned crewmen wrapped themselves in greatcoats and slept on sofas in the mess, rather than freezing in the Nissen huts. The stores provided bicycles, but navigator Norman Pittam soon decided that it was easier to walk. "The only time I saw a vehicle," he said, "was when they took us to the aircraft for an op. We trudged around in Wellies, wearing gloves, scarves and great-coats. It was a bloody awful place."

Equally awful and no less muddy was the base at North Killingholme, on the north coast of Lincolnshire, where the on-shore winds, straight from the Arctic circle, were cold enough to emasculate brass monkeys. In the bitter winter of 1944, a laden Lancaster of 550 Squadron strayed off the runway and sank into the quag-mire. Jimmy Bennett, the squadron commander, called a friend at the Eighth Air Force fighter field at Goxhill. "The Yanks had a lot of practice at that sort of thing when they first moved in," said Bennett, "and they turned up not long after-wards with all sorts of magnificent machinery and aids, including some pierced steel sheeting which they could just unroll and turn into a tem-porary runway. They had that Lanc back on the

concrete in no time at all."

Melbourne and Killingholme were but two of many contenders for the title of the RAF's most bloody awful base. High amongst the rest stood Blyton, the Lincolnshire home of No. 1662 Heavy Conversion Unit, where the aircrews were introduced to four-engined planes in the shape of the docile if unwieldy Handley-Page Halifax. The contractors who built Blyton in 1941 were still trying, four years later, to repair its worst defects. The strength of the concrete in the runways, hardstands and taxiways proved to be unequal to the constant impact of the heavy airplanes, and the water in the wash-rooms seldom ran hot and often not at all. Other disadvantages were that the food was remarkable only for its tastelessness, and the medical facilities were totally inadequate to the demand upon them. The casualty rate in train-ing accidents frequently exceeded that of the squadrons bombing Germany, due largely to the fact that Blyton's Halifaxes were all well past their prime. Worst of all, the nearest town was Gainsborough—probably the dreariest metropolis in Lincolnshire, if not in the whole of England. Despite all this, No. 1662 con-trived somehow to match the other HCUs in turning out an average of thirty crews a month to maintain the bomber squadrons at full strength. And there was this about Blyton— after two months there, to serve on even the most desolate of No. 1 Group's bases was, as the airmen said, "a piece of cake".

On the well-paved, permanent bases, where cycling was possible, there were seldom quite enough bikes to go around, and men of hitherto unblemished character adopted a philosophy of "finders, keepers" overnight. Radio operator Roger Armstrong of the 91st Bomb Group, who had paid no less than five pounds ten shillings for his personal transportation, took the precaution of padlocking the chain. During the course of one early morning stampede from quarters to the mess hall, an attempted larceny was frustrated by this measure; gratified, Armstrong removed the padlock and rode on, only to collide with another cyclist and tumble to the ground. In his jacket pocket were three fresh eggs, which he had been looking forward to frying for his breakfast. They did not survive the fall.

In addition to the padlock, Armstrong's bicycle was equipped with a headlamp. More remarkable still, the lamp had a battery—a rare acquisition in those days. So, on the occasions when it was his turn to fetch supper for his crew from the village fish-and-chip shop, he would find, on the homeward ride, that he was acting as pathfinder for the group.

It was not unknown for members of the 351st Bomb Group, returning to Polebrook, Northamptonshire, from the local pub, to ride on bicycles that were not their own. Sometimes the bikes were returned to, or recovered by, their owners in the village, and sometimes they were not. It was the latter that increasingly weighed on the conscience of veteran Roger Johnson as the years went by, and he has moved, at last, to make some recompense. In the summer of 1991, he returned to Polebrook and presented fine new bicycles, complete with three-speed gears and all the latest fittings, to ninety of the village boys and girls. The gesture did not pass unnoticed by the British media; indeed, it was the subject of a leader in *The Times*. Shakespeare recorded that "conscience doth make cowards of us all": not so with Johnson; for the people of Polebrook, and for all who read the story, it made him a very nice American.

Some of the crews based at Linton-on-Ouse, in Yorkshire's North Riding, were comfortably

top: This air raid shelter on the Lavenham, Suffolk base of the 487th Bomb Group now shelters an old yellow Volkswagen; left: The Flying Fortress pub sits on the northern edge of the 94BG Rougham airfield.

Wednesday, 24 March 1943

I've already put in four hours and must fly another 40 minutes tonight sometime to complete my six hours of night flying prior to a two-hour cross-country to be flown tomorrow night. By tomorrow all the flying I'll have to do in basic will be a check ride with the Army, two hurdle stages, and the two-hour night cross-country. Then, if I can get by code, I'll be ready for advanced. I wound up my instrument flying in glory. Cohen finally said I have the makings of a good instrument flyer. This, after all the trouble I've had with Link and instrument, made me feel good.

Friday, 26 March 1943

I flew my last two hours in a BT last night, to complete this course. This morning I passed code, so I'm ready and waiting for advanced with its grief and woes. The night was beautiful and clear. The ship I had flew nicely, but I had a mechanic check it before I left because of an oil leak in the belly and underneath. It was never found, but the servicings didn't show much eating of oil, so he OK'd it. Every crock here seems to have several things wrong with it. I made up my mind that if something went wrong, I had a new 'chute and would head the glide into the darkest spot I could find away from any town and go over the side. After I was clear of Augusta and had settled down, howev

billeted in Beningborough Hall, ancestral home of the Countess of Chesterfield. Their only problem was that the nearest pub, The Alice Hawthorn, lay on the far side of the River Ouse. The ferryman charged two pence to row them across but, to bring them back after nine o'clock at night, he was likely to raise his fee to half-a-crown. Since the alternative was swimming, or a ten mile detour via Aldwark Bridge, the ferryman was usually paid.

Strange as it may seem to those unacquainted with the weird anomalies of military life, it was possible to find, here and there in England, a certain type of individual whose rigid views on discipline, formed in pre-war service, remained unaltered by the circumstances of war. Such a man would be affronted by the sight of people walking, or merely standing still, with their hands in their pockets: if it pleased him to address them he would insist that they assumed a position of attention (or "took a brace"); he would expect to be saluted by those of lower rank on every possible occasion, and would be constantly distressed by the casual attire adopted by some aircrew. One such commander decreed that all ground staff, before they entered the airmen's mess for lunch, should change out of overalls and into regulation dress. Bravely and sensibly, the "erks" ignored the order and, faced with charging a thousand men with disobedience, the despot rescinded it.

Air Vice-Marshal Donald Bennett, the RAF Pathfinder chief, calling unannounced on the CO of one of his airfields, came upon another instance of this dinosaurian attitude. The CO was about to hear a disciplinary charge against an airman who had contravened standing orders by walking on the grass on his way from the photographic hut to the squadron office. Bennett, a no-nonsense Australian, took it on himself to

intervene. "Tell me," he said, "what is the direct route between these two places?" That, it was admitted, lay across the grass. Bennett made it known that in his view any man in No. 8 Group who did not take the shortest route between two points was guilty of sabotaging the war effort. The charge was dismissed.

Let us imagine that a veteran has decided to undertake a journey. Call it sentimental, call it a nostalgia trip—one last look, perhaps, at the field he used to fly from. The folks at home have tried to talk him out of it. "Never go back," they said, "you'll be disappointed. It's best to keep your memories." Maybe they were right, and he can't explain the reason for his pilgrimage: there is no shrine to kneel at, no healing waters, no special anniversary, but he has set his heart on it, and here he is. At least, he thinks he is. According to the map, this is

the airfield road, but where is the airfield? He drives slowly on, looking for a signpost. There is none. Suddenly, he recognizes something in the landscape: the hulk of a windmill on the rising ground to westward, the steeple of the village church and the line of poplars leading to the manor house. He has found his airfield. It is quite a moment. He pulls onto the verge and steps out of the car.

Standing at the roadside, while the sparrows chirrup and dart from hedge to hedge beside him, he finds it hard to believe that the months he spent here, in this peaceful, pastoral part of England, were the most demanding, the most frightening, and the most exciting of his life. Sure, there have been some moments since, some thrills and frights and traumas, but nothing to compare with what he went through then. That wartime experience was of a different order, and it all happened to him here.

er, it turned into a lovely joy ride. Just purred along. I followed the course lights to Steedman and then did 180 degrees back to Augusta and went out to Greensboro. This town is right near Silvan, where there is an airport. Checked by radio with Silvan and came on back. The whole trip took two hours and five minutes, 240 miles. I doubt if I'll ever be content with a car again!

Monday, 5 April 1943
An announcement came over the P.A. system that Class 43-E will be measured for uniforms in the next three evenings, so someone is gambling that most of us will qualify. Now that I'm over the physical exam and will be checked out tomorrow as a pilot, I feel fairly sure of making the grade.

far left: The 1944 Pub Crawler, a clever creation of these ground-pounders on an American air base in Britain; left: Bikes often proved to be the most useful way to cover the vast distances on a World War Two airfield.

Thursday, 8 April 1943
The AT-10 is a Beechcraft manufacture. Each engine develops 280 hp at 2,200 RPM at sea level. It is underpowered and doesn't have sufficient wing area. If a man is careful and watches his glides and air speed, he shouldn't have any trouble. Two boys were killed this noon, and a half hour later both engines went dead on take-off on another ship from the main field and the boys came in on the belly with no physical damage to themselves. Either they weren't careful in this cockpit procedure or there was something wrong with the gas lines. I'm the checkingest guy on the field!

Friday, 23 April 1943
What a swell way to see the country. Of course, Georgia is monotonously just the same. Fir trees, poor farms, heavier trees following river beds and swamp land. There is a perpetual haze and then the dull grey of soft coal smoke hangs over all up to around 5,000 feet.
  Night flying in the crate will not be so hard once I get on to it. My first landing last night was so hard my teeth still ache from the jar. I flew it right into the runway. The next time I came in too hot and used up the full runway for landing, whereas in a good landing about one-third of the strip should be sufficient. I also grew lax on one of my take-off checks and took off with full flaps. There is a danger of not getting off at all with so much flap because of the

He walks along the road a way and tries to find his bearings. He recognized the landscape, but all the rest is different. The paths he used to follow are no longer here. He seems to remember that his billet stood beside a copse of trees—oak, he thinks, and alder, or was that at some other place? Anyway, he finds no copse like that. Okay, perhaps he'll find the mess. It was an H-shaped structure, he recalls, two big huts connected by a smaller one, lying about a half-mile from where the airfield taxiway passed between the ops block and the flying control tower. Surely, there will be some sign of that. There isn't.

Baffled for the moment, the veteran takes a rest. He leans against a fence and tries to remember the way things used to be. It isn't easy. So many things have happened since those days. He was a single man then, barley nineteen years of age. Boy, he was green, and so were all the other guys—they had no conception of what they'd gotten into, flying in heavy bombers. That first briefing! Really scary. Matter of fact, they were all pretty scary. And that CO, the tough one. "Forget about the future," he told them, "because you don't have one. What you've got is this day, this squadron, and this mission." Something like that. What the hell was that guy's name? He can't quite remember. The operations officer, he remembers, the chaplain, the ground crew chief—who else? Not many, apart from his own crew. He remembers them, and always will—the way they stuck together, the way that they came through. They did have a future, after all. He was really close to them. Apart from his mother, and Mary Ellen and the kids, he had never been so close to anyone. He wonders if anyone nowadays ever feels that way about a bunch of other guys.

increased drag. After that, there is the danger of one flap tearing off. In this case the plane spins in. It is not a habit-forming procedure and the instructor was disgusted.

far left: A lovely field of linseed fronts the old control tower at RAF Wickenby in Lincolnshire, England, wartime home to the Lancaster crews of No 12 Squadron; left: The officers' mess at Scampton; lower left: A 100BG crew just back to their Thorpe Abbotts base after a raid.

Wednesday, 16 June 1943 Five men burned to death just off the end of the SE runway. It happened early this morning on take-off. Some say it got into the air, others say it never left the ground. At any rate, before it could be stopped, the nose wheel folded, and it piled up on its nose. A fire started in the number three engine, but didn't spread for fifteen minutes.

The way those fifteen minutes were wasted by the crash crew and the fire department was nothing short of murder. The civilian firemen wouldn't go near without asbestos suits and these weren't handy. The crash crew debated on how to get the men out. It is known that at least the flight engineer was alive because he talked to a sergeant who finally took an axe and started to chop a hole in the fuselage. This sergeant hardly got started when the fire exploded an oxygen tank. He is in the hospital severely burned. The engineer was blown out and lived to reach the hospital.

The fire spread with a vengeance after this explosion. The Goddamn civilians ran back to start spraying their chemical foam. Naturally, it was too late. Three captains and two enlisted men are dead because of such bungling. We can only hope that investigation from Southeast Headquarters will help to remedy this idea of having disinterested, yellow-bellied civilians running the fire department on Army fields.

I didn't know any of the men involved. They were upper classmen in another squadron. But we are all feeling badly about it. We only hope that, because accidents run in threes, the end of this cycle came today. There have been two other bad ones in the past month. One just before we came.

"Navigators came out to the flight line and picked up their equipment after everybody else had been and gone. They'd load us in a jeep and take us out to the airplanes. One night the driver had delivered everybody and I said 'Hey, what about me?' And the driver said 'You mean I've still got somebody?' He had this little walkie-talkie, and he found out my plane was way over on the other side of the field. It was ten or fifteen minutes before take-off. I've never been so scared, going around that field with the jeep's lights blacked out and the driver going like a bat out of hell. I got in the airplane through the waist door, while they were warming up the engines, and I lost my hat. When we got back I asked the crew chief, but he hadn't found it. I walked back about 150 feet behind the plane and found it in the grass."
- W.W. Ford, 92nd Bomb Group

"I bought a bike about a week after we arrived. I paid £11 and had to buy the accessories, lights, pump and a couple of tools. I was robbed, but it is new, and we haven't had any use for money . . . today was actually sunny and we did some cycling. These English saddles just don't give, and my fanny is in a delicate condition. Have to build up callouses, I guess."
-Keith Newhouse, pilot, 467th Bomb group

"It was so muddy at Deopham Green that you had to carry your bicycle."
- Sam Young, bombardier, 452nd Bomb Group

The corporal rides in a jeep,
The sergeant rides in a truck,
The captain rides in a limousine,
But we're plumb out of luck.

KEEP 'EM FLYING

Monday, 21 June 1943
I can now say I've really flown the B-24. O'Leary and myself were checked out this morning. Dillman, our instructor, spent the better half of the morning, making us land with two and three engines. He'd pull back a throttle on take-off and make us gain altitude and fly that way for a time. It was a workout in this heat, but surely made our solo hop, with everything functioning, seem simple. We even shot a no-flap landing. This means you fly the ship to the ground at 150 mph and stall out just over the runway at about 130. It is a pretty hot proposition, and burns up a lot of brakes and rubber stopping on the mile-plus runway. Of course, we just set it down, and took off, following through.

Saturday, 26 June 1943
Yesterday was an all-round red letter day. I was visiting one of my friends in another barracks where I discovered two vacant rooms. He offered to help me move, so move I did. I now have a pillow, a chair, a lovely bed, quantities of boiling hot water, better showers, better wash bowls, a barber shop right across the hall, a

When the first contingents of the US Army Air Force arrived in England in 1942, they were met with friendship, every possible assistance and a certain scepticism. The Americans made it known from the start that they intended to pursue a policy of precision bombing, essentially in daylight, trusting in the fire-power of their massed formations to fight their way through the defenses, and in the accuracy of the Norden bombsight to hit their targets on the nose. In this, they were determined to succeed where the RAF bomber crews, with their weaker armament and less effective bombsights, had gallantly tried but admittedly had failed.

Despite all British doubts, a few early setbacks and some appalling losses, the Americans persevered and, once their escort fighters were equipped with extra fuel tanks to extend their range, succeeded in attacking targets throughout the length and breadth of Germany. While the unescorted British bombers, apart from some spectacular attacks on pin-point targets at low level, steadfastly sustained their long campaign of saturation bombing in the hours of darkness, the USAAF grew in potency and strength. It mounted, conjointly with the RAF, the massive "round the clock" onslaught which increasingly dislocated the German war economy and cleared the Luftwaffe from the skies of Europe so successfully that the allied armies were able to land in Normandy without a crippling death toll, to thrust on into Germany and eventually, with the massive assistance of the Russian Army, to bring the Third Reich down.

The effort was colossal, the outcome was decisive, and the fliers who achieved it have been rightly wreathed in glory. It should never be forgotten that the administrative, technical and logistic effort it took to keep them flying was just as important and equally successful.

The crumbling
flying-control tower
at RAF Bovingdon
in Buckinghamshire.

Each heavy bomber was serviced by a ground staff—a flightline crew of fitters and mechanics working on the hardstands where the aircraft were dispersed—and a second echelon of specialists in engines and airframes, radio and radar, armament and ordnance, gasoline, oil and oxygen, instruments and emergency equipment, operating from hangars and workshops on the technical sites. For the more sophisiticated engineering operations, such as major overhauls, the base personnel were supported by another echelon of technicians at designated rear depots, provided for the Eighth Air Force by the Air Service Command, and for the RAF by Maintenance Command.

Supporting the technicians who worked on the aircraft were all the other services on base—flying control and weather staffs, interrogators, operations and intelligence officers, administrators, parachute packers, photo technicians, doctors and dentists, storemen, fire fighters, chaplains, military police, butchers, clerks and orderlies. For every bomber in the air, at least a hundred and fifty men and women were working on the ground.

"In terms of men and machines, the Eighth Air Force was the largest air striking force ever committed to battle." So wrote Roger A. Freeman, doyen of the Mighty Eighth's historians, and he continued: "The complexities of putting two thousand bombers and fighters in a single day over Hitler's Reich were extraordinary and might involve, directly and indirectlly, one hundred and fifty thousand men and women. The daily logistical requirements could be enormous: some three million gallons of fuel, four thousand tons of bombs and four and a half million rounds of ammunition to give just the major items."

Target Germany (one of the earliest and best

phone at the end of the hall, a coke machine, and this is a cooler barracks, having some insulation. Then I went over and got my friend, Sully. He is now in the room next to me.

Sunday, 11 July 1943
My buddy O'Leary and I rode as copilots the other night with a major who has more hours in the B-17 than any man living. He was checking himself out in a B-24 after fifteen hours. He handled the plane beautifully, had lots of stories about flying in combat areas and told us much about emergency procedures. He was rather cocky, but knew his stuff, so we sat back and listened, learning all we could. The B-24 is this Army's bomber until something bigger is perfected.

Lt Garlington, Lt Gettings, and Capt Riggs, their instructor, were all killed yesterday morning about two. No one knows what happened but the ship struck a hill southeast of the field and exploded. All the men were married. Hunt, the kid across the hall from me, got his this morning in the plane just ahead of me as we were taking off.

clockwise, far left: US president Franklin Roosevelt; 8AF CO Gen. James Doolittle; Col. Dale O. Smith, CO of the 384th BG; target planning files at 8AF HQ; and 8AF Gen. Ira Eaker.

Thursday, 22 July 1943, Gowen Field, Boise, Idaho Few of the Smyrna boys have flown since arrival. Neither Sully nor I have had the honor. We are going to get only ten hours a piece to be checked out, then given a crew, and on to second phase as first pilots. We may go to Wendover, Utah, a desolate place on the salt flats 120 miles south of Salt Lake City. Or maybe Pocatello, Idaho or Casper, Wyoming. The present push is for bomber pilots at all costs. Two hundred single-engine men just reported from Tallahassee, Fla. We left Smyrna as a bunch of B-26 pilots came in to learn to fly the B-24. Those single-engine boys are filled with righteous wrath as they are slated for copilot jobs. It is fun to hear them talk. They believe the '24' flies itself. I can hardly wait for their comments when they first try to taxi it. Some of them are waking up. I overheard a group discussing an introductory show they'd seen on cockpit procedure and the checklist. One said that it made the P-40 look like a kiddie-car. I hope none of them make the mistake of letting this job fly itself to a landing.

Monday, 26 July 1943 I flew with a 1st Lt Good. He was a wonderful guy who put the ship in my full control. I got the crew together, saw that the ship

right: B-17Gs of the 381st Bomb Group, over the English midlands.

official histories of the USAAF in Great Britain), provided a selection of statistics: "If one man eats six pounds of food a day (and he does on a bomber station), 150,000 men eat 450 tons of food a day. If one man consumes one-half pound of candy and cigarettes a day (and he does on a bomber station), 150,000 men will require more than thirty-six tons a day. If one man needs three ounces of soap a day to keep himself, his socks and his dishes clean (and he does on a bomber station), 150,000 men will need more than sixteen tons of soap a day."

Many of these products had to be transported over thousands of miles, and the air forces depended on a multitude of manufacturers and carriers to maintain supplies. Without the workers in the factories, the oil wells and the farms, without the ferry seamen who brought the cargoes across the dangerous Atlantic, the great air offensive could never have been mounted, and there would have been no missions for the bomber men to fly. The supply never faltered, despite the deprivations of the prowling U-boat packs, and the air campaign went on.

At a USAAF bomber base, the first indication of a pending operation is the "mission alert" message: it comes through in the late afternoon on the scrambler telephone from Wing Headquarters to the duty officer in the group operations centre. The duty operations clerk relays the message to all the people on the base who have the need to know: in turn, the Group commanding officer, the air executive, the intelligence and operations officers, the navigation, bombardier and weather officers, flying control, the ordnance, armament and engineering sections, the signals and photographic units, the mess hall, the motor pool, and the CQ (charge of quarters) on each aircrew living site. Military police are posted at the ops and war

room doors, the telephone exchange clamps down on outside calls, and squadron personnel are restricted to base.

Soon, more mission data clatters through the teleprinters; the squadron operations officers assign crews and airplanes to their formations, and the technical officers plan the allocation of materiel. The mission is beginning to take shape, and every man and woman on the base has a part in mounting it. The assigned airplanes, plus a couple of reserves, are serviced and loaded with fuel and oxygen, bombs and ammunition; the combat crews are warned to expect an early call, their pre-mission meals are planned and the in-flight rations are prepared; transport is ordered for the pilot, navigator, and bombardier of the group lead plane and their deputies to attend initial briefings at the Wing Headquarters, while the specialist group officers make ready for the main briefing on the base; runways and taxi-ways are inspected and cleared of any debris; decisions are made about take-off and assembly times;

top left: 8AF HQ at Wycombe Abbey; top centre: London statue of RAF Bomber Command CO, Sir Arthur Harris; above: German U-boat pens at La Pallice, France.

was serviced and then wound it up. There were a few things different about procedure, but we discussed the merits of each system, and there was no feeling of there being only one way to do a thing. I did a fair job of flying and at all times felt at ease. After a couple of landings, Good got out and let the copilot sit in his seat. After we got in the air, I turned it over to the copilot and got to talking to Good. He had put ten months in in the Aleutians. No wonder he was so confident and at ease; he knew what he was doing! He's flown the B-24 for a year now and thinks it's the best. This from a man who has flown the B-17 proves again why the Army has decided on '24s for time.

Then, I let the copilot take the ship down to pattern altitude, and I landed it. I had a complete crew today, but it was only for the day. Good said he would mark me as being checked out, so in a few days I will get a crew.

radio codes, emergency procedures and pyrotechnic signals are selected; the crash, fire and ambulance teams are alerted; the chaplains are notified, so are the public relations officer, the motor pool, the airdrome defence force . . .

The bombers leave the ground at thirty-second intervals. The air reverberates with the sound of their engines as they climb in race track patterns through the lowering cloud banks to join the other bomb groups at the wing assembly points. The roar of the Wright Cyclone engines becomes a heavy drone as the air armada sets course to the east; gradually it dwindles to a distant hum, until at last it dies away. Comparative silence falls upon East Anglia, and the base comes back to life.

Now is the time for everyday affairs: for patching damaged aircraft and overhauling others, for a replacement crew to fly a practice mission, for catching up on paper work and domestic chores, for calibrating instruments, for replenishing the bomb dump, the fuel tanks and the ammunition stores, for cleaning up the mess halls and preparing the next meal, for distributing the mail and reading *Stars and Stripes*, for putting fresh flowers in vases at the Aeroclub, for pasting amendments into service manuals, for chewing out the men who have offended against Army Regulations, for responding to complaints about the noisy airplanes (and possibly a few about the noisy airmen), for mending fences and re-painting gate-posts, foraging for coal supplies, clearing snow or mowing grass (depending on the season), for inducting new arrivals, for the chaplain to visit patients in the sick bay, for the adjutant to write to someone's grieving parents, and for all the other matters that are the daily business of the base. It is also, for some, a time for silent prayer.

The hours pass, the time draws near for the bombers to return; again, the sky is the focus of attention. Men congregate at the flying control tower, leaning on the railing of the balcony and standing on the roof, crew chiefs and mechanics squat on dispersal pans all around the field, and ground staffers gather outside hangars, offices and workshops; the crash crews man their vehicles and the ambulance stands by. All eyes are turned towards the east, and everyone is waiting for the first sight of the bombers and the words "They're coming in."

They come over the horizon, squadron by squadron, element by element, still in their formations, although there are some gaps; they peel off in sequence, join the traffic pattern and slide down the approach. The watchers start counting: six, twelve, eighteen . . . they count up to thirty, and then there are the stragglers. One comes in with the starboard outer engine out, another with a tail-plane fluttering in shreds, and the last with only half its landing gear. It touches down beside the runway, skids sideways for a while and slithers to a halt: the fire truck, the ambulance and a pair of jeeps are alongside as soon as it has stopped.

Telling one another that the missing bombers may have landed some place else, the watchers turn away, and the base goes back to work. It will be the same tomorrow, and for many more tomorrows. They must keep the warplanes flying for as long as they are needed, for as long as it takes to set the lands of Europe free.

"Power is not revealed by striking hard or often, but by striking true." -Balzac

"If you are not receiving my transmissions, please fire a red flare." -Pilot Officer Prune, on approaching base.

left: Headquarters of Third Air Division, Eighth Air Force, at Elveden Hall near Thetford in Norfolk; above: The bomber's view of the sub pens at La Pallice under heavy attack by B-17s of the Eighth.

TAKE GOOD CARE OF MY AEROPLANE

Thursday, 5 August 1943
The PDI (pilot's directional indicator) is a simple instrument. It has a blunt pointer and a dot. When I'm exactly on the bomb run, the pointer rests on the dot. It is very delicate, and takes very little skidding movements of the rudders to get off or on. Besides keeping the PDI centred, the pilot has to maintain his altitude within forty feet and his air speed can't vary five mph either way. It was smooth this morning, so I didn't have much trouble. But in rough weather and through flak . . .

right: Fitting tail fins and fuses to bombs on a 91st Bomb Group B-17 at its Bassingbourn base in Cambridgeshire.

When a crew were first assigned to a bomb squadron from an Eighth Air Force Combat Crew Replacement Center or an RAF Heavy Conversion Unit, they seldom flew the same aircraft twice in succession. They might like one better than another: no one cared. They flew whatever came along. But once they were established, after maybe ten or twelve missions, they rated more consideration: same aircraft, same ground crew, same hardstand or dispersal. They might have to fly another aircraft while their own was being repaired or under major servicing but, thereafter, it was generally accepted that *Piccadilly Lady* or *C for Charlie* was their plane. Technically speaking, she might not be the finest on the field: she might try to ground-loop in the slightest cross-wind, she might wallow like a lugger at certain heights and airspeeds, her number three engine might always run a little warm, her magnetic compass might need swinging after every trip, but none of that could matter less. Hadn't she brought them home from Schweinfurt (or from Nuremburg or Berlin) through all kinds of trouble? The aircrew were agreed: she was the best damn aircraft on the base.

The flight line mechanics knew she wasn't that. But they, too, had a stake in her, and they understood the way the fliers felt. True, they never knew the icy stab of fear in her, and they didn't have to bleed in her—at any rate, not much—but she was as much their aircraft as she was the fliers', and they used all their skill to ensure that she never let either of them down.

The Australians of No. 460 Squadron had an aircraft which never disappointed any of the twenty-seven crews who flew her to war: between December 6th 1942 and April 20th 1944, when she was at last put out to grass, the Mark 1 Lancaster G-George completed ninety operations. She was hit twenty times in combat,

and once, above the target, by an incendiary from a bomber overhead, but her worst injuries were suffered standing in dispersal on July 3rd 1943, when the detonation of a "cookie" falling from the bomb-bay of a nearby aircraft began a conflagration; on that occasion, the damage to G-George took six weeks to repair. By the end of 1943, G-George had flown 76 missions, and the legend had developed among the Aussie crews that if you flew G-George you were certain to return. The RAF technician who checked her over on arrival, and kept her flying from then on, was Flight Sergeant Harry Tickle. "I took a personal interest in G-George," he said, "She bore a lot of scars, and no one ever counted all the flak holes."

G-George, however, was by no means the champion survivor: 103 Squadron's M-Mother, for example, completed 140 operations, including ninety-eight to Germany and fifteen to Berlin. A grateful nation broke her up for scrap in 1947. 550 Squadron's *Phantom of the Ruhr* survived 121 missions, and her fate was the same. The Aussies made sure that the G-George legend didn't end that way. When the war was over, they flew her to Canberra, where she was proudly mounted in the Aeroplane Hall of the Australian War Memorial, and she stands there to this day.

For reasons of security, the ground crews were not told the location of the target (although sometimes it leaked out), and even USAAF combat gunners didn't always know where they were going until they were in the air, but the mechanics could judge the flight duration from the fuel load, and sometimes the demeanor of the fliers gave a clue as to what sort of mission they expected it to be; certainly, the preparations for a "milk run" over France and for a long flight into Germany created different

top left: Maintenance on Lancaster; top right: Refuelling a B-17G; right: Women at work assembling B-17Gs in 1944; far right: RAF armourers lugging a trolley-load of bombs to a waiting Handley Page Halifax bomber on an RAF station in Cambridgeshire; overleaf: Views of the *City of Lincoln* Avro Lancaster.

atmospheres. But be the target near or far, difficult or easy, the ground crew's preparations were the same—the aircraft had to be just right.

In line with the British tendency to establish clear distinctions between the high and low born, the vocations and professions, and between the skilled and semi-skilled among the manual workers, the RAF perpetuated the ground crew grades it had inherited from the days when aeroplanes were made of wire, wood and canvas, and when the "aircraftmen", in their khaki uniforms of high-buttoned tunics, breeches and puttees, attended either to the engine or the airframe, and were fitters or mechanics, according to proficiency. There were regulations as to which grade was qualified to undertake or supervise each technical inspection, and to sign the aircraft log to that effect. The USAAF, on the other hand, less inhibited by precedent, assigned a ground crew to each airplane and relied upon their initiative to keep it in good shape; if the crew chiefs were satisfied, it didn't really matter who did what.

Although their tasks might be confined to changing spark plugs in a Wright Cyclone, a Rolls-Royce Merlin or a Pratt & Whitney Wasp, to cleaning the oil filters and bleeding the hydraulics, to filling oil and fuel tanks, loading the bomb-bay, balancing the gyros, servicing the pneumatic and electric systems, or checking out the fuses and the circuit breakers, many an engine mechanic or an airframe fitter, an armourer or an electrician, an instrument, radar or radio technician, having carried out those tasks, would go on to fly the mission with the aircrew in his heart; many a mechanic stayed out on the hardstand, sitting on his tool-box, waiting for his aircraft to return; sometimes he stayed there until somebody told him it was no use waiting any more.

Friday, 6 August 1943
I'm gradually getting a crew. The way I began to realize it was by the fact that I started going up with the same copilot and radio operator. We checked up and sure enough, they were the nucleus. The copilot's name is Coyle. He struck me at first as being a rather argumentative gent, but I'm getting used to him, and he isn't a bad sort. We made our first flight solo this morning, and I think he'll be O.K. It was really his first time in the copilot's seat. Here, the instructor pilot always rides in the co-pilot's seat and that poor gentleman has to learn his job by standing back of the seats. Naturally, I was a little dubious of how he'd do, but all went well. I took things slow, he was rather clumsy and had too many thumbs, but didn't get excited. A couple rides will make him all right.

The radio operator is a fellow named Wentz. He knows his radio and is a hard, plodding worker. I believe he will do a good job. I'll have no complaints about him, I'm sure.

Yesterday afternoon I was trying hard to catch a few winks when a fellow came in and asked if I was Newhouse. After I said, 'Right', he introduced himself. 'I'm Simpson, your bombardier!' Surprise. I hadn't even heard I had a bombardier. He is a slender-built guy and is from St Louis. He moved in when he found I had plenty of room (Sully and my other two roommates

The assistant engineer's name is Twogood. He's from Spokane, and just a short while ago I signed a 24-hour pass for him. His folks and girl friend are in Boise until tomorrow. I like him. A good, conscientious kid whom I'll gladly groom for first engineer if Wilhite doesn't pan out.

It's great for the morale. The day I leave here, if I have a full crew, I will then begin to think maybe we can stick together. All except the copilot. If he is any good and wants it, I have to recommend him for first pilot. Which means leaving this country with a very green man or some lesser sort of guy. Am I growing a little bitter? I can still laugh and think, 'Oh, what the hell! Maybe it's for the best.'

Thursday, 12 August 1943
Wilhite, the first engineer, was in his glory. He knows the guns, thank God, and loves to fire. The radio man was having fun with the nose gun, but everyone else was sick. Three men were making use of the toilet. Walking through, I thought of the street scenes after a battle. Men grotesquely sprawled in every position.

The rounds had to be fired, so I crawled into the rear turret and got pretty good with it before I was through. Then I tried the flexible waist guns. They're hard to operate because of the pitching and tossing and the pressure of the slipstream against them. The only casualty was the

guess a few of them were new. The only way you'd know was if you looked at the form. That would tell you how many hours were on the airplane, who had checked what and what was wrong with it, but you never looked. There were other things to worry about."

Warplanes, like people, had their own personalities and their own peculiarities. Some were models of behavior: if you filled them with gas and lubricants and sent them off to fly they gave no trouble at all; some needed more than average attention: every flight seemed to bring another little problem; others were peculiarly vulnerable to weather—ice in the carburetors, freezing up of gun oil, moisture causing the radios to act up. And there were recidivist aircraft, which constantly reverted to vices that nothing and nobody could cure. The aircrew would report a static-ridden intercom, an overspeeding prop, or a tail-wheel shimmy, which somehow failed to happen when the mechanic, having done all he could to fix it on the flight line, at last asked if he could try it in the air.

No matter how much care the ground crew might take of an aircraft, some flight crews were always prone to accidents—they were forever breaking pieces that needed replacement or repair. Worse, a show-off pilot could undo all their work. Crew chief Ira Eakin witnessed such an incident when he was based at Atcham, deep in rural Shropshire. "One of the hangars stood out there by itself, and we had the doors open to air it out. This Spitfire came over—it was before we got the Thunderbolts—and he made a couple of passes at that hangar, and pulled up before he got to it. He dragged the field twice, and then the third time he was right on the ground with that Spit and he was really throwing the coal to it, heading straight towards the hangar. Just before he got to it, I

guess he chickened out, and tried to pull up. He hit that thing just above the doors and it really wiped him out. There were some English Clerk of Works people—kind of like our civil service and they were out there putting in the runway lights. They were watching this Spit, and one of them turned around and said 'Well, that would have been a bloody good trick, if he'd pulled it off.' "

The USAAF crew chiefs and their RAF equivalents not only provided skilled supervision on the hardstands but a vital link between the air and ground crews. The fact, however, that they were generally older and with longer service than the combat fliers, and their experience of life considerably greater, did not always guarantee that they were models of rectitude. "Our new crew chief", pilot Keith Newhouse noted, "is a capable fellow and loves engines. He has been in the Army eighteen years, but he has a record for losing stripes because of bottle bouts. He's been a Tech and a Master Sergeant a couple of times, and at present he's a Corporal—I think. He never wears chevrons, because of all those sudden changes, I imagine. The ground crew are all a man could ask, and that is half the battle, so we should do all right."

There are many instances of an Eighth Air Force crew chief flying on a mission with the combat crew; his RAF colleague, however, very rarely did. Space was more restricted in an RAF heavy bomber, and everybody had to earn his keep. While the American could make himself useful with a machine gun in a Flying Fortress or a Liberator, the RAF man's only option was to act as flight engineer. That would not find favor with the regular incumbent, who would miss the operation, and so have to fly as a "spare bod" with another crew to complete his tour.

radio antenna. The top gunner shot it away on one of his first bursts.

Each time we work together I get to like my crew better. Wilhite, the chief engineer, is proving himself to be quite capable and is learning rapidly about the '24. I kind of lead him on each day by going over something I'm not quite sure of myself and seeing how little or much he knows. We both learn this way. I'm anxious to have the best engineer possible.

Friday, 13 August 1943
I was assigned two gunners today. A big, blonde, West Chicago boy named Kobel. About twenty years old and still growing. He will be huge when he stops. Meanwhile, he sort of gets in his own way with his new large frame. The other new man will be our Tail-end Charlie. Ravetti is a small, dark, sinewy Italian. Just right for the turret. I think he is a real addition to the crew. Knows the guns inside out and worked on the line with B-26s.

top: Gunners of the 388BG cleaning their .50 calibre weapons after a raid; left: The Consolidated B-24 *Shoot Luke*, a veteran of 27 missions with the 93rd BG based at Hardwick, Norfolk in April 1943.

above: A B-24J instrument panel; right: A J-hangar at the Chelveston base of the 305th BG; top right: A cotter pin and tag from a 379th BG bomb; centre right: A squadron patch from the A2 flight jacket of an 8AF airman; One of four Wright 1820 engines of the B-17G Flying Fortress.

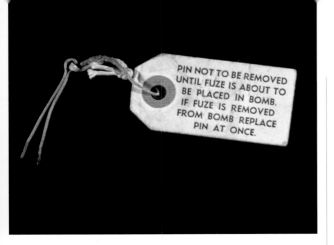

The aircrew, furthermore, had together practiced the procedures for bailing out and ditching, and in those emergencies a ground crew man, unfamiliar with the drills, might jeopardize the safety of the crew. There was also this harsh but inescapable consideration: an experienced senior noncom in a technical trade would be harder to replace than a flight engineer.

There have always been loners in any human group, and there always will be, but most men like the feeling of belonging to a team, of mutual endeavor, of sharing together in hardship and in danger. We call it the team spirit or *esprit de corps*, and it is conducive to a high morale. The feeling of comradeship in a front-line ground crew was probably as strong as within a flying crew, and their sense of loyalty to the unit—the squadron or the group—was likely to be stronger, because the fliers' combat tour seldom lasted longer than six months (and sadly often less), after which they would be "screened" or "rotated" and assigned somewhere else, whereas, apart from training, the ground crew men were likely to spend all their wartime service with one unit and sometimes on one base.

When at last the bombs stopped falling and the guns fell silent in 1945, thousands of aircraft became redundant overnight, while technology, preternaturally developed in the forcing house of war, continued to march on. More advanced aircraft, already on the drawing board, moved through production lines and into squadron service—bigger, better bombers, more formidable fighters. Gradually, the Fortresses and Liberators, Lancasters and Halifaxes, Marauders and Mosquitoes, Lightnings, Thunderbolts and Mustangs, Spitfires and Hurricanes were rendered obsolescent and, in due course, obsolete. Third world governments

Sunday, 15 August 1943
On this night check-out, I had a fine fellow as an instructor pilot. He turned it over to me, telling me to make a landing, then he'd make one, and then we'd cruise about a bit. Just as we made our first pass at the field, the tower told us to go around because of traffic. On the next try, our electrical system went out on the base leg. No radio or landing lights, so we had to go around again. When we got the lights on again, I greased one in. Lt Brown just said, 'Well, I won't be able to duplicate that, but we'll see.' He took over and did a fine job, but mine had been perfect. I felt mighty fine about that. After flying around for a time, letting the new copilot handle it a while, I brought it in for a landing that equaled Lt Brown's, just good, not perfect. I'm beginning to feel a lot of confidence about my landing ability, I guess now that I'm checked out at night, too.

Monday, 16 August 1943
Kobel was checking the bomb racks this morning and found a bad release. This was easily fixed on the ground and saved us much trouble in the air. Little things like that make us all feel more confidence in each other. Ravetti can really handle those gun malfunctions. I appointed Wentz, the radio operator, to check parachutes. The other morning he found three chutes out of twelve not right. We had eleven men flying that trip. It could have been embarrassing in the air. That's the

motto: 'The more trouble found on the ground, the less in the air.'

Thursday, 19 August 1943
I'm waiting for Will to come back and we're taking off for a full night in town. We have much to celebrate: completion of first phase, I passed an instrument check this morning, and we have a complete crew minus the navigator. We ship Saturday to Wendover, Utah, as I've predicted all along.

Sunday, 22 August 1943, Wendover, Utah
From Salt Lake City to Wendover is only a three or four-hour trip ordinarily, but we were hooked behind a freight and shunted back and forth between yards. Eleven hours later we reached Wendover with no breakfast, to find that due to some Goddamn inspection, only two trucks were there to meet us. They took our hand luggage and we marched to camp! The men were fed a half hour after reaching here, but what an introduction to this forlorn hole.

We're stuck up against some mountains that have all the romance and color of a slag pile. There is quite a railroad freight yard here with the camp close enough to catch the full benefit of the soot and coal. The enlisted men are assigned to tents, with the officers having charming 30-bed tarpaper shacks. These shacks are arranged around a community latrine affording all the privacy of Grand Central. Home Sweet

bought a number to form the nuclei of their emergent air arms; some hulks were posted as "gate guardians" at the entrances to bases, to stand at the mercy of the elements and as targets for bombing raids by every passing bird; a precious few were preserved in air museums. Most of the famous warplanes, however, were consigned to the scrap heap—"struck off charge". Melted down, the metal of many bombers was used in the construction of pre-fabricated homes for the millions of servicemen recently demobilized, and in the replacement of houses destroyed by enemy attack.

Of the great bombers, only two still fly from English fields. The RAF's Battle of Britain Memorial Flight, based at Coningsby in Lincolnshire, delights millions every summer with majestic, careful fly-pasts by the Lancaster *City of Lincoln*, usually escorted by a Spitfire and a Hurricane, and a private company, B-17 Preservation Limited, at Duxford near Cambridge (wartime home of the USAAF's 78th Fighter Group), proudly displays the Flying Fortress *Sally B*. From their appearances at air shows, on TV and in the movies, these veteran warplanes more than earn their keep.

"The good carpenter measures twice and saws once."
- Anon.

"Mechanical excellence is the only real vehicle of genius."
- William Blake

"The test of a vocation is the love of the drudgery it entails."
- C.P. Smith

Home for the next two months, prior to going overseas. As a fond remembrance of what we're fighting for, we can look out on these gray, soot-bedecked hovels, with alleys of gravel between them, the ugly rocks and smoke rising behind, and beyond that miles upon miles of dirty, salt-white desolation. Not a tree or blade of grass, with no life in view except an occasional buzzard, a scavenger who will be defeated in his search for putrified carrion because this waste is too dead even to furnish corruption. Even the lonely telephone poles are refusing to stay by shriveling away from the salt base they've been stuck in. There is a sickening feeling when one looks at so vast an area without scamper of some small animal or the bowing and waving of some vegetation. Just dull, stark white with abortional lumps rising here and there. I'll be here for about two months.

top and left: Two fine views of B-17s being cared for on their hardstands in World War Two England.

D FOR DOG

Last night, some of the young gentlemen of the RAF took me to Berlin. The pilot was called Jock. The crew captains walked into the briefing room, looked at the maps and charts and sat down with their big celluloid pads on their knees. The atmosphere was that of a school and a church. The pilots were reminded that Berlin is Germany's greatest center of war production. The intelligence officer told us how many heavy and light ack-ack guns; how many searchlights we might expect to encounter. Then, Jock, the wing commander, explained the system of marking, the kind of flares that would be used by the pathfinders. He said that concentration was the secret of success in these raids; that as long as the aircraft stayed well bunched, they would protect each other. The captains of aircraft walked out. I noticed that the big Canadian with the slow, easy grin had printed Berlin at the top of his pad and then embellished it with a scroll. The red-headed English boy with the two-weeks'-old moustache was the last to leave the room.

Late in the afternoon we went to the locker room to draw parachutes, Mae Wests and all the rest. As we dressed a couple of Australians were whistling. Walking out to the bus that was to take us to the aircraft, I heard the station loudspeakers announcing that that evening all personnel would be able to see a film: Star-Spangled Rhythm. Free.

We went out and stood around the big, black four-motored Lancaster, D for Dog. A small station wagon delivered a thermos bottle of coffee, chewing gum, an orange and a bit of chocolate for each man. Up in that part of England the air hums and throbs with the sound of aircraft motors all day, but for half an hour before take-off, the skies are dead, silent and expectant. A lone hawk hovered over the airfield, absolutely

Monday, 23 August 1943 These 2nd Air Force despots are the same ones who mapped the 24-hour program that was forced down our throats at Boise. The plan was this: starting at midnight until 4:00, we were to fly. From 4:00 to 8:00 was for Link training, Bomb Trainer or Navigational Trainer work. 8:00 to 12:00 was flying time. 12:00 to 13:00 was all our own time. From 13:00 to 17:00 was school. From 17:00 to 24:00 (midnight) was for sleeping. Maybe we could also eat in that seven hours, although it was never mentioned. That was the program our operational officer had to try to rationalize. And, by God, they followed it as closely as human and machine endurance would allow. Some men actually turned themselves in to the flight surgeons, refusing to fly because they lacked sleep. At times I was ready to give up too.

left: The crew of Joe McCarthy, third from the right, the only American on the famous May 1943 Ruhr dams raid by No 617 Squadron.

above: A Merlin-28 Lancaster III in late 1944; above right: Sergeant Pilot Nick Kosciuk, a Polish member of RAF Bomber Command, with his Wellington aircraft.

still as he faced into the wind. Jack, the tail gunner, said, "It'd be nice to fly like that." D-Dog eased around the perimeter tract to the end of the runway. We sat there for a moment. The green light flashed and we were rolling . . . ten seconds ahead of schedule.

The takeoff was as smooth as silk. The wheels came up and D-Dog started the long climb. As we came up through the clouds I looked right and left and counted fourteen black Lancasters climbing for the place where men must burn oxygen to live. The sun was going down and its red glow made rivers and lakes of fire on the top of the clouds. Down to the southward, the clouds piled up to form castles, battlements and whole cities, all tinged with red.

Soon we were out over the North Sea. Dave, the navigator, asked Jock if he couldn't make a little more speed. We were nearly two minutes late. By this time we were all using oxygen. The talk on the intercom was brief and crisp. Everyone sounded relaxed. For a while, the eight of us, in our little world of exile, moved over the sea. There was a quarter moon on the starboard beam and Jock's quiet voice came through the intercom, "That'll be flak ahead."

We were approaching the enemy coast. The flak looked like a cigarette lighter in a dark room: one that won't light–sparks but no flame–the sparks crackling just below the level of the cloud tops. We flew steady and straight and soon the flak was directly below us. D-Dog rocked a little from right to left but that wasn't caused by the flak. We were in the slipstream of other Lancasters ahead and we were over the enemy coast. Then a strange thing happened. The aircraft seemed to grow smaller. Jack in the rear turret, Wally the mid-upper gunner, Titch the wireless operator, all seemed somehow to draw closer to Jock in the cockpit. It was as though each man's shoulder was against the others. The understanding was complete. The intercom came to life and Jock said, "Two aircraft on the port beam." Jack in the tail said, "Okay, sir. They're Lancs." The whole crew was a unit and wasn't wasting words. The cloud below was ten-tenths. The blue-green jet of the exhausts licked back along the wing and there were other aircraft all around us. The whole great aerial armada was hurtling toward Berlin. We flew so for twenty minutes, when Jock looked up at a vapour trail curling above

above: Outdoor engine maintenance on a Lancaster; top right: An October 1941 drawing by William Rothenstein of Sergeant P. Kirk, No. 226 Squadron, which operated the Blenheim bomber from RAF Wattisham, Suffolk, in late 1941; right: A messenger pigeon trained to return to its RAF base carrying a message from its downed bomber crew about their location relative to a rescue effort.

remarking in a conversational tone that, from the look of it, he thought there was a fighter up there. Occasionally the angry red of the ack-ack burst through the clouds, but it was far away and we took only an academic interest. We were flying in the third wave.

Jock asked Wally in the mid-upper turret, and Jack in the rear, if they were cold. They said they were all right and thanked him for asking. He even asked how I was and I said "All right so far." The cloud was beginning to thin out. Off to the north we could see lights and the flak began to liven up ahead of us. Buzz, the bomb-aimer, crackled through on the intercom, "There's a battle going on over on the starboard beam." We couldn't see the aircraft but we could see the jets of red tracer being exchanged. Suddenly, there was a burst of yellow flame and Jock remarked, "That's the fighter going down. Note the position." The whole thing was interesting, but remote. Dave, the navigator, who was sitting back with his maps, charts and compasses, said, "The attack ought to begin in exactly two minutes." We were still over the clouds.

But suddenly those dirty gray clouds turned white and we were over the outer searchlight defences. The clouds below us were white and we were black. D-Dog seemed like a black bug on a white sheet. The flak began coming up, but none of it close. We were still a long way from Berlin. I didn't realize just how far. Jock observed, "There's a kite on fire dead ahead." It was a great, golden, slow-moving meteor slanting toward the earth. By this time we were about thirty miles from our target area in Berlin. That thirty miles was the longest flight I have ever made.

Dead on time, Buzz the bomb-aimer reported, "Target indicators going down," At the same moment, the sky ahead was lit up by bright yellow flares. Off to starboard another kite went down in flames. The flares were sprouting all over the sky, reds and greens and yellows, and we were flying straight for the center of the fireworks. D-Dog seemed to be standing still, the four propellers thrashing the air, but we didn't seem to be closing in. The cloud had cleared and off to the starboard a Lanc was caught by at least fourteen searchlight beams. We could see him twist and turn and finally break out. But still, the whole thing had a quality of unreality about it. No one seemed to be shooting at us, but it was getting lighter all the time. Suddenly, a tremendous big bloc of yellow light appeared dead ahead; another to the right and another to the left. We were flying straight for them. Jock pointed out to me the dummy fires and flares to right and left, but we kept going in. Dead ahead there was a whole chain of red flares looking like stoplights. Another Lanc was coned on our starboard beam. The lights seemed to be supporting it. Again we could see those little bubbles of colored lead driving at it from two sides. The German fighters were at him. And then, with no warning at all, D-Dog was filled with an unhealthy white light.

I was standing just behind Jock and could see all the seams on the wings. His quiet Scots voice beat in my ears, "Steady lads, we've been coned." His slender body lifted half out of the seat as he jammed the control column forward and to the left. We were going down. Jock was wearing woolen gloves with the fingers cut off. I could see his fingernails turn white as he gripped the wheel. And then I was on my knees, flat on the deck, for he had whipped the Dog back into a climbing turn. The knees should have been strong enough to support me, but they weren't, and the stomach seemed in some danger of letting me down too. I picked myself up and looked out again. It seemed that

Friday, 27 August 1943
I don't imagine some of the older Army men would approve of mingling so intimately with enlisted men, but by doing so I have found out several things I want to know. The boys all call me 'Sir' even now. A couple of times I've been approached about problems, personal things, that is, and I believe I'm gaining the respect I want from the crew. They are a swell gang, and as long as we're going to work so closely together when things get hot, I think many of the officer-enlisted men barriers have to be lifted.

Tuesday, 31 August 1943
There seems to be something wrong in the 2nd Air Force. Eighty-four men have been killed in the past ten days. Crack-ups at Pocatello, Boise, Mountain Home and Wendover.

Friday, 17 September 1943
This place is driving us all mad. It is a hell of a place to have little or nothing to do. But that is the situation. We are scheduled for some ground training. There are no instructors around, no organized classes, so we try to pick up a little here and there. This morning we got some good pointers on radio equipment. I put in two hours on Link. We tried to get a little engineering this afternoon and wound up playing pool and bowling. No one is doing much flying. I wonder what the devil it is all

about and when we start getting to work!

Wednesday, 22 September 1943
We wound up a terrific day yesterday by flying only three hours. It was another new ship but had a few things wrong with it, nevertheless. The co-pilot's instrument light wouldn't work so we had to use a flashlight to read the engine instruments. The left-hand nosewheel door wouldn't close. This caused a vibration in the ship that was disconcerting and dangerous for the boys who had to climb into the nose compartment. Engines number one and four ran quite hot.

Thursday, 23 September 1943
Try wearing an oxygen mask for three or four hours at 20,000 feet with the temperature around zero. It is anything but comfortable. Heavy clothes, parachute harness, mask, earphones, safety belt, throat mike, all make you feel like you are wound up in Government red tape.

one big searchlight, instead of being twenty thousand feet below, was mounted right on our wing tip. D-Dog was corkscrewing. As we rolled down on the other side I began to see what was happening to Berlin.

The clouds were gone and the sticks of incendiaries from the preceding waves made the place look like a badly laid-out city with the street lights on. The small incendiaries were going down like a fistful of white rice thrown on a piece of black velvet. As Jock hauled the Dog up again, I was thrown to the other side of the cockpit. And there below were more incendiaries, glowing white and then turning red. The cookies, the four-thousand-pound high explosive [bombs], were bursting below like great sunflowers gone mad. And then, as we started down again, still held in the lights, I remembered that the Dog still had one of those cookies and a whole basket of incendiaries in his belly, and the lights still held us, and I was very frightened.

While Jock was flinging us about in the air, he suddenly yelled over the intercom, "Two aircraft on the port beam." I looked astern and saw Wally, the mid-upper, whip his turret around to port, and then looked up to see a single-engine fighter slide just above us. The other aircraft was one of ours. Finally, we were out of the

top left: The crew of a Short Stirling heavy bomber; A Lancaster pilot and his flight engineer.

cone, flying level. I looked down and the white fires had turned red. They were beginning to merge and spread, just like butter does on a hot plate. Jock and Buzz, the bomb-aimer, began to discuss the target. The smoke was getting thick down below. Buzz said he liked the two green flares on the ground almost dead ahead. He began calling his directions. Just then a new bunch of big flares went down on the far side of the sea of flame that seemed to be directly below us. He thought that would be a better aiming point. Jock agreed and they flew on.

The bomb doors were opened. Buzz called his directions: "Five left, five left." And then, there was a gentle, confident upward thrust under my feet and Buzz said, "Cookie gone." A few seconds later, the incendiaries went, and D-Dog seemed lighter and easier to handle. I thought I could make out the outline of streets below, but the bomb-aimer didn't agree, and he ought to know. By this time, all those patches of white on black had turned yellow and started to flow together. Another searchlight caught us but didn't hold us. Then, through the intercom came the word, "One can of incendiaries didn't clear. We're still carrying it." And Jock replied, "Is it a big one or a little one?" The word came back, "Little one I think." Finally, the intercom

Friday, 24 September 1943

From all I can gather, we are going to fly all missions from here on at high altitude. This means, generally, around 20,000 feet. Flying at altitude is simply hard labour. It is awfully cold, for one thing. The cabin and nose are supposed to be heated, but the heaters are forever blowing fuses and, if working, smoke and fume so that they give no comfort. Then, as I have mentioned, there's the oxygen mask, which must be tight to be good. This causes a squeeze and discomfort after a few hours. Ice has the habit of forming around the edges of the mask. To keep from frostbite, it is necessary to rub the face under the rubber every so often. Too, a constant check on the oxygen supply and the regulator must be made. A heavy rubber hose with a clasp attachment to be clipped on the clothes is the carrier of the oxygen from the regulator to the mask. This often gets in the way of quick movement. If a man needs to walk around a little he gets a 'walk-around' bottle. This is a small supply of oxygen in a metal container, which lasts from five to twenty minutes, depending on the altitude and the amount of work the man does. But there isn't much moving done. The clothes necessary to keep warm are so cumbersome that you just sit as much as possible.

The other night I had to go up with a new helmet that was too tight when I put the earphones in the

announced that it was only a small container of incendiaries left, and Jock remarked, "Well, it's hardly worth going back and doing a run up for that." If there had been a good fat bundle left, he would have gone back through that stuff and done it all over again. I began to breathe, and to reflect again that all men would be brave if only they could leave their stomachs at home, when there was a tremendous *whoomph*, an unintelligible shout from the tail gunner, and D-Dog shivered and lost altitude. I looked to the port side and there was a Lancaster that seemed close enough to touch. He had whipped straight under us; missed us by twenty-five, fifty feet, no one knew how much.

The navigator sang out the new course and we were heading for home. Jock was doing what I had heard him tell his pilots to do so often–flying dead on course. He flew straight into a huge green searchlight, and as he

cups on the side of the helmet. My ears were pressed so hard against my head that I had to take the damn thing off after a couple of hours. I've remedied that. Then there is the throat mike. This little gadget has to be pressed against the Adam's apple to get a good transmission. Another annoyance.

The interphone systems aren't always in good shape and even the best ones are affected by high altitude. It is often necessary to repeat an order two or three times so a man can understand. The radio generates a great deal of static up there, too, which makes bombing range contact difficult. Sometimes the static garbles things so badly it is next to impossible to distinguish the words. Or maybe someone's throat mike has been damaged. This ruins transmission. Then, if a transmission button sticks in the 'on' position, the static and whistling gives you the screaming jitters.

top left: The air crew memorial at RAF Wickenby; top right: The control tower at RAF Tholthorpe, a Halifax base in Yorkshire; far left: The art deco tower at RAF Lindholme; left: Gooseneck flares at RAF Elvington, used to light runways.

Friday, 1 October 1943 Today we completed our clothing issue for overseas. We even got some field equipment, A small first aid kit, a super bandage in a metal kit, and our tin helmets. The helmet has a plastic liner which allows the metal to be slipped on or off easily. This way it can be used as a wash basin or a container. In completing the clothing, I had to get three sets of long winter woolies, the kind I used to laugh at Grandpa for wearing–a shirt stuck into a drawstring pair of pants.

rammed the throttles home he remarked, "We'll have a little trouble getting away from this one." Again, D-Dog dove, climbed and twisted, and was finally free. We flew level then. I looked out on the port beam at the target area. There was a red, sullen, obscene glare. The fires seemed to have found each other . . . and we were heading home.

For a little while it was smooth sailing. We saw more battles. Then another plane in flames, but no one could tell us whether it was ours or theirs. We were still near the target. Dave said, "Hold her steady, skipper. I want to get an astral sight." Jock held her steady. And the flak began coming up at us. It seemed to be very close. It was winking off both wings, but the Dog was steady. Finally, Dave said, "Okay, skipper. Thank you very much." A great orange blob of flak smacked up straight in front of us, and Jock said. "I think they're shooting at us." I'd thought

so for some time. He began to throw D for Dog up, around and about again. When we were clear of the barrage, I asked him how close the bursts were and he said, "Not very close. When they're really near, you can smell 'em. That proved nothing for I'd been holding my breath.

Jack sang out from the rear turret that his oxygen was getting low; he thought maybe the lead had frozen. Titch went scrambling back with a new mask and a bottle of oxygen. Dave said, "We're crossing the coast." My mind went back to the time I had crossed that coast in 1938, in a plane that had taken off from Prague. Just ahead of me sat two refugees from Vienna–an old man and his wife. The copilot came back and told them that we were outside German territory. The old man reached out and grabbed his wife's hand.

The work that was done last night was a massive blow of retribution, for all those who have

Tuesday, 5 October 1943
Lou Bober, the navigator, is grounded for 48 hours with a heavy cold. Wilhite also has a cold but is taking a ground engineering course this week anyway, so we're flying with Twogood as first engineer. Ravetti is complaining of ear trouble. In a couple of days we should know how he'll stand this altitude stuff. And to top it all, Simpson has turned himself over to the flight surgeon, a major, to get a verdict on his ears. Will has been having headaches and buzzing in his inner ears for the last several trips. Audiographs proved a 20% loss of hearing in his right ear. Tomorrow morning the major will give the verdict on whether my bombardier will be grounded or not. We're supposed to bomb at 20,000 feet tonight for four hours. If there is any trouble due to altitude it will surely show up for the major tomorrow morning.

fled from the sound of shots and blows on a stricken continent.

We began to lose height over the North Sea. We were over England's shores. The land was dark beneath us. Somewhere down there below, American boys were probably bombing up Fortresses and Liberators, getting ready for the day's work. We were over the home field. We called the control tower and the calm, clear voice of an English girl replied, "Greetings D-Dog. You are diverted to Mulebag." We swung round, contacted Mulebag, came in on a flare path, touched down very gently, ran along to the end of the runway and turned left. And Jock, the finest pilot in Bomber Command, said to the control tower, "D-Dog clear of runway."

When we went in for interrogation, I looked on the board and saw that the big, slow, smiling Canadian, and the red-headed English boy with the two-weeks'-old moustache hadn't made it. They were missing.

There were four reporters on this operation. Two of them didn't come back. Two friends of mine, Norman Stockton of Australian Associated Newspapers, and Lowell Bennett, an American representing International News Service. There is something of a tradition amongst reporters, that those who are prevented by circumstances from filing their stories, will be covered by their colleagues. This has been my effort to do so. In the aircraft in which I flew, the men who flew and fought poured into my ears their comments on fighters, flak and flares in the same tone that they would have used in reporting a host of daffodils. I have no doubt that Bennett and Stockton would have given you a better report of last night's activity.

Berlin was a thing of orchestrated Hell—a terrible symphony of light and flames.
– Edward R. Murrow

top left: A Canadian Halifax crew at its base in England; top: A Stirling bomber about to be loaded for a mission.

PADDLEFEET

Friday, 15 October 1943
Ours was the highest air-to-air gunnery score of the squadron that last time. The crew as a whole has a fine record in all departments. The radio operations lieutenant is always telling me what a good man Wentz is. Ravetti and Kobel are demons at checking over the ship. When we come back from a gunnery mission, I know the guns will be stowed properly and the ship cleaned of all empty cartridges, etc. This new man, Hollick, is fitting in beautifully and learning fast. Smitty is landing the ship now and doing a good job. I couldn't ask for a better copilot. While we haven't been able to give him a real workout, Bober seems to know his navigation and is a little beaver. His missions in the navigation trainer have been above average.

top: Illustrator Philip Brinkman and one of his Zodiac paintings on the nose of a 486BG B-24 at his Sudbury base; right: Remains of a parachute packing hut at RAF Marston Moor.

The American fliers called them ground-pounders, paddlefeet or gravel-crunchers, in the RAF they were penguins or wingless wonders, and they were sometimes known by names less felicitous and sometimes more pejorative. They were the multitude of officers and men who did not fly. They included engineers and administrators, controllers and technicians, caterers and equippers, transportation and ordnance men, doctors and dentists, PR men and chaplains, ground defence and military police. They all had a job to do, and an essential one, and despite their irreverence the flying men knew that to be so.

Among the men who stayed behind when the bombers headed east, the fliers felt they owed the most to the front line crews—they felt it every time their plane was safely airborne with all the systems working as they should. The feeling was natural, because of the ground crew's proximity, their availability at the crucial moments of departure and return, and because their work was evident and vitally important. Equally important, but not so clearly evident, and so less likely to receive acknowledgment, were the labours of the men who loaded bombs and ammunition, fuel and oxygen, who serviced instruments, radio and radar.

Among the most essential and active members of the ground staff were the squadron armourers, who took the bombs to the hardstands, and cranked them up into the bombbays. It was an early morning job, physically strenuous, but not normally particularly dangerous. "Around six o'clock," said Sam Burchell, "just before the flight crews arrived, the ordnance men would come out and put the fuses in the bombs. We never did that—the bombs were completely safe while

Thursday, 21 October 1943
The rumors are flying fast about our departure from Wendover and where we'll be going. The most prevalent, persistent guess is that we are going to be out of the United States by the second week of November. All of the pilots feel we've been short-suited on training, and even to hear we may be gone before the date we were originally scheduled for leaving may be the reason for my low mental attitude.

Saturday, 6 November 1943
I'm writing this with my chin in hand and my eyelids like lead. Was up at 5:30 this morning, flew 5 hours and fifteen minutes at 20,000 feet in a 24-plane formation and it knocked me for a loop. Same routine tomorrow only I'll have two hours of bomb-trainer and four hours of navigation trainer piled on that schedule.

top left: The bombing teacher building at Podington, home of the American 92nd Bomb Group; left: Administrative offices at the 401st Bomb Group airfield, Deenethorpe in Northamptonshire.

right: The barber shop at the 381st Bomb Group air base, Ridgewell in Essex.

we were handling them."

The RAF method was similar, but rather less orderly. The bombs came to the aircraft, not as packaged loads, but piecemeal, the way they had been loaded onto trolleys by the bomb dump crews: first the 4,000 pounders, then the 1,000 and 500 pounders, and last the SBCs—the small bomb containers packed with incendiaries. Each aircraft's bomb-bay had to be loaded with a certain lethal mixture. The armourers were required to hurry to and fro, following the trolleys and carrying their winching gear from dispersal to dispersal, sometimes half a mile apart, and back to where they started, loading each aeroplane in turn. When one failed to pass its run-up checks, they had to load a spare aircraft in a hurry, and unload the sick one when the rest had taken off. On those occasions, or when a mission was cancelled for some reason, the regulation was that the bombs should go back to the dump; understandably, that instruction was occasionally ignored, and the loads were stacked on the dispersal, ready for the next time.

Another ordnance chore arose when a aircraft came home with a "hang-up" in the bomb-bay, either on account of electrical malfunction or because the release-gear had frozen up at altitude. This rarely happened in an Eighth Air Force bomber, because the bombardier had internal access to the bomb racks (albeit with difficulty and at no small hazard), and could usually contrive to free the bomb himself. It was a fairly rare occurrence in a Lancaster or Halifax, which was just as well, because the process for dealing with it, as described by Alan Ashmore, an armourer at a 1 Group base in Lincolnshire, sends a shiver down the spine.

Sunday, 21 November 1943
I'm fairly certain now we won't go to England. The latest dope is that we won't be out of here until March 1st. Things that are expected to bring the European mess to a head will be underway by then, so it looks like the Pacific for us. I'm happy about that.

Thursday, 25 November 1943, Thanksgiving Day
We really had a beautiful spread this afternoon. Plenty of candy, nuts, fruit, fruit cake, mince pie, cranberries, and turkey. A new hostess has charge at the club now. She is French, with quite an accent. She is influencing a lot of changes for the better. Many corners that were never dusted since the place was built now have a lustre. The girls who serve the food have been given red-and-white checked aprons which at least changes their appearance, if it doesn't help their manners. A sloppy bunch.

Saturday, 27 November 1943
The rumors are getting more persistent that this group will be permanently stationed here. If that happens, chances are that I'll become an instructor pilot and fight the 'Battle of Wendover' for some time. What a Goddamn break that will be.

"We had to decide what, if anything, was laying on the bomb doors, and where, by shining a torch and looking in the bomb-bay through a little window behind the bomb-aimer's position. The next step was for four men, holding a blanket, to stand below the doors. The blanket only covered a third of the area, and as soon as you touched the bomb-door lever, they crashed wide open. It was all or nothing. These Heath Robinson scenes were taking place all over Bomber Command, and usually in darkness.

If they were sensible, ground staff men and women would try to be dispassionate about the men who flew the warplanes. They would try not to get involved with them personally, emotionally, or in any other way. To try, however, was not always to succeed: it was difficult for the flying controllers and the operations staff, for the squadron clerks and orderlies, and especially for the ground crews, who were all in daily contact—difficult not to care about the fate of men whose faces, names and voices they came to know so well; for the Red Cross girls, the WAAF R/T operators, crew-bus drivers and parachute packers, it was practically impossible. They were bound to have their favourites—that tall pilot who looked like Robert Taylor, the little tail gunner who played the harmonica, the red-haired navigator who was always ready with a joke . . .

Of course, they wanted everyone to come home safely from Merseburg, Hannover, Frankfurt or wherever (although from experience they knew it was unlikely) but, try as they might, they couldn't help hoping that, if anyone went down, it wouldn't be those guys in *Naughty Lady* or *F for Freddy*. Then came the

Sunday, 28 November 1943
I finally flew as an instructor this morning. Five hours—four of them at 20,000 feet with the temperature 20 below. I've been cold all day. My feet felt like they were asleep all afternoon, but are only cold now. I'll have to wear more tomorrow.

It was a formation-gunnery mission. The fellow I was with is O.K., but needs a lot of formation practice. I don't know yet how his gunners made out on the target. We led the flight for gunnery. The tow-target ship was late getting off and we had quite a time contacting it. This shortened the time so I don't believe all the ammo was expended. It wasn't our fault, so nothing was said. The more I fly high altitude, the more respect I have for those guys over Germany. God, that's a rugged ordeal. No wonder a man is through after 25 missions over Europe.

top: Few buildings remain at Ridgewell, the base of the 381st Bomb Group in World War Two; left: The handsomely restored control tower at RAF East Kirkby, Lincolnshire.

24 June 1943.
Ground personnel of
the 91st Bomb
Group sweat out the
return of the group
from the day's mission.

right: In the tower at Deenethorpe; far right: A B-17 of the 388th Bomb Group; below: The remains of a Nissen hut at the Rattlesden home of the 447th Bomb Group; A Military Police sign from the B-24 base at Bungay, Suffolk.

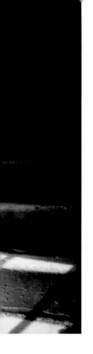

Thursday, 30 December 1943

We've been fogged in here so long that there is talk of moving to another field for third phase. Yesterday a group of eight ships got off through a very low ceiling to fly to Pocatello for some training. They were skeleton crews of pilot, copilot, bombardier, navigator, engineer and radio operator. So each ship carried two crews, so to speak.

They were flying formation when one dropped back and down. He knocked the wing off the lower plane and went down out of control himself. Two ships and four crews were lost. Just to show how fate works, a friend of ours had begged to go along as navigator but was turned down cold. He was mad all afternoon until the report came back, naturally. Two of the crews were supposed to be on leave but had that joy cancelled in order to get this time in.

There were a couple extra passengers along. One was a ground crew chief who'd never flown before and had requested a bus ride instead. He was a family man and that morning had turned down the opportunity of boosting his insurance to $10,000. He was to busy getting ready for this flight and was going to increase the $1,000 he did have as soon as he got back. You try to figure out why these things happen the way they do.

These accidents are really getting out of hand. Thirty-nine men have been killed in ten days from Wendover alone.

problem: the anxious time of waiting for the news, the awful empty feeling when the crew was overdue, the lingering chance that they had landed at another field, and at last the sickening knowledge they had not—that they would neither be seen, heard nor spoken of again. The most contented paddlefeet were those who didn't know one flier from another: it was really better not to get involved.

There were many instances of ground staff officers (non-rated, to the USAAF) accompanying a flight crew on a combat mission. Usually, these ventures had official sanction: they were regarded as offering valuable

top: Laying a concrete runway; right: The 388BG bomb dump.

experience, beneficial to morale and tending to bridge the gap between the men who flew and those who didn't have to. Following this principle, many specialist officers, including USAAF flight surgeons and RAF medicos, flew on operations—maybe not the toughest ones, but real combat missions. Occasionally, however, the venture was unauthorized: the would-be passenger made a covert arrangement with the crew—sometimes with the help of an alcoholic bribe—and crept on board the aircraft when the top brass weren't around. That kind of escapade was likely to be frowned on, because of what might happen if the plane went down and the crew were posted missing. Next day an officer would not appear for duty and, in due course, the administrators checked. He was not on leave, he hadn't gone AWOL, and in a way he was.

The average GI on a USAAF bomber base, squelching through the mud in boots and shapeless overalls to perform his duties, rejoiced in the sobriquet of "sad sack"; his RAF equivalent, similarly occupied, knew himself to be an "erk". They did not have to share the aircrews' mortal danger, nor know the fear of death in the embattled skies, but neither could they share the strange, fleeting glamour of the fliers' lives. There was no great excitement in unpacking and re-packing parachutes, driving the ration truck, filling tanks with gasoline, greasing Browning guns, loading film in cameras, crystalizing radios, charging batteries or cleaning blood and waste products out of fuselages; there was no sense of achievement to be had in guarding bomb dumps, mopping kitchen floors, peeling potatoes, trying to make

something edible from a pack of powdered egg, or counting vouchers in the clothing store; no medals were awarded for lancing boils in sick bay, pulling jack-plugs in the PBX, typing Routing Orders or stacking coins in pay accounts.

Not for them, with wingless tunics, the smiling welcome of the barmaid in the local pub, the free drinks from the customers, the admiring glances of the dance-hall girls, the travel petrol ration, the Nuffield leave money; for their labours, they got "more kicks than ha'pence", as the saying went. But every flier knew, if he paused to think of it, that without those gravel agitators, GI Joes and erks, there would be no bombs in the bomb-bay, no bullets in the guns, no parachutes, no rations, no pay, no billet to fly home to—no allied bomber force to take the war to Germany.

"Small deeds done are better than great deeds planned."
-P. Marshall

"The secret of all victory lies in the organization of the non-obvious."
-Spengler

"It is the fate of those who toil at the lower employments of life . . . to be exposed to censure without hope of praise; to be disgraced by miscarriage, or punished for neglect, where success would have been without applause, and diligence without reward."
- Samuel Johnson

"All delays are dangerous in war."
- Dryden

Then today, another went down. The weather conditions have a lot to do with it. Icing conditions and all.

Wednesday, 5 January 1944
I've surely been lucky, getting Smitty as a copilot. We get along fine and he seems content as a copilot. Here is a poem he wrote about it:
I'm the copilot; I sit on the right;
I'm not important, just part of the flight.
I never talk back lest I have regrets,
But I have to remember what the pilot forgets.

I make out the flight plan and study the weather,
Pull up the gear and stand by to feather;
Make out the forms and do the reporting,
And fly the old crate when the pilot's a-courting.

I take the readings, adjust the power,
Handle the flaps and call the tower;
Tell him where we are on the darkest night,
And do all the book work without any lights.

I call for my pilot and buy him cokes.
I always laugh at his corny jokes.
And once in a while when his landings are rusty,
I come through with, 'Gawd, but it's gusty!'

All in all I'm a general stooge
As I sit on the right with the man I call Scrooge.
I guess you think that is past understanding
But maybe some day he will give me a landing.

WHAT A CLIMATE

Monday, 10 January 1944
Tonight we're to have a conference and a POM inspection, that is Preparation for Overseas Movement. Tomorrow we draw our .45s and the damndest looking toad-stabber you ever saw. We are under orders to wear these at all times. The enlisted men have been asked to turn in all their sun-tan uniforms, so England looms again. There is definitely a big push to get us out the end of this month.

Tuesday, 25 January 1944
Staging for the group will be at Topeka, Kansas, and there will not be the series of tests promised us earlier. Merely an overseas processing. This shouldn't take more than five days.

right: A fog-shrouded control tower at the former base of the 487th Bomb Group, Lavenham, Suffolk.

Flying in the English climate, especially in winter (which often seems to last for eight months of the year), was and remains an interesting experience: often enjoyable, sometimes deadly dangerous, and hardly ever dull. Those cold, clear mornings, ideal for aviation, with the sun shining palely in a turquoise sky, could quickly change to afternoons so misty that even the boldest sparrow would not fly; those perfect nights, when you could see a million stars from 20,000 feet, might end in a ground fog back at base in which you couldn't quite make out your wing-tip navigation lights, let alone the runway.

In the 1940s, for landings at night or in poor visibility, all British bomber fields were equipped with the Drem lighting system—so-called for the Scottish airfield where it was evolved. The equipment included fifty yellow sodium lamps, mounted on poles in a pattern-wide circle round the field. Downwind of the field, this yellow circle was broken by a tapering avenue of blue lamps (known as the "funnel" lights), which outlined the approach path to the runway threshold. So, even on nights when the flarepath could not be seen clearly from pattern height, homecoming pilots could follow the yellows until they found the blues, then turn gently upwind and descend, through the "funnel" to the threshold. On the approach, the GPIs (glide path indicators) came into view, showing amber if the aircraft were too high, red if it were low, and green for the recommended angle of descent., For the pilot, one problem still remained: it was necessary first to find the field.

On the night of December 16/17 1943, four hundred and eighty-three Lancasters set out to bomb Berlin. The city was cloud-covered but the sky-marking was good, and important railway installations and administrative centres

When the weather was fine for flying in England it was often terrible over the Continent and ops would be postponed. Then we did local flying. Either a "bull's-eye" exercise that put you over English towns at night on a dummy raid, complete with searchlights but no flak, or practice bombing runs without bombs. During the day we had gunnery practice, fighter practice against friendly Spitfires, compass swings, or air tests to check various pieces of equipment. The best of all was local flying practice. Those were the times that presented an opportunity for low flying, which was strictly forbidden. But over the Yorkshire moors or over the North Sea, who was to know? It was the pilot's only chance to really throw the Lanc all over the sky and discover just what a beautiful machine he had.
–from *Boys, Bombs and Brussels Sprouts*
by J. Douglas Harvey

were destroyed, but the cost was high. Twenty-one bombers were shot down by the enemy—about the average loss rate for the "Battle of Berlin"—and four were destroyed by collisions on the bomb run; an English "pea-souper" did the rest: twenty-nine returning Lancasters and a mine- laying Stirling either crashed or were abandoned when their pilots could find no place to land. The squadrons based in Lincolnshire had the heaviest losses on "Black Thursday", as it was later called, and No. 97, with seven aircraft down, suffered worst of all.

A device known as FIDO (Fog, intensive dispersal operation), which could have saved a number of those aircraft, had just come into service at Graveley, a PFF base in East Anglia, where the chief pathfinder, Air Vice-Marshal Donald Bennett, had himself tested and approved the installation. According to Bennett, it had first been offered to his brother group commanders in the northern counties, but they, in their wisdom, had declined it. The system consisted of perforated pipes, 2,000 yards in length, laid on each side of the runway and the end of the approach; the pipes carried petrol which, when ignited, produced sufficient heat to burn off the lower layers of fog. Proved successful at Graveley, FIDO was eventually installed at Woodbridge and Carnaby, the emergency landing strips near the eastern coastline, and at a dozen other fields (including some of those commanded by the early doubters).

FIDO was thirsty—in one operation it consumed enough fuel for an hour's flying by fifty Lancasters—and in action it provided an unusual experience for the crews—the glare and the turbulence could be quite alarming, and the runway looked like the highway into Hades. But in one day alone, sixty-five Eighth Air Force bombers set down safely at Carnaby and, from FIDO's inception, nearly 2,500 bomber crews used it and made landings which, without it, they might not have walked away from.

Bomber captains inclined to the opinion that fighter pilots as a breed wouldn't fly at night and couldn't fly in cloud—an opinion which was shared by a highly experienced Eagle Squadron flier, Carroll "Red" McColpin, Commanding Officer of No. 133 Squadron: "I had studied instrument flying," McColpin stated. "I got a lot of Link hours in, and I flew at night whenever I could. I flew in all kinds of weather, and I never had any trouble with it, but I felt that most of our pilots were leary of instrument and night flying, mainly because they didn't get enough of it."

If to fly in winter was occasionally unpleasant, to live in it was worse. Most US Army Air Force men suffered from the cold. Of their days in the UK, they would always remember "those damp winters", "that bone-chilling weather", and shaving in icy water was never a happy way to start the day. "It got pretty cold in the huts at Grafton Underwood," said pilot Lawrence Drew, "and that hard English coal wouldn't make a hot enough fire. Every once in a while someone would go out in the forest and chop down a tree. But the Duke who owned the land, he inspected the condition of his property regularly and if he found any damage he would send our government the bill."

"I was stationed at Molesworth," said Calvin Swaffer, "from October 1942 until the end of July 1943. The weather was 'El Stinko', as we used to call it. Lots of fog and rainy days with a few good days for flying. The four officers in my crew slept in one room; we had no heat in it at all. I slept under seven blankets."

Saturday, 29 January 1944
I'm now the proud possessor of $350,000 worth of B-24 airplane. Nothing pretentious, sort of olive drab color, has four engines, three new tyres, in fact, looks a great deal like any other H-model except, of course, that it belongs to crew W-32. It will be known as 'Army 421' until the crew decides on a name. The ground crew is giving it an acceptance check and we may be able to fly it this afternoon if it is completed in time.

Sunday, 13 February 1944, Herington Army Air Base, Kansas
We are going to take the south Atlantic route. This means, Miami, Trinidad, Natal and some point in Africa. From there we don't know, and won't until arrival. It's beginning to look like the real thing. Just returned from another lecture, all about different routes to almost every theatre. Men who have actually made the trips several times gave us the dope.

left: A B-24 Liberator crewman finds a fresh snowfall on returning to his Norfolk base from a mission in early 1944; overleaf: Examples of Eighth Air Force painted A2 leather flight jackets.

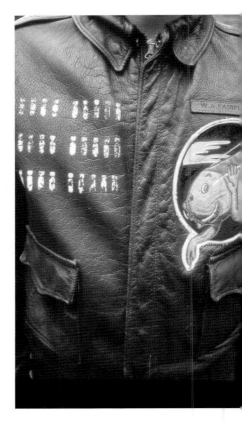
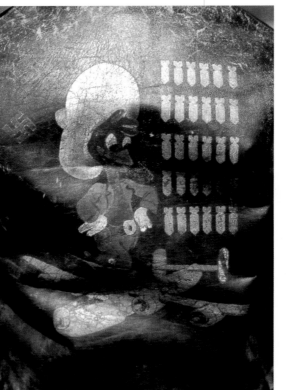
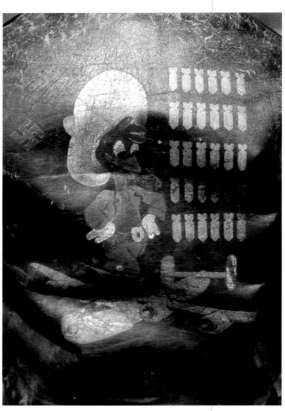

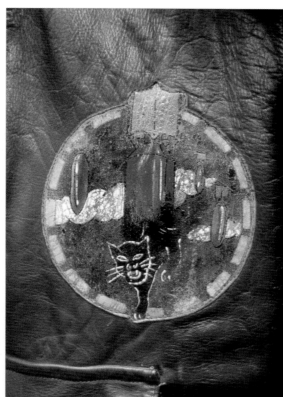

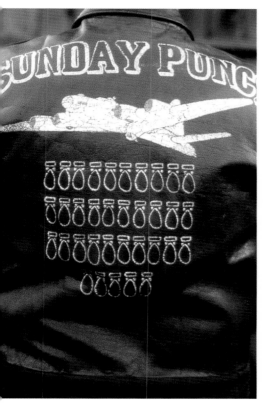

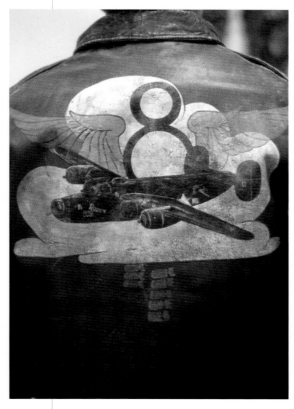

Monday, 14 February 1944
Finally got enough time off to go check up on my airplane. It is being well taken care of. I've never run into such wonderful cooperation on the line. There are technical experts for everything. There is a very competent crew chief assigned for our stay here. We went over some of the things that needed looking into, and before I left the ship, many of the items were done. I felt sure the remainder would be well taken care of.

Snow, at least, had the effect of exciting the Australians, into whose lives it had hitherto not fallen. On first sight of it, these sun-tanned, narrow-eyed sons of the Antipodes, casting aside their customary cool, ran out of their billets to throw snowballs and build snowmen, like a bunch of children in a kindergarten playground.

Airmen have it in common with farmers that their activity is affected and their planning influenced to a great extent by weather: rainfall and sunshine, barometric pressure, temperature and wind all have their effects. English weather in the short term is never difficult to forecast: there is always a fifty-fifty chance that you will get it right. As a countryman would tell you: "If you can see them hills yonder, that means it's gonna rain; if you can't, it's raining already." But a glance at yonder hills was of little help for long term forecasts, covering the time it took to

prepare, mount and fly a bomber operation, the success of which depended on the pressure distribution and frontal dispositions across the length and breadth of European skies.

The problem for the weather men of the USAAF and the RAF was that the international exchange of meteorological information had ceased when hostilities began and that, from then on, no more forecasts were issued by the warring nations. The Allies did their best to fill the gaps by aerial reconnaissance and reports from ships at sea, but the forecaster's task, always more an art than a science, was bound to include an element of guess-work.

In selecting objectives for their bombers, the USAAF commanders were influenced by two main considerations. The first was their directive from the Chiefs of Staff, which listed target systems in order of priority; the second was the weather in the target area. Air Chief

Both: Views of the 401st Bomb Group heavy bomber base at Deenethorpe, Northamptonshire in January 1945.

Marshal Harris was subject to the same criteria, but he tended to allow himself a measure of autonomy, and it was not unknown for him to put the weather first and the directive second or, on occasion, to take account of neither. As to that, it must be said that General Spaatz once did the same: in February 1944, ignoring the forecasts and defying his orders, he launched "Big Week" against the German Air Force; he lost 250 bombers, but he cleared the skies of Normandy for the allied armies to go ashore on D-Day.

None of the air commanders liked to scrub a mission on account of weather: they would rather postpone it and have the crews stand by in the hope of an improvement. Ira Eaker was especially concerned that they should fly whenever possible—Henry H. Arnold, the USAAF Commander, had unfavourably (and as Eaker thought unfairly) compared the hours flown by the Eighth's bombers with those flown by training units of the Second Air Force in the States. What "Hap" Arnold and those guys flying desks back in Washington didn't seem to understand, Eaker felt, was that it made no sense at all to send the bomb groups on a mission if they couldn't find their bases on return.

Eaker considered that the weather was a greater danger to his bombers than the enemy defences, and used this as an argument at the Casablanca summit conference when Churchill, Roosevelt and some of his own superiors wanted him to give up daylight bombing and join the night offensive with the RAF. "We'll lose more people," he told Arnold, "coming into that fog-shrouded island at four o'clock in the morning than we lose over Germany in the daytime."

It was the English weather which convinced General Arnold (and which he used in turn to

Thursday, 16 February 1944
Yesterday afternoon I took the opportunity of talking to the POM inspector, a major. He was sitting alone in the club, so I went up and had quite a chat before anyone interrupted. My primary concern was to find out what he could do for us as a crew if the group is ordered to split up. The boys all want to stick together and feel we're ready for combat. I knew the inspector had singled us out as flying good formation, so I approached him. He promised us to do what he could and added that before any crews were sent back through phase work or broken up, the pilot would have a chance to talk for himself and his crew.

Tuesday, 22 February 1944
As nothing better has turned up, I guess the ship will be named 'Wallowing Wilbur', 'Willie' for short, of course. It was Smitty's suggestion and surely describes the sonofabitch. So far, we haven't received any equipment that would place us in a specific theatre, so we're still guessing.

Sunday, 27 February 1944, West Palm Beach, Florida
We've had our passes taken away and aren't allowed to phone or telegraph anyone. An MP meets us at every turn, 'Have you your AGO pass, sir?' It stops us cold. So, we sleep, go to our airplane, eat, and attend scheduled meetings. We're preparing ourselves for what's ahead.

Sunday, 5 March 1944
Our first hop from the States took us to Trinidad. The flight was not too eventful. The weather was excellent, and while we worried some about fuel consumption, we landed with quite a bit to spare.

Wednesday, 15 March 1944, Rackheath, England
I've been cold since we left Africa, and don't think I'll warm up until I get home. The stoves here are small and coal is strictly rationed. We look on these little heaters not to warm us up, but to keep us from freezing to death.

right: Another fine painted A2 jacket; top centre: A plug-in point for the heated suit of 8AF gunners; The CO's quarters at Shipdam in Norfolk; The B-17 *Ruby's Raiders* of the 385th Bomb Group.

Tuesday, 28 March 1944
The weather has been dev-ilish for the past couple of days. The damp cold just can't be driven out of the barracks, so we haunt the club where it is some-what warm. The chow has improved after much determined bitching on the part of the air crews. The ground personnel were eating better and in much grander style than we. It caused a hell of a lot of ill-feeling. Can't say it is all ironed out yet, but it is on the mend.

Thursday, 6 April 1944
There is always a heated discussion going on in the hut. Everything is talked about, argued, and kicked around. Food has held the center of atten-tion lately. The chow here is pretty good but no matter how much we eat, we always feel hungry. I've just had a cheese sandwich and a piece of rationed chocolate. A couple of the boys are grilling cheese and bread. This goes on night after night with variations, depending on what we can get hold of.

convince the Chiefs of Staff in October 1943) that half of Eaker's bomber force should be based in Italy, so doubling the chances of favorable conditions for take-off and return—if necessary by flying shuttle operations. Eaker had misgivings, and it turned out he was right: the Italian climate was certainly warmer, but low cloud and fog were just as much a problem as they were in England. By then, however, twenty-one of his bomb groups had been whisked away to form the Fifteenth Air Force, flying from bases in Apulia.

Once the bomber commanders had made their targeting decisions, such details of the baromet-ric pressures, humidities and temperatures on the projected route as the met. staffs had either estimated or obtained from reconnaissance were collated, and passed down the wire to the group and squadron bases. There, in their offices in the flying control towers, the section weather men transcribed the data onto synoptic charts, added what they found from their own instruments, and did their best to provide the kind of information needed by the fliers: local cloud base and ceiling (this was crucial for the USAAF crews who, unlike the RAF, had to assemble in formation), icing index, visibility, wind speed and direction, and hazards of fog or electrical disturbance. They drew diagrams to show the profile of the cloud that would be met en route for screening at the briefing.

The forecasters tried to send the fliers off well-briefed, but it tended to be a somewhat thankless task. Few pilots or navigators would remember to congratulate the met. man when his forecast turned out right, and many would be quick to let him know when it did not. "Duff gen, Cloudy," he was likely to be told, "you were all wrong about the goddam cloud base, freezing level, con-trail height, turbulence, et cetera . . ."

The "weather spies", too, did their best to help, and flew round the clock to provide the information needed by their comrades in the bomber fleets. Their long-range recce flights over the Atlantic gave warning of the fronts which were approaching Europe with the inex-orable rotation of the earth and the subsequent south-westerlies; squadrons of Mosquitoes, later joined by Mustangs, covered the routes to European targets; when adverse conditions were expected, B-17s from selected bases made pre-mission checks of cloud and icing levels in the assembly areas, and from the fall of 1944 each Eighth Air Force division had its own weather scouting force.

Meanwhile, RAF Mosquito crews of No. 1409 Flight, based at Wyton with Donald Bennett's Light Night Striking Force, flew long-range mis-sions over Europe and the western approaches. As one of the pilots wrote: "Not the smallest cloud, from the Russian front to the Atlantic, from Norway to the Alps, from mean sea level to 40,000 feet, was left in privacy. A blue Mosquito would be sniffing round it, seeking out its secrets, and running home to tell—to Bomber, Fighter, Transport, 2nd TAF and USAAF, to anyone who was prepared to listen."

On the way home from PAMPAS (pre-attack met recce flights) over target areas, the Mosquitoes met the heavies coming in for the attack and, from high above them, radioed their findings to the master bomber. I often wonder," wrote Bennett, "whether it was appreciated at HQ Bomber Command, or for that matter by any other senior officer who called for a PAMPA, that in doing so they were asking an unarmed aircraft to proceed deep into the heart of enemy territory, often in broad daylight. The ease with which they called for PAMPAS was sometimes quite frightening. No. 1409 Flight, on the other hand, never hesitated for one moment, and never failed to do their job with absolute reliability."

Of course, England had, and continues to enjoy, its gorgeous days. The old folk will recall long summer holidays when they were kids in school and, if they are to be believed, the sun shone all the time and the sky was always blue. It is true that July, August and September are often warmly pleasant, and it only takes a week or so of that kind of weather for the Water Board to proclaim a drought, and to issue dire warnings to anyone so wicked as to hose a flower-bed or wash a car.

With November there would sometimes come a fog so dense (it was before the time of smokeless fuel) that it brought all movement to a crawl, if not a halt. A Mosquito pilot, the proud owner of an Austin Seven, had to persuade his navigator to walk ahead with a flashlight when they were returning to the mess from an evening at the village pub.

The next two months were normally so cold that radiation fog could not occur, but a mist was always possible, both at dawn and dusk. It was not uncommon to experience every kind of weather—days of drenching rain, stinging showers of hail, drifts of gleaming snow which turned to slush in daylight and froze hard at night—all within the time span of a week. There could be days of pristine clarity, when the landscape looked so clean and the sky so brilliant that you could believe the world had just begun; then there were days so dank and colourless it seemed that the sun had forgotten how to shine.

"February fill-dyke" was how the English knew the next month, when the snows of winter, melting on the hillsides, flowed down to the lowlands and made the ditches overflow. Then, "March winds and April showers gave way to May's spring flowers", and the unpredictable, fascinating cycle started over again.

In the "Times" of Thursday, April 1st 1993, this paragraph appeared: "The biggest flypast since the Coronation will greet the Queen today when she presents new colours to the Royal Air Force to mark the 75th anniversary of its formation. Nearly 150 aircraft, representing every type in current service as well as the historic Lancaster and Battle of Britain veterans, will sweep the skies above RAF Marham, Norfolk, in what will be only the fourth full-scale royal review in the service's history . . . Last night service chiefs were casting anxious eyes at an overcast and rainy sky. The flypast requires a cloud base of not less than 1,500 feet and visibility of five miles . . ."

That anxiety was fully justified. An intense low pressure zone, slowly moving north-east from the coast of Sussex, had arrived over Norfolk, bringing low cloud and pouring rain which persisted throughout the day. The great flypast, six months in the planning, had to be abandoned, and Her Majesty presented the colours in the shelter of a hangar. "Such a shame," she commented, to a few of the thousands who had come to see the show. USAAF veterans of the European war may rest assured: the English climate hasn't changed a bit.

"Systems and opinions change, but nature is always true."
-Hazlitt

"We actually saw the sun late this afternoon for the first time in a week."
- Keith Newhouse, pilot, 467BG

Friday, 7 April 1944
We actually saw the sun late this afternoon for the first time in a week. If that is any indication of good weather things should be popping around here in short order. I guess most of the boys feel as our crew does—as long as we're here, we might just as well get going to finish this thing off in the shortest time possible. The risks involved are definitely less than they were several months ago. The enemy is showing signs of wear and the escorting fighters make it far easier for us in the Big Boys.

The mud was atmosphere: you breathed it even if you didn't want to, it was under your nails, it was in the grooves of your hands. We took off in it, flew in it, often had to abort because of it. On takeoff the mud would be splashing and whirling over the Plexiglas; it was sticky, and wouldn't drain after the airplane had climbed aloft. The guck interfered so severely with visibility that no one could see anything. You couldn't bomb, you had to come home. It would have been like trying to sight a target from inside a blown-up football.
–from *Mission with LeMay* by General Curtis E. LeMay with MacKinlay Kantor

A GENTLE REPAST

Wednesday, 12 April 1944
In the evening we rode our bikes to a small town nearby and drank a couple of beers. This English stuff is rather bitter and flat, but has a goodly quantity of the spirits within. Pubs close by 10:00 pm so we were in bed by 11:00. The countryside is growing beautiful. Trees are popping buds, flowers in bloom, and fruit trees are all a-blossom. It is lovely and growing more so.

Sunday, 16 April 1944
In the towns one can't help noticing the enormous number of baby carriages that crowd the walks. These Englishmen may be away to the wars most of the time, but they surely aren't wasting any leave time nor shooting many blanks. Women with perambulators and two or three little mits swarm through the streets. Shopping is done by sweating out long lines to buy whatever is left over. Mid-afternoon finds long queues winding for a block from a shop's door. Which reminds me, over here one doesn't wait inside a restaurant or tea shop for a table. Oh, no, no, can't be cluttering up one's establishment with customers. 'Wyte outside,

For men accustomed to living in America, or in any country where the availability of foodstuffs was relatively unaffected by the war, the diet in Great Britain, after three years of blockade, was liable to come as quite a shock. Although the rationing regime for the civil population ensured that no one starved, it also meant that few people ever sat down to what in peace-time would have been regarded as a truly satisfying meal. Every type of foodstuff that Britain had imported from Europe or the Commonwealth and Empire before the war began were either non-existent or "in short supply"; that included most of her lamb and bacon, a lot of cheese and butter, much of her wheat, fruit and sugar, all her tea and coffee, and a high percentage of the seafood her fishing fleets had always netted. Ice cream was non-existent for five years. Only bread, among the staple foodstuffs, was never "on the ration", although restrictions were considered at the height of the U-boat threat in 1942. You could be fined ten shillings for indulging in the Londoners' lunch-time habit of throwing breadcrumbs to the pigeons in Trafalgar Square, and white bread was virtually unknown: when America's First Lady, Eleanor Roosevelt, dined at Buckingham Palace, she ate the grey-colored "national wheatmeal loaf", as did Their Majesties and everybody else.

To meet the emergency, farmers and their labourers were exempt from military service and, in the "Dig for Britain" campaign, every householder with the smallest plot of land was directed by the government to uproot his flower beds and, in their place, to grow his own potatoes, cauliflower and cabbage. He was further encouraged to rear pigs and chickens (the catch was that if he did so he was liable to lose the official egg and bacon ration).

By measures such as these, there was never a

cawn't yew?' And, by God, you do! Especially if they have inviting-looking sweets to go with the tea or burnt coffee they serve.

The shops are rather sorry affairs. They have little to sell. What they do have is valued in coupons. Not 'How much is it?' but 'How many coupons does it cost?' I've done some scouting in second hand stores and antique shops to find some little thing to send home, but so far have discovered nothing of value. When a country has been at war as long as England has, there just isn't much left from the war effort. It makes a me wonder what the situation must be in Germany.

Friday, 21 April 1944 We are living in Nissen huts, which aren't bad but are rather cold. The coal we're issued burns like paper and gives little heat. Also, the quantities allow a fire only in the evening. But then, we're here only after supper. The chow was awful at first. It has gradually improved, but surely is not interesting. We get some eggs, steaks about once in ten days, but in the interim things are monotonous. The 8th [Air Force] must have bought the entire U.S. output of orange marmalade, and, of course, we get our quota of

overleaf: A former mess hall at the Horham base of the 95th Bomb Group.

disastrous dearth of protein or of mineral, but of certain vitamins there was. It was no wonder, by the end of 1942, that incoming Americans noticed spots and poor complexions on the faces of the children and the adolescents, especially in the industrial cities far from farming land.

Farmers, too, had problems. The early marks of Halifax, for one reason or another, were more prone to accidents than the other heavies. At one northern bomber base, a pilot overshot the runway and crash-landed in a field. The crew scrambled out, and the farmer ran to meet them. "It's all right," the pilot told him, "we're not hurt."

"You may not be," said the farmer, "but what about my bloody turnips? I've had six of you buggers landing on them in a week."

Servicemen, of course, had a supplementary ration, and cooking for large numbers was

always more economical than for individuals, but on the far-flung wartime airfields, the quality of cuisine and of comestibles could be infinitely variable. The cooks, some of whom were at best half-trained, did what they could with limited provisions under primitive conditions, but their efforts would seldom have been approved by Mrs Beeton, let alone an epicure. For several months of the year, the only fresh vegetable readily available was a small variety of cabbage known as a Brussels sprout. "We ate a lot of sprouts," said a pilot based in Lincolnshire, "with sausages, potatoes, and little dried peas like buckshot. When we had a pie, the pastry was like cardboard. You needed a good appetite. Fortunately, we were usually ravenous."

Halifax navigator Norman Pittam was rather less complimentary about the sergeants' mess food at his base in North Yorkshire. "Totally

inedible," was his opinion. "I ate breakfast and flying meals in the mess, and went out to cafés for the rest."

Pittam's view was understandable. There were occasions, standing at the counter waiting to be served, when the smell from the kitchen was like a whiff of noxious gas. Dimly, you might wonder what could cause those fearful odors. In a sour mood—perhaps that last mission had been nasty—you could imagine that it was the smell of death: dead cattle-meat and dying cabbage, putrefying cooking fat and long-expired tea leaves, decomposing dish cloths and maybe the cadaver of a suicided cook. The meal, when you got it, was not unappetising, and yet there was that smell. They could have bottled it and sold it to the chemical warfare branch at Porton Down.

Having survived a tour with No. 4 Group,

Norman Pittam was awarded a Distinguied Flying Medal and commissioned rank; he flew his second tour on Mosquitoes from a permanent PFF base near Huntingdon, where he noticed a considerable improvement in the food: "It was first class grub. They ran a twenty-four hour service for the weather flight, and we got a good meal whenever we wanted it. I had an arrangement with my pilot: he liked eggs and I liked bacon, so we used to swop."

Ball turret gunner Ken Stone was equally satisfied with the chow at Ridgewell. "It wasn't like what we had in the States, but the meals were good. We ate the same as the officers. Every time we came back from a mission, we could have extra food if we wanted it. I used to have a huge bowl of pineapple—I loved pineapple. Breakfast was regular food: real eggs, and lots of spam."

Breakfast at Lavenham didn't amount to

Spam and powdered eggs. No fresh milk. Coffee has a peculiar green taste and coloring, and everything is flat.

Today was a bad one. We were scheduled for a mission, but had to assemble above some clouds. 'Wallowing Wilbur' really lived up to his name. From 12,000 feet we began icing up. We just about reached 14,000 when we stalled out. Smitty put on all the coal and we dropped eight degrees of flap to get a better lift from the wing. By this time we were back to 12,000. But the ice was heavy on the engine cowls and props, the tail assembly was thick with it, and the de-icer boots were just clearing immediately on themselves, so the stuff was building up fast. The left wing whipped down, and we lost altitude again. Tried twice more to get above the crap, but no go. It finally got so bad we couldn't maintain level flight, to say nothing of climbing.

I was forced to turn back. Shortly after, the mission was called off because of weather. It felt damn good to get on the solid earth again. If the weather is better, we try again tomorrow. Saturday, 22 April 1944 On mission ratings we

far left: American Red Cross doughnut girls; left: 1943 Thanksgiving dinner at the 385BG base.

have to get shot at, drop our bombs, or encounter flak before we receive credit. Hence, many times we sweat out two- and four-hour flights for nothing. In almost every respect, this heavy bomber stuff is a tougher racket than pursuit; I believe 'most anyone will concede that.

We blew hell out of the target [Hamm, Germany] yesterday. Visibility was good so we had a good run, although there was some confusion getting lined up. Coming back, it was dark and some clouds added to our trials. Then too, Jerry was raising hell at our field when the first of us arrived. First time we had to fight our way in. There were B-24s crashing all over England last night. Lack of gas, enemy planes and British ack-ack were the causes. The four officers who've shared our barracks were killed in a crash landing a short way from the field. It all adds up to the fact that one doesn't know when he is in for curtains. As the RAF says, 'He had it', and it seems a lot of fellows 'had it' last evening.

much," said navigator Frank Nelson of the 487th Bomb Group. "Not many guys ate a lot, anyway. Maybe the time of morning had something to do with it. And powdered eggs, after you'd had them for a while, you sort of lost your taste for them. If they had hot cakes, which they did on occasion, that was different, but usually we didn't eat much breakfast, a couple of pieces of toast and some coffee."

The Eighth Air Force bomber crews frequently included men from widely different regions of the USA ("Where'd you say you came from? Where'n hell is that?"), and many crews in RAF planes were from yet more distant parts. There are grounds for believing that such mixed crews turned out better than the average: no right-thinking Englishman would wish to be found wanting by a Canuck or Aussie, no more than a good New Yorker would care to be unfavourably compared with, say, a Texan or a

Californian. For the inter-mingled British crews, there was also the advantage that the overseas members were likely to receive food parcels from the folks back home, and those sumptuous luxuries—fruit, cakes and sweetmeats—scrupulously shared, always gave a welcome fillip to the mess hall diet.

Certain types of foodstuff could give rise to gastric problems when men flew at high altitude, and it was for this reason that, for the combat crews, the Eighth Air Force established separate mess halls, where a non-starch diet was the rule. Fresh eggs, seldom seen in other mess halls, were provided at most bases before and after missions, boiled, poached or fried, according to taste.

In RAF messes there was no segregation between fliers and non-fliers. This had its advantages in the way of social intercourse, but pre-mission mealtimes could sometimes be

right: An American mural on a mess hall wall at Shipdam, near Norwich; far right: Examples of C-type rations used in World War Two.

embarrassing. Envision four combat men seated at a table in the dining room: with them are an engineer and a flying controller. The waitress comes by with plates of egg and bacon. "Are you all for flying meals? she asks. The ground staff officers confess that they are not. They will be on duty through the night, they may have to work like dingbats, but they don't rate an egg, no more than they rate a tin of orange juice and a bar of chocolate to sustain them through the watch. "I'll bring yours," says the waitress, "when I've served the aircrew gentlemen." Their meal, when it arrives, consists of spam, mashed potatoes and Brussels sprouts. A sensitive pilot or navigator (not a bomb-aimer—few bomb-aimers were prone to sensitivity) might feel as though he ought to make an offer: "I say, old boy, would you care for half my egg?" The thought would quickly pass: after all, it was virtually impossible to bisect a fried egg "over easy."

Keith Newhouse of the 467th Bomb Group was a cultured man—one who could appreciate the good things of this life—and he took a liking to a certain condiment that was briefly served at Rackheath. "There is a steak sauce called HP," he noted, "which really stands for 'Houses of Parliament', but we call it 'Hot Pilot' and so feel obligated to eat it. The flavor is a delicious blend of the best from A-1, Lea & Perrins and India chutney. We only had it for a short time, and now it is impossible to get."

For sheer style, you had to hand it to the French. In the early summer of 1944, the Free French Air Force formed two heavy bomber squadrons to operate from Elvington, near York, with the RAF. Each man serving on those squadrons, Nos. 346 "Guyenne" and 347 "Tunisie", was historically entitled to a glass of wine at every meal and, one way or another,

that tradition was observed (the fact that the rate of flying accidents at Elvington exceeded that of other bases was probably only a matter of coincidence).

It was the RAF custom on December 25th for the caterers and cooks to put out a special effort. The countryside was scoured for every kind of poultry, the mess halls were festooned with paper chains and holly, baby fir trees were uprooted, decorated and re-planted in fire buckets, the kitchens turned out mince pies, Christmas cakes and puddings, and booze was available on tap. For this one day of the year, no "erk" stood in line to get his chow: the men were served at table by their commissioned officers, some wearing aprons, others funny hats or Santa Claus beards, and all entering warmly into the spirit of the season. Greetings were exchanged, there was a lot of kidding, second helpings were encouraged, and when the meal was over everyone pulled Christmas crackers. The veterans, of course, had seen it all before; they knew and enjoyed it as a part of service life; a new man was surprised by the atmosphere of bonhomie—why, some of those officers weren't such bad blokes after all. But he suddenly felt homesick—perhaps it was the booze—and a lump came to his throat when they all sang "Silent Night", the way the family did back home.

With minor variations, the same kind of seasonal festivities were observed in USAAF mess halls. Children were collected from the nearby villages, to be generously fed and entertained. For them the Christmas party on the base was something to remember all their lives. GI Joe might not always be a paragon of gentlemanly behavior, but for many English children in the 1940s he was a great ambassador for Uncle Sam. Christmas time, to him, was essentially

for kids; Thanksgiving Day, however, was strictly for Americans, and it had to be marked by a traditional feast, largely imported from the States. Roast turkey would be served, with stuffing and potatoes, accompanied by cranberries, candied yams and corn bread, followed by a luscious pumpkin pie. Tomorrow, the menu would be back to normal: leathery mutton or insipid spam, and the inevitable sprouts. But the first harvest of the Pilgrim Fathers had been duly celebrated.

"Go to your banquet then, but use delight, so as to rise still with an appetite."
- Herrick

left: A war-weary B-24 crewman has a quick bite on his return from a raid over Germany; below: B-17 air crew at table on their 390th Bomb Group base at Framlingham, near Parham, England

CURRIE'S NIGHT MOVES

Sunday, 23 April 1944
This afternoon is a beautiful, sunny Sunday. Makes all of this stuff seem unreal and rather far away. We had interrogation and the ship to get ready before we went to bed last night, so it was 3:00 am before we bunked. I've that done-in feeling of a harrowing physical workout. I mention this only as a statement of fact on behalf of the many guys who were on that mission, and not as a complaint. When a fellow gets through this theatre he is a very humble man. I know this to be true of heavy bombardment men because I've talked to many of them. They gain a quiet confidence but they realize how much depends on chance. It makes men, and I'm glad to be a part of it.

The more I work with the crew the more satisfied I am that I've been extremely lucky. The way they take care of their guns and how anxious they are to learn more makes me very happy. Wilhite and Twogood have been able to do something about almost every mechanical trouble we've had. Every man can handle any turret. Sam has gained my confidence more than Will ever did. We still haven't a permanent nav-

In the winter of 1943-44, two Lancaster heavy bomber squadrons were based on an airfield in the flat, fertile farmland ten miles north-east of Lincoln. The base took its name from the near-by village of Wickenby— "a place of reeds" in the language of the vikings. The senior squadron was No. 12 which, with "A", "B" and "C" flights of eight aircraft each, had operated from the field since it opened in 1942. My crew and I, fresh out of training, had been assigned to "C" flight in the early summer of 1943.

When, late that autumn, Air Chief Marshal Arthur T. Harris expanded his Command with a view to mounting the Battle of Berlin, some existing squadrons provided the nuclei of new ones, and the air and ground crews of 12 Squadron's "C" flight became founder members of 626 Squadron overnight. The new code letters were painted on our Lancasters, we moved them to more distant dispersals, transferred our kit to yet more distant Nissen huts, and tried to assimilate our new identity. The task remained the same: once, twice, three times a week, depending on the weather, we dropped bombs on the enemy.

At seven o'clock in the morning of January 2nd 1944, emerging from the overcast at fifteen-hundred feet, I saw the airfield beacon flashing dead ahead—just as navigator Cassidy had predicted that I would. I called flying control, and the WAAF they called the Duchess (she had a somewhat haughty manner) instantly replied: "Orand Charlie Two, you're clear to join the circuit, runway two-six, Queenie-Fox-Easy (QFE—code for barometric pressure at airfield level) one-zero-one-four. Call down-wind, over."

I adjusted the altimeter, reduced the airspeed, and reminded wireless-operator Fairbairn to retract the trailing aerial—the mechanics tended

below: The control tower at RAF Waltham; overleaf: RAF bomber crews awaiting transport to their aircraft at a Lincolnshire base.

to complain if you left it wrapped around a tree. "Give me ten degrees of flap, engineer, check supercharger 'M' gear, rad shutters open. Brake pressure?"

"Flap going down," said Walker, "shutters open, 'M' gear pressures OK. Hey, look! It's snowing."

I never ceased to marvel at his powers of observation. Charlie Two floated down the approach, rounded out nicely and settled on the runway with a muted squeal of rubber. At the upwind end I turned onto the taxiway and headed for dispersal. "Charlie Two clear, over."

The crew piled out into the darkness and sheltered beneath the starboard wing. Sergeant Donovan was waiting in his hut. He pushed the form 700 across his desk (fabricated from an engine crate), and offered me a pen. "Everything all right?" (Donovan didn't hold with calling Pilot Officers "Sir": you had to be at least a Squadron Leader before he brought himself to that.)

"Apart from a few little holes in the fuselage," I said, "she's fine." (No matter how masculine the call sign, aircraft to flying men, and ships to sailors, are always feminine.)

"Gee-box okay?"

"Yes, for what it's worth. When are we going to get an H2S set?"

"When am I going to get my Chiefy's crown?"

"You know what they say—you'll get no promotion . . ."

". . . this side of the ocean. Yeah, bless 'em all. The crew bus is on its way."

Outside, the sky was even darker, and the snow was still falling, muffling the sound of the Lancasters— one on the runway, one on the approach, another downwind and a dozen in the "stack". Wickenby's birds were returning

igator, but we've had some excellent substitutes, and as a lead crew we should get a good one. Our chances of coming through are good, I believe.

Monday, 24 April 1944 Over here, probably because of the larger number of men endangered [than in the Pacific air war], it is the policy to have the unfortunate drop out of the formation. Can't slow up for ten men when it involves the lives of hundreds more. So here a fellow either rides hell out of his remaining three engines and stays in, or peels out to take a chance on getting fighter escort back or not meeting Jerry at all. If he's really hurt, he'll probably 'hit the deck' to come home on three at about 100 to 500 feet of altitude. This puts the plane out of flak and fast fighters have only the topside to shoot at and just one pass at a time to do it with. There are three pilots in our squadron who have come back across Germany on three engines. One chap lost No. 2 on the way into the target, dropped his bombs with the group, got another bad flak hole in the tail, and came home alone. Another lost an engine earlier on a different mission. He stayed at altitude, bombed some airfield coming out and returned. These 'exploits' are jokingly mentioned when we're fanning the breeze, but there is no thought of something warranting a medal having been done.

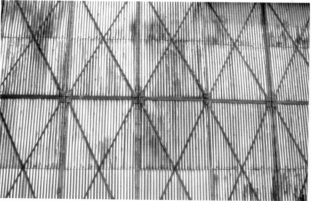

above: The main runway at the former RAF Bardney base in Lincolnshire; right: A memorial window for Royal Canadian Air Force air crew at Great Gransden in Cambridgeshire; top centre: T-2 hangar doors at the RAF Syerston base; below centre: Nissen huts at Bruntingthorpe in Leicestershire.

LET LIGHT PERPETUAL SHINE UPON THEM

405 SQUADRON 401 ESCADRILLE

THIS WINDOW COMMEMORATES THE EIGHT HUNDRED AND ONE AIRMEN OF 405 SQUADRON ROYAL CANADIAN AIRFORCE WHO GAVE THEIR LIVES ~ 1941-1945

to the nest.

It had been our twenty-sixth operation, our sixth to Berlin, and it hadn't started well. Someone had burst a tyre on the taxiway, and it took so long to clear the obstruction that a lot of engines overheated and had to be shut down. Seven aircraft hadn't made the take-off deadline of thirty minutes after midnight; we had missed it by three minutes but we took off anyway, and Charlie Two had missed another Lancaster by inches on the climb. In an attempt to catch up with the stream, we had been obliged to cut some corners on the route to Germany. That had involved us in another problem.

Now the snow was falling thickly. "We'll be all right if this keeps up," said mid-upper gunner Protheroe. "There'll be a stand-down tonight." The crew bus whined round the taxiway and crunched to a halt below the aircraft's nose. The crew climbed in at the back and, by *droit de seigneur*, I sat with the driver. I was telling myself that maybe the reason why I hadn't queried Cassidy's message, when we had two hundred miles to run before our time on target, was because of all those short cuts, but I knew that wouldn't do: I should have checked it anyway. The course had been more or less due east when he came through on the intercom: Nav to pilot, can you make it one-five-five?"

It was a major course change, but what of that? He was the navigator. "One-five-five, roger." Ten minutes later, our nice dark piece of sky had been suddenly illuminated by a score of searchlights and a fusillade of flak—clearly the defences of a major city where no major city should have been. A brief discussion had elicited the facts: Cassidy had wanted a small increase of airspeed, I had responded

with a change of course—a course which had brought us directly over Hannover.

"Sorry about that, Hannover. Didn't mean to disturb you. You can stop shooting now—we'll be on our way." Despite using full power in an effort to catch up with the stream, we had been seven minutes late, and I had expected the sort of warm reception that greeted late arrivals, but the Big City had seemed almost quiescent after the Hannover fracas. It had been my fault—it was I who insisted on minimum use of intercom while we were over Germany. That part of the regime would have to be re-jigged. "MPH or degrees," I muttered, "we've got to have that clear."

The driver turned her head. "What was that, sir?"

"Nothing, just talking to myself. Don't you ever do that?"

"Oh, yes, often—when I'm on my own."

She braked to a stop outside the briefing room. The cab was warm and comfortable, the WAAF's voice was pleasant. It would be nice to stay there, to chat of this and that, maybe smoke a cigarette . . .

"Wakey, wakey, skipper, let's be having you. They want us for debriefing."

We left the flying kit in the locker room, handed in the parachutes, and accepted mugs of cocoa, tots of rum and a smile of welcome from the chaplain. Usually, I gave the rum to Myring, our regular bomb-aimer, who had a liking for it, but he was on commissioning leave, and his stand-in looked too young. I drank the rum and Cassidy's as well. It may have been the snow that prompted the indulgence—or maybe it was Hannover.

Briefing and debriefing were held in the same room—they just rearranged the furniture while we were away. The CO and the Squadron

Friday, 28 April 1944

I've heard of fellows getting all hopped-up about this game of war, but by gosh, I can't see it. When I finish this tour, I'm going to do all in my power to get a non-operational job. If I can't do that, I'm going to work like hell to get in with the 'buzz boys', either P-47s or P-51s. The mission yesterday qualified me for the air medal. I'm now a beribboned veteran.

Sunday, 30 April 1944

We ran into flak so thick it appeared like a cloud ahead. Jerry's interceptors met us before we reached Berlin and because our timing was off and we had no fighter protection, he accompanied us all the way back across Germany. Twogood and Ravetti each got one. Sam missed the most marvelous shot. An Fw-190 was making a head-on attack. Sam had him in his sights for a dead shot, pressed the triggers, and—nothing happened. He broke into a cold sweat, felt that he'd shrunk to a fly speck size on his sight view but still wasn't small enough. That German just fanned the ship so his guns sprayed the whole formation. He got an engine and the stabilizer of the fellow flying next to me. My only view of the pass was a flash of silver with a red nose spinner and a yellow stripe around the cowl. For that split second I seemed to stop the Jerry in my sight. I had the instantaneous feeling that he was aiming at me personally. Then he was gone and this ship alongside was smoking and falling back. The boys saw seven 'chutes come out before the winged ship disappeared in the clouds.

It was a hell of a trip. There were contrails to confuse formation flying, constant attacks even during flak, and because of the length of the trip and our loading, we had to sweat out gas.

Flak has a terrible fascination. There is a five-ball burst, and the black smoke rolls out like a plume dancing in a heavy wind. Then it is caught in the slipstream and disappears. If it is close enough to hear, it is a rather subdued 'pooh'. The pieces sound like hail on the plane.

But when the flak first starts it is generally low and ahead. Step by step it advances up. Then you find yourself saying, 'The next one is it. Can't miss this next time. This is it. Next one.' Well, so far, the next one hasn't done all it was expected to do. Perhaps there hasn't been a 'next one', although we've had damage on the bomb doors. A fellow gets a detached air while watching those angry, black puffs. Can't do a thing about them so you relax and observe,

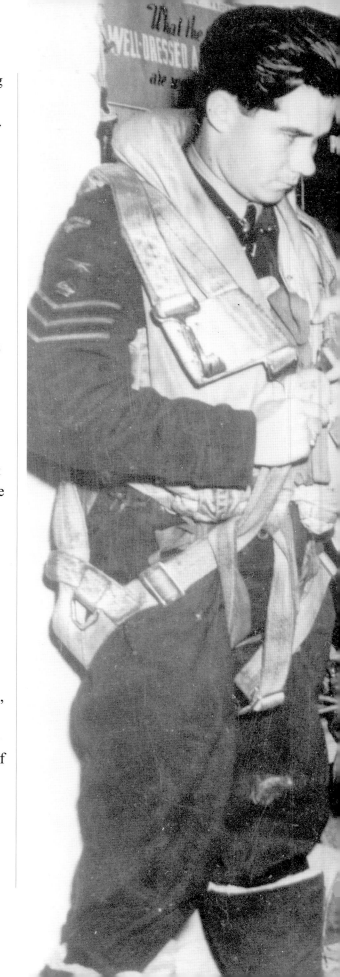

right: Lancaster crewmen of No 467 Squadron in their locker room at RAF Waddington.

Commander moved among the tables, listening in on one interrogation or another; WAAF clerks brought cigarettes and plates of biscuits. The CO caught my eye and gave a flicker of a smile; the Squadron Commander was rather less demonstrative. Their well-pressed uniforms and freshly-shaven faces contrasted sharply with the appearance of my crew, who looked like the survivors of an unsuccessful Himalayan expedition.

I was hoping that one of the more experienced IOs would make himself available, but the only free table was presided over by the blonde WAAF officer known to all as Clueless Kate, and at her debriefings I had often felt that she didn't understand the questions, let alone the answers.

Willy-nilly, we grouped ourselves around her and went through the motions: yes, we had bombed the primary target, at least we thought we had: George Wilson had aimed at the centre of a vivid orange glow, but you couldn't really tell with ten-tenths cumulus below. No, we hadn't heard the Master Bomber, nor had we seen the target indicators—ten-tenths cloud, remember, ma'am—but three sky markers, red dripping green, went down just astern of us only seconds after bomb release. That's right, after. The gunners had seen a few fighters on the run-in to the target, but we hadn't been attacked; we had observed the odd shoot-down, and their locations were noted in the navigator's log; yes, we had collected a few flak fragments, but nothing to worry about—that sort of thing was bound to happen now and then . . . We'd rather like to move along now, ma'am, if that's all right with you.

The snow was ankle-deep, and the temperature was lower than a grass-snake's belly, but the mess was only three-quarters of a mile

hypnotized by them. If I'm flying, I can't resist a corner of the eye glance to see how close they are.

Condensation trails make lovely photographs but are like clouds to formation flying. Ducking in and out of them adds to the terror or crashing into a friend. They were dense at one point when we were under direct attack, so it was necessary to fly close for fire power. Those moments are almost unbearable. A man feels like screaming or sobbing, but instead he hopes.

It was rough and we came home sweating out gas and weather. The ground under our feet never felt better. We are alerted again for tomorrow and I've been assigned a new navigator. Have to get him settled.

Wednesday, 3 May 1944
It is not uncommon for crews to fly formation without navigators. Another thing that has proven to be a lot of hooey is crew solidarity. Crews are literally thrown together when needed. Tomorrow we'll fly a nine-man crew with a substitute radio operator. What can you do? Wentz is in the hospital with ear trouble, and we're scheduled. We haven't had a real tryout as a lead crew, but are flying all the time as deputy lead. We are quite content with this setup. We fly without a command pilot and don't have so many 'foreigners' in the ship. Lead crews are always being split up to carry specialists.
Saturday, 13 May 1944

away and the walk didn't bother me at all. I had reached a condition in which neither pain nor pleasure meant a thing. We ate the baked beans, sausages and eggs, and trudged another half-mile to our beds. At half-past eight, having reinforced the blankets with a greatcoat and an Irvin jacket, I slipped between the sheets, while Cassidy, as always, knelt to say his prayers. Good show, Jimmy, say one for us all.

The Merlin engines still droned in my ears, the flak bursts flashed before my eyes, I could still taste oxygen and traces of the rum, but that was quite all right: the snow was falling. Let it fall all day, let it fall all week, let it bury Wickenby, the runways and the Lancasters.

Sixty seconds later—according to Cassidy it was six hours, but that just wasn't credible—the news that our ineffable CO had equipped every non-flying officer, NCO and aircraftman with spades, brooms and shovels. He, they and the Sno-go had worked throughout the morning, and would continue until they cleared the duty runway and the taxiways. "Really," I enthused, "I hope they all get frostbite and double pneumonia."

"That reminds me," said Cassidy, "Fairbairn has a cold, and the doc grounded him. Oh, and George Wilson is flying with his own crew. We'll need a couple of spare bods."

"Splendid. And the bad news?"

"They've patched Charlie Two up, and the fuel load is maximum. You'd better get a move on, or we'll miss late lunch."

"Is it all right if I brush my teeth?"

Lunch was a bowl of thin, grey soup, a piece of hard, flaky fish with mashed potatoes, carrots and the eternal Brussels sprouts, followed by jam tart and a slop of yellow water advertised as custard. It wasn't all that appetising but a man had to eat. From the table talk it

seemed that, of four hundred Lancasters in last night's operation, twenty-eight—two of which belonged to Wickenby—had not been seen again. That, too, was bound to happen now and then.

The question was what to do with the two-and-a-half hours before the evening briefing. In our early days at Wickenby, we would have flown an NFT—a night flying test—in Charlie Two, but all that had ended with the Battle of Berlin. Now we accepted the Lancasters on trust. I wasn't in the mood for writing letters home, and the Taylors' farm, where we might expect a welcome, would mean a three mile route march through the snow. "Anyone fancy a game of billiards?" I asked, and was overwhelmed by silence. "Or ping-pong?" More silence. "Or tiddly-winks?"

There was nothing for it but to quit the comparative comfort of the mess for the small, dank hut beside the airfield perimeter which served as the flight office. This was where the Flight Commander did his paper work, assigned crews to the battle order and arranged the training programme; he had the desk, the armchair and the telephone. Non-commissioned aircrew had access to the crew-room and their section huts for these inactive moments, but it was accepted that commissioned pilots used the flight office as a meeting place, somewhere to shoot the breeze, exchange the current rumours, and scan the latest issue of *Tee Em* or *Aircraft Recognition*.

Of the assembled pilots, three were Australians (as were Cassidy and Myring), and eight were Britishers. We got along all right, and I liked the Aussies' style. They had their mishaps in the air, the way we all did, but they retained an air of competence and common sense that rang a bell with me, and they

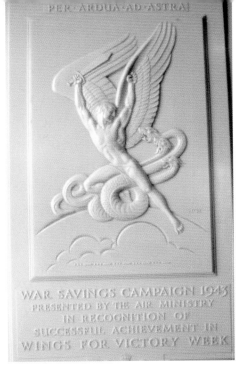

PER · ARDUA · AD · ASTRA

WAR SAVINGS CAMPAIGN 1943
PRESENTED BY THE AIR MINISTRY
IN RECOGNITION OF
SUCCESSFUL ACHIEVEMENT IN
WINGS FOR VICTORY WEEK

far left: The RAF bomber station at Binbrook; left: A War Savings Campaign plaque; below: The little control tower at Great Gransden.

I'm very much afraid this damn war will last longer than 90 per cent of the people at home think. Naturally, we combatants get a more direct look at things, but this very fact can give us a limited view. Maybe our sector is tougher than others, and so our overall picture would get distorted. Men here are sure of victory, of course, but it will take time. Germany knows it will lose everything, so everything will be tossed in before giving up.

The London leave was perfect. We arrived at noon on Thursday. The number of cabs and the crowds on the streets impressed us at first. I've never seen as many cabs, even in Chicago. We never had any trouble getting one, and they were cheap until blackout time. Then the sky was the limit. A trip that cost about 30 cents in daylight ran about $1.00 after dark. We didn't have much trouble getting a good hotel room and had excellent food at one of the officer's clubs. We bought some clothes at the big PX and then went in search of liquor. Finally bought Booth's dry gin and some good scotch at $13 a fifth for the gin and $17 for the whisky. Saw 'Something for the Boys' the following evening. It was a fair show, but the chorus saved the day. What seductive legs, and of course, we were only three rows from the front.

I bought five more records. Then we tried to buy a pipe from Dunhill's. The shop had

seemed to be devoid of pretentiousness and guile. It would have been easy to make a friend of any one of them, but I had learned my lesson about that. When fellows I had trained with, such as Scotty Walker and Dave Garrett, had gone down, and then McCleod, Davison and Buzz Marshall, it had seemed as though a part of me had gone along with them. There had been enough of that: relationships now, except for those with the crew of Charlie Two, were kept on a strictly epidermal level.

I stared out of the window. The snow had stopped and the visibility was excellent. Black and glistening, with their bomb-doors gaping and turreted nose pointing into the wind, the waiting bombers were spaced around the field. The little scrub trees beside the Snelland road crouched, white and ghostly—like Napoleon's soldiers on the great retreat from Moscow. Silhouetted on the south-western skyline, the great cathedral towered over Lincoln, serene and symmetrical. It was a satisfying sight. If anybody needed a symbol of England and the things that we were fighting for, it would fill the bill.

"They're still out on the runway," said Tony Wright, "the Old Man and his labour gang." Wright was a tall, fair Englishman with a feathery mustache, and a living rebuttal of the theory that flying was incompatible with booze. Wright never spared himself in his attempts to drink the pubs of Lincoln dry, and yet he persistently survived. "Jolly fine show," he continued, "don't you think so?"

"No."

The Flight Commander lit a cigarette, and asked if anyone had reported sick. I mentioned Fairbairn, and he scanned the crew list. "Sergeant Colles is spare until Smithy comes back. You can have him."

"And I need a bomb-aimer."

"Goodness me, what a nuisance you are. You'd better take the new chap—just arrived from Flying Training Command."

I boggled at him. "Straight out of training, sir?"

"He's been an instructor, old thing, a bombing instructor."

That did not enthuse me: the sort of bombing runs they taught in FTC were significantly different from those we made on Germany. "Thanks very much, sir."

"Don't mention it."

No one liked to have a spare bod in the crew, nor did anyone like being a spare bod in someone else's crew. Often, it seemed that one jinxed the other. "We lost our mid-upper," you would hear, "flying spare with so-and-so when they all got the chop."

Belay that thought, I told myself, it's supersti

tious crap. John Colles is a nice chap, and a capable wireless-operator; this bomb-aimer might be just as good. It's not fair to condemn him because he is a sprog—we all began that way.

The sky was dark before the timings filtered through: main briefing at 2100 hours, flying meal at 2145. That meant transport to dispersal would be at 2230 and take-off one hour later. The CO's work force had completed their assignment: the runway and the taxiways were clear. They hadn't quite managed to clear the Drem lighting system, so they marked the runway with good, old-fashioned gooseneck flares instead.

"If they'd only made briefing half an hour later," said Cassidy, "we could have gone to the cinema."

"They never seem to think of things like that. What's on, anyway?"

"Errol Flynn in something. Does it matter?"

In the crew room, Walker, Protheroe and rear gunner Bretell were playing pontoon for pennies. Their conversation was restricted to "I'll take another card," "Give me one more," and either "Stick" or "Bust". Bretell was never garrulous, but Protheroe usually chattered on happily, and Walker seldom stopped. The silence was abnormal, but waiting for late briefings had never been much fun.

At last it was over, and we filed into the room we had vacated some thirteen hours before. Observing the convention that you always sat where you did at your first briefing, like a church-going family taking the same pew every Sunday, we occupied the third row on the right of the aisle. No one actually went down on his knees, but most men sat in momentary silence, and it may be that some of

suffered a direct hit one time, and was now quite modernized. But to buy a pipe one has to arrive at 8:00 am and hope that the 12 to 24 briars for that day will last until they get to him. The queues number about 50 people every morning, so until I get a seven-day leave, I don't get a pipe. Vital labour needed elsewhere is the answer.

Tuesday, 16 May 1944
We have a brand new ship assigned to us now. It is quite an improvement over 'Willie' and if she'll fly as well as she looks, we'll be very happy with her. I met the crew chief only today. He seems like a good man, and his other ship has gone twenty missions without a balk, so we can only hope for a duplicate performance. If there is no mission tomorrow we hope to make an acceptance flight. There are several modifications that will make things easier for the crew to out their duties, so if she'll fly, we all ought to be happy. By coincidence, the call letter on the tail is N.

top: A fine daylight image of an Avro Lancaster in flight.

Thursday, 18 May 1944 My newly assigned ship was flown on a test hop by another pilot this afternoon. I'd hoped to do this myself, but the weather was bad until noon, at which time I was stuck with this job, so for a time I'll just have to take this chap's word for its flight ability. He raved about it being one sweet aircraft. Flies beautifully, trims up so nicely that very few corrections have to be made when the automatic pilot is switched in, and that so-convenient mechanism works fine. His test hop wasn't what I'd call a thorough check, but it surely makes me eager to get up in that plane. And it is confirming what I was led to believe about the ship, judging from the paperwork that came along with it. Looks like we once more have a good, clean airplane. Knock on wood and fingers crossed.

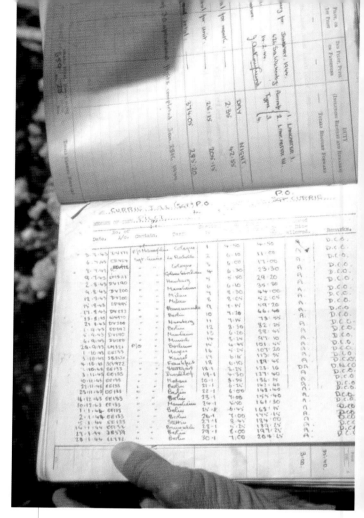

top left: Former Lancaster and Mosquito pilot, Jack Currie; top centre: Jack's logbook; top right: The Bomber Command Memorial window in Lincoln Cathedral; right: The No 617 Squadron memorial in Woodhall Spa, Lincolnshire, based on a breached dam in the Ruhr after the famous raid of May 16-17 1943.

them offered up a prayer. Then, like me, they started looking round to see who was or wasn't present.

There were many faces I didn't recognize—replacement crews, recently arrived. We would get to know them if they stayed a while. The trouble was they didn't always do that. The crews, for example, who had not come back this morning—I could bring none of them to mind.

Statistics showed that the first few operations were those most likely to ensure you gave up smoking—permanently. Get through five or six, and the odds against survival shortened quite a bit. You began to learn the tricks they didn't teach in training schools: stay with the bomber stream but don't bump into other aircraft, don't look

into searchlight beams, forget the "standard corkscrew", turn into fighters if they are coming at you, don't chatter on the intercom, don't fly over hot spots like Texel, Terschelling, Amiens or Chartres, don't make dummy runs on well-defended targets, don't eat baked beans before you fly . . .

There was another crucial phase around the twenty-five mission mark—when you thought you knew the score. You and the crew and the Lancaster were one and indivisible, and neither flak nor fighters could ever bring you down. Last night, that fallacy had been chillingly revealed. Thanks a lot, Hannover, we'll be more careful now.

At one minute to nine, give or take three seconds, the Commanding Officer, followed by his retinue, strolled down the aisle. "Please, don't get up," he drawled, as soon as he was sure that everyone was standing. A redcap shut the doors, and the lights were dimmed. The Squadron Commander mounted the rostrum and went through the performance of drawing back the curtain. All eyes were focused on the map. A murmuring arose, a groan or two, a chuckle. "No surprises, chaps," he said, "the target is Berlin."

There were no surprises in the briefing either. Three hundred and sixty Lancasters, plus a few Halifaxes and PFF Mosquitoes, would fly the operation. Cloud was expected in the Berlin area, with good visibility above. If the cloud hid the target, the PFF would use Wanganui marking—slow-burning, parachuted flares. The route passed over the Zuider Zee, continuing east across the rivers Ems and Weser, with a north-east turn above the Mecklenburg plain to attack the target heading south-south-east. The outbound route was southerly, leaving Magdeburg to starboard, over the Harz moun-

Wednesday, 24 May 1944 We're listening to a German program for Yanks in the ETO. Lots of good music interspersed with ditties about D-Day meaning Death, Defeat, Destruction, Dunkirk and Dieppe. Anti-Jewish propaganda and threats of all sorts. They like to dwell on sore spots between Yanks and Limeys. Rotten weather in England, terrible tasting beer, girls expecting U.S. soldiers to have gold pockets, and the mud at most bases. The idea is good but they generally put it so coarsely that one either laughs or is disgusted. Bing Crosby, Frances Langford, and good, name bands are featured on records with a German band supplying accordion, sax and piano native music. It is also interesting to get the German side of our bombings and attacks. Apparently our bombs are hitting only hospitals, churches, cathedrals, old women and kids, just like theirs did and do.

Sunday, 28 May 1944
The layman can't possibly imagine what thrills, narrow escapes and heartbreaking things occur when assembling at, say, 17,000 feet. The ships are loaded to the point of it being physical effort to keep them in the air. As each smaller unit is formed, it has to join with a larger mass on practically a seconds schedule. When the biggest formations are falling into line, seconds still count, and if they're wrong, whole formations sift through each other. God-a-mighty, what turbulence, and what a sickening feeling to see two big bombers tangle and start tumbling earthward. If each man didn't have

tains, to rejoin the inbound course at the coast of Holland. The leading PFF crews would drop green spot fires to mark the turning points (and show everyone in Germany exactly where we were; Hermann Goering ought to give them all Iron Crosses). The total distance was 1,237 miles, and the flight was timed for seven hours.

The SIO made one of his little jokes: this one was about the flak guns in Berlin being fired by fifteen- year-old members of the Hitler Youth as fast as Russian POWs could load them. One or two chuckles greeted the remark, but I forbore to smile. Maybe I had lost my sense of humour. I was more concerned with the new men in the crew. The bomb-aimer was leaning forward in his chair, listening intently and nibbling a pencil. I made a mental note to have a cheery word

and , in passing, to discourage dummy runs; big John Colles, impassive and relaxed, was serenely gazing at the ceiling. I decided not to worry about him.

The section leaders spoke their familiar pieces, we all checked our watches on the navigation leader's mark, and the CO rose to give his valediction: "Your meal will be ready in five minutes. Good luck to you all, and I'll see you at debriefing."

Sixty minutes later, Charlie Two halted at the runway caravan. Down there, in the snow, stood a group of muffled figures—airmen and WAAFs who had loyally braved the cold to see us off. "Trim tabs set," I said, "pitch fully fine; fuel, Johnny?"

"Contents okay, skipper; master cocks on, number two tank selected, cross-feed off, booster pumps on."

"Air intake."

"Cold. Radiator shutters auto."

The caravan's Aldis lamp shone green; I released the brakes and Charlie Two rolled onto the runway. Suspended in her bomb-bay were a 4,000 pound "cookie", three 1,000 pounders, a dozen cannisters of incendiary bombs and a photo-flash. All we had to do was carry them to Germany and drop them on the centre of Berlin—well, somewhere in Berlin. It was really quite a simple exercise. "Stand by for take-off, everybody. Follow me through on the throttles, Johnny. Here we go again."

We came back from that trip more or less unscathed, and from another four—Stettin, Brunswick and two more to Berlin. We touched down from the last one in the early morning of January 28th 1944, and it was not until a fine September day in 1992 that I landed at Wickenby again. Cassidy was with

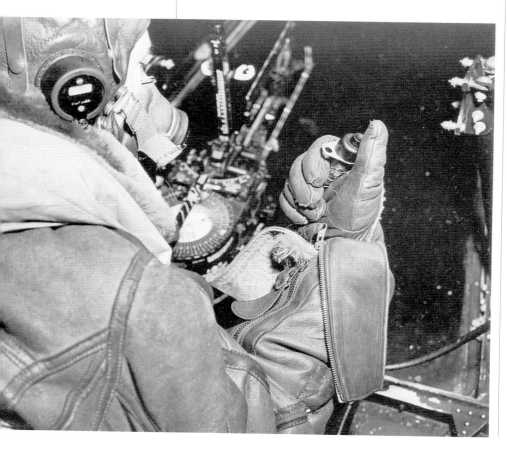

me in the single- engined Cessna when we flew in for the open-air service annually mounted by ex-squadron members in memory of their comrades who never would return.

Half the airfield had reverted to the land, and the rest was in the hands of a civil flying club. Coach-loads of veterans and relatives arrived, among them Johnny Walker; an ATC band played, the chaplain gave a sermon and favourite hymns were sung, while the sun shone down on the Icarus memorial. The service ended with the Requiem, and someone touched my arm. "You won't know me," he said. "I'm Frank Taylor's son—your crew used to come down to Dad's farm."

I looked him over. It was difficult to see the lively infant I remembered in this solid citizen—as difficult as it was to see the far-flung bomber base in the little airport, or the fresh-faced aircrew in the grey-haired men around us. Even the village pub was unrecognizable, and as for The Saracen's Head in Lincoln . . .

Two Buccaneers of the present day 12 Squadron roared fast and low above our heads. The pilots rocked their wings and everybody waved. "Hey," exclaimed Walker, "that's some aeroplane! How would you like to fly one of those?"

I considered for a moment. Meanwhile, the Buccaneers flew half-way back to Lossiemouth. "Not particularly," I said. "That sort of aircraft is flown by a computer. The Lancaster was different—it needed a real pilot." They smiled at each other, and I knew what they were thinking. They were absolutely right: the years had taken something as they passed. I could no more fly a Buccaneer than run a four-minute mile. But at least we were at

Wickenby, standing in the sunshine, while a thousand men who flew from here were not.

ROYAL AIR FORCE
WICKENBY
No 1 GROUP BOMBER COMMAND
1942-1945
IN MEMORY OF
ONE THOUSAND AND EIGHTY MEN
OF 12 & 626 SQUADRONS
WHO GAVE THEIR LIVES ON
OPERATIONS FROM THIS AIRFIELD
IN THE OFFENSIVE AGAINST GERMANY
AND THE LIBERATION
OF OCCUPIED EUROPE
Per ardua ad astra
The "Icarus" Memorial at Wickenby

so much to think of immediately it would take the heart right out of him.

far left: The bomb aimer in an RAF Lancaster; below: A 'sparks' or wireless operator in a Lanc.

129

Apart from combat injuries, frostbitten feet and fingers, the inevitable head cold and the self-inflicted injuries sometimes known as hang-overs, the flying men of the USAAF and the RAF were seldom troubled by physical disorders. They had been thoroughly examined by doctors on enlistment and routinely ever since. They were young and healthy, and their regimen was well-planned if austere. If they did develop symptoms, they often faced the sort of situation defined for all posterity, in another context, by the writer Joseph Heller as "catch-22": the sick bay was located so far from their quarters that only a well man could ever make it there.

It was, however, comforting to know that doctors, nurses and orderlies were there to give immediate assistance when a bomber brought a wounded crewman home. His comrades would have done what they could with field dressings, tourniquets and morphia while the plane was still in flight, but many limbs and lives were saved by expert attention as soon as the engines were shut down. Blood transfusions were given and instant surgery undertaken, often in the shadow of a bomber's wing.

Sometimes, when a pilot knew that urgent treatment was required, he would set down at the first field he came to after making landfall; at other times he would make a bee-line for his base. At one Eighth Air Force field, far from any hospital, *Ball of Fire*, a veteran B-17, too beat-up for further combat duties, was always standing by. When a red smoke cartridge, fired by Very pistol from a returning bomber, indicated wounded men on board, *Ball of Fire* was ready to provide a lift to hospital that was faster and less painful than a slow, jolting journey in a motor ambulance over country lanes.

A page extracted from the sick bay log at Grafton Underwood, dated April 25th 1945, shows some of the injuries sustained by crewmen of the 384th Bomb Group on the Oberpfaffenhofen mission and treated on the base; others, more life-threatening, required the resources of a hospital.

Anstead, William W., wounds right arm and forearm, penetrating, multiple, moderate severe.

Matican, Sigmund, wound left hand, dorsum, penetrating, moderate severe.

Bonanaza, John J., fracture right ankle, simple.

Wyatt, Kenneth A., sprain, left shoulder, moderate severe.

Perrone, Michael J., sprain, back, moderate severe.

Kanclewski, Edwin J., fracture, external malleolus, right, simple.

Cleland, Deston K., wound, penetrating, right thigh, moderate severe.

Helm, Gerard A., wound, penetrating, both legs, moderate severe.

Barad, Robert L., wound, penetrating, right knee, slight.

Brooks, James J., wounds, multiple, penetrating, right cheek and right arm, moderate severe.

Williamson, James E., wound, penetrating, plantar surface, right foot, moderate severe.

Sacco, Salvatore R., wounds, multiple, penetrating, right leg and right forearm.

Gowder, Charles F., burn, second degree, sole of right foot.

Leber, Richard E., contusion, right knee, moderate severe.

Baird, James J., wounds, penetrating, right chest and neck, moderate severe.

Although the men who crewed the warplanes were medically rated as "fully fit for flying", not every one of them could be regarded as a perfect specimen. There was a Lancaster gunner who had an artificial leg, and a famous fighter pilot

left: An Eighth Air Force B-17 crew member in full flying gear at his 91st BG base, Bassingbourn.

Friday, 9 June 1944
Today we were faced with what we all rather expected, but secretly hoped would never come to pass. There is no such thing as only thirty missions any more. We will keep on going over until this thing is finished. So, unless the Germans say 'Uncle' before then, we haven't much hope of getting home in September. It surely makes this mess look endless right at the present moment. We'll just have to keep hoping for an early finish.

Sunday, 18 June 1944
London was going through these 'pilotless planes' bombings with alert following alert. Gave us a creepy feeling to be under the stuff instead of above it. We never did see one of the 'planes' but heard them and their resulting explosions many times.

right: The hospital ward at the 388BG base, Knettishall in Suffolk.

by the name of Douglas Bader who had two. Many other airmen were afflicted with significant, if lesser, disabilities. One long-surviving bomber captain suffered from such chronic flatulence that he constantly passed wind while his aircraft climbed to altitude. So vile were his emissions (he was a dedicated drinker) that his crew formed the habit of putting on their masks and turning on the oxygen as soon as they were airborne. An Australian navigator, who flew two tours of operations, always spewed into a sick-bag shortly after take-off, and rejected all suggestions that medication might be helpful with these words: "No thanks, skipper, the doc might ground me." A member of W.W. Ford's crew in the 92nd Bomb Group had a similar debility, and coped with it as stoically. Many an American came back from a mission with a lesion or a laceration which would have merited medical attention (if not a Purple Heart), but which he did not mention for fear of missing the next trip.

Men flew with headaches and stomach pains, chilblains and boils, sore throats and running noses, just as their comrades in the other services with similar afflictions had to fight their battles on the land and sea. The only minor ailments that kept fliers on the ground were blocked sinuses and, possibly, acute cases of diarrhoea.

Virus infections were relatively few, but pilot David Parry was unfortunate enough to catch the dreaded English "flu" within days of his arrival to join the 390th Bomb Group. He spent his first week overseas in an improvised infirmary, which was largely staffed by volunteers. "I've often wondered," he said, "where they recruited all those beautiful American girls from. I think a lot of them may have been daughters of commanding officers, and people like that. They were just first-class."

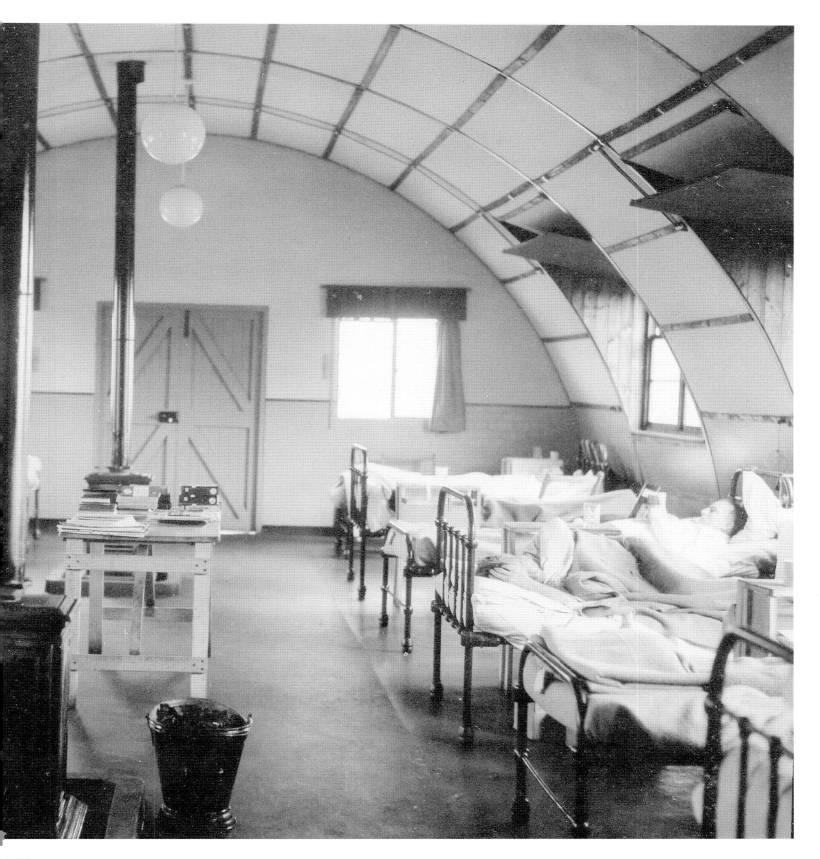

right: B-17s of the 100th Bomb Group at Thorpe Abbotts, Norfolk; below: An ambulance crew standing by on the airfield at Hardwick in Norfolk; below centre: A mossy leather flying glove found near a B-17 hardstand at the 384th BG base, Grafton Underwood, Northamptonshire; bottom right; A throat microphone found at Polebrook, Northamptonshire.

The occasional head cold which, for a ground staff man, might merely be a nuisance, could be a serious matter for a bomber crewman. Descending from high altitude in normal circumstances, he could equalize the pressures on either side of the aural membrane by yawning, swallowing or even chewing gum; with blocked sinuses, those simple measures were seldom so effective, and a perforated eardrum could result. "I got ear trouble over Munich," said RAF navigator Ted Richardson of 463 Squadron. "It was when we were diving. It was very painful, and I went to see the MO next day. He didn't ground me, but he restricted me to flying below ten thousand feet, which came to the same thing, because our Lancs were bombing from over twenty thousand. It was two months before I got right again."

There were certain fliers who mistrusted doctors, and would never voluntarily go inside a sick bay. A Lancaster rear gunner, a hardy Australian, was one such man. "He'd been constipated for days," his pilot noted, "but he wouldn't go to the MO. He said he didn't trust quacks. He took four pills the wireless op. gave him, a bar of Exlax and, not being one for half measures, drank half a tumbler of Andrews Liver Salts, all in quick succession. As an operation, it was totally successful, but the bomb doors opened just before he reached the target."

The USAAF's flight surgeons and the RAF's medical officers could help a lot in keeping up morale. They were trained to notice signs of "combat fatigue" and take remedial action. For the crewmen of the Eighth, a week of R and R (rest and recuperation) in comfortable surroundings was often enough to meet the case, and some dozen country houses or hotels in the quieter parts of England were provided for the purpose. These rest homes or "flak farms", staffed by the American Red Cross, offered a variety of leisure pursuits and the sort of service you would expect to find at a good hotel. A man could go walking or fishing, riding or shooting, or simply sit around and take it easy; he could go to bed late or early and, best of all, there would be no Charge of Quarters to rouse him for breakfast and a mission briefing. He could get up when he wanted to and, for a while, forget the bomber war.

The air commanders, however, never could forget it. No rest home could help them disremember that their frequent duty was to send, unwillingly but knowingly, a number of young men to their deaths. It required an unusual degree of moral hardihood to accept that duty, and fulfil it without flinching as the months went by and the lists of "Missing in action" or "Failed to return" grew longer with every mission flown. It was especially demanding on the sort of commander whose human instinct was to know and like his men, to feel for them as people, not as cogs in a machine. Such an officer, however tough mentally, however determined to prosecute the war, might at some point find the strain too much. Two fine motion pictures—*Twelve O'Clock High* and *Command Decision*—have portrayed this dilemma and men's reactions to it. It was usually resolved by the reassignment of the officer in question to less agonizing duties. It is known of Curtis E. LeMay, one of the Eighth Air Force's most successful and far-seeing commanders, who himself flew many missions, leading first a bomb group and later a division, that he deliberately avoided personal relationships with the men he led. "Ole Iron Ass" recognized the moral danger, and was careful to avoid it.

Returning from a mission, a B-17 of the 92nd Bomb Group was ditched in the English Channel, and the pilot nearly drowned; two

Tuesday, 20 June 1944
Our nice new airplane is now in the sub-depot getting patched together. We had a hot trip this morning and landed with one elevator control shot away. Kobel had a narrow escape when a flak piece hit a caliber .50, firing it through his pants leg. But our luck held and no one got hurt. Naturally, the briefed weather was all false. Instead of scattered clouds at 5,000 feet, we had complete cloud cover. As we came in for the landing, we almost hit a seagull. I'm sure I saw him thumb his nose at us. We've flown in weather here when the birds lined the runway and silently folded their wings over their eyes as we took off. They're no fools. Wish we could say the same for ourselves.

Saturday, 24 June 1944
A typical mission? What they all have in common is a 'sweat', varying in degrees from beginning to end. It all boils down to a mental anxiety that can be controlled, but is the governing factor every time. A mission is tough, often times, not from the enemy's action but from the fact that you know he is there and may add to your constant troubles of weather, assembling in a small area with hundreds of other sluggish-flying, overloaded, high-explosive freights, scratchy, squealing, static-charged headphones, and the plain 'dragged down' frustration of hanging equipment from your

bundled-up self.

We are alerted the night before. This has finally come to mean little. If during the night the High Command decides to use more airplanes the next day, you will be awakened, prepared or not. Or, if weather proves bad, you may not fly because the effort will be smaller or the mission scrubbed entirely. So, being alerted means nothing because one is practically always 'on the alert.'

Next is the awakening. Here the two types of sleepers are catalogued. Some boys can snore away no matter what is pending. It takes a good shaking or some sort of horseplay to wake them. Unfortunately, I'm a light sleeper, so I can hear the CQ open the outside door, or lean his bicycle against the hut. A shiver runs down my spine. Just anticipating how chilly it will be when I throw my legs over the edge of the cot to dress in those wee small hours of pre-briefing. At this time of the year, it is usually shortly after midnight. Sitting on the edge of the bed, yawning and shivering, the thoughts are, 'Here we go again.' Unconsciously, each man is convincing himself that he is not really as tired as he feels and that all those aches, pains and stomach flutters are in his mind. But he can't help wondering why the hell he didn't take that instructor's job, at least, or stay on the ground.

Shaving and washing was all completed a few

days later, with another damaged airplane, he barely made it back to a field close by the coast. Understandably, that pilot was in a state of shock. Ray Wild was his friend: "After that, as soon as he got near an airplane engine running up, he started vomiting. He just couldn't stop. The medics worked on him there a bit, then they sent him to a flak farm and put him into what they called a deep sleep. You just sleep all the time, and you're supposed to wake up feeling like a million dollars. Then he came back to the group and the same thing happened. All of a sudden he was gone from the group, and that was the last we heard of him."

During his tour with 103 Squadron at Elsham Wolds in Lincolnshire, pilot Alan Forman had little need for contact with the medicos. "They weren't much in evidence unless you had a problem. There were some sinus troubles, but I don't remember many colds. I suppose if chaps were worried or depressed they could go and see the MO, but they kept it quiet if they did. I remember one or two people being hauled before the CO and told they'd be classed as LMF [Lack of Moral Fibre] if they didn't get on with it. That must have been a terrible thing—very difficult to overcome."

Part-way through his tour as a lead navigator with the 94th Bomb Group, Sidney Rapaport enjoyed six days R and R at Stockport's Palace Hotel, near Blackpool in Lancashire (incidentally, the only rest home which catered for both officers and enlisted men). "It was a marvelous Victorian edifice," said Rapaport, very well-to-do, middle-class people. All the women from Stockport came in for the dances almost every night. We were completely sexually emancipated. You might get no sleep at all, but it was a very joyous kind of thing."

Colonel Dale O. Smith, on a few days' break

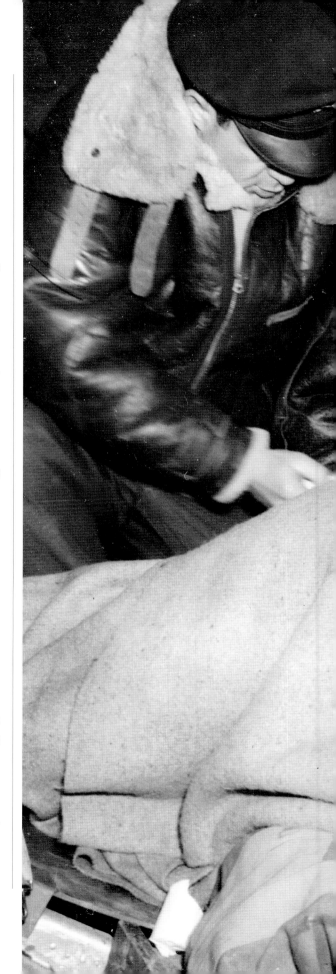

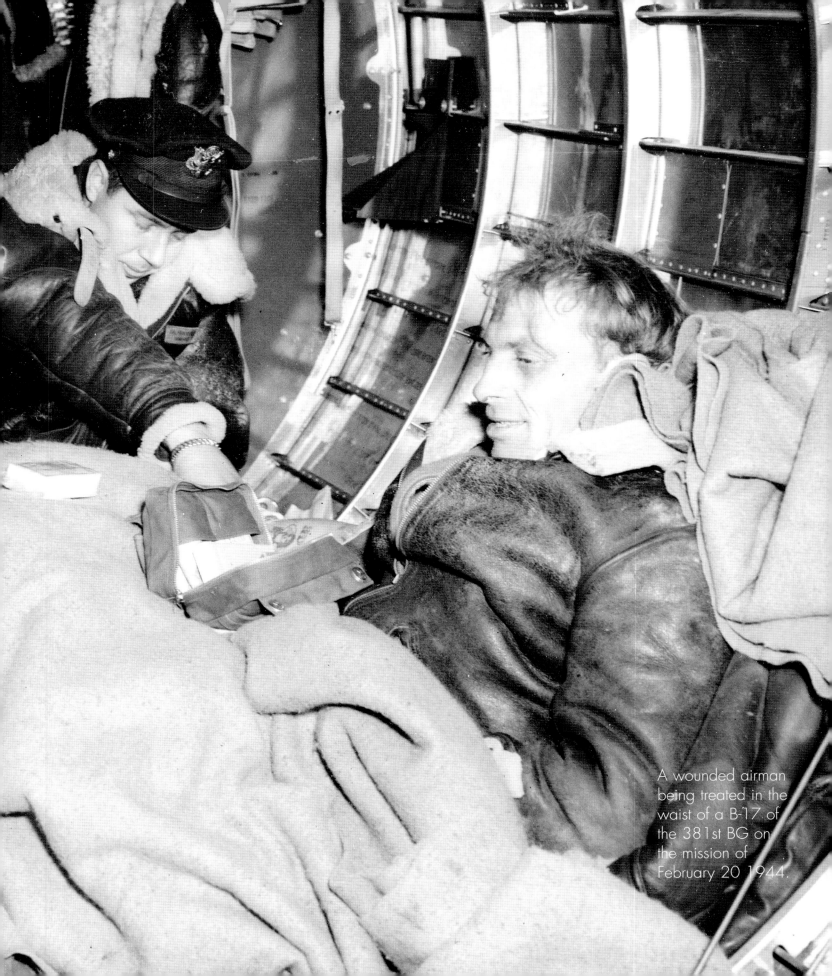

A wounded airman being treated in the waist of a B-17 of the 381st BG on the mission of February 20 1944.

hours before. Not having been in bed long enough to ruffle the hair, we stumble off in the dark immediately after dressing. At the mess hall the men are positively catalogued again. Those that can eat heartily at any hour, and those who have butterflies in the belly so early in the morning. Luckily, I can eat OK, although I feel as hungry as ever by take-off time.

Chow finished, we pile into trucks to go to the briefing. In the locker room, friendly razzing and the same corny jokes are gone through every day. Fellows greet each other with 'Hello Milk Run. Didn't think they'd call you in on this one. We may see some fighters.' 'Joe, are you bothered with constiption or dysentery when those 109s come in?' 'How many *real* missions have you got in now, ol' boy? Weren't you ashamed to take credit for that last recall?' 'Boy, that Focke Wulf puckered me up for a week with his pass yesterday.' 'They'll never get an extra mission out of me. No, sir, I'll get me a mess officer's job, so help me God!' This banter never changes much.

When the route is unveiled in the briefing room, there are chuckles or groans, depending on the length of the route and the territory where the penetration is being made. The flak maps bring their unrestrained comments, too. The weather officer gets a certain number of catcalls, depending on how

from Grafton Underwood, agreed—at least, about the comfort and the staff: "Living was easy at the flak house, with clean sheets in soft beds, and charming but entirely proper Red Cross girls as managers and hostesses."

Charles Bosshardt's crew were due for their only R and R on May 10th 1945. "Then VE Day occurred," he remembered, "and we didn't go. I always felt cheated about that. And we didn't get any celebrities or USO shows visiting us at Horsham St Faith. They may have felt we had it so good we didn't need entertaining."

Calvin Swaffer of the 303rd had slightly better luck than Bosshardt. "I received one week of leave while I was over there, and I went to Torquay, on the southern coast of England. Believe it or not, they have palm trees there. It's right in line with where the gulf current comes up. We played some golf and laid around until it was time to go back."

When attempts are made to compare the present day with an earlier time, the device is sometimes used of imagining that an observer, say, from Mars, visits all the other planets twice in every century to check on developments, and report back to the appropriate Martian government department. Supposing that this visitor last came to planet Earth in 1944, it is interesting to speculate on what might be included in 1994's report. He (maybe "she" or "it", but "he" for convenience) would surely note the ability to fuse the nuclei of certain atoms, the progress in space and supersonic flight, the invention of the micro-chip, the laser beam and organ transplant surgery. He might comment on the decline of communism, the rise of women to positions of authority, the rather greater rise in general criminality, but if his remit were to check, not just the main developments, but other changes in the way that people live, he might include such matters as the advent of pre-packaged foods, the ball-point pen and electronic music, the mass addiction to the television screen, the extraordinary renown of certain entertainers . . . and in passing he would notice that the average male in the developed world, from adolescence to early middle-age, is noticeably heavier and larger than his predecessor of fifty years ago.

It is true that there were tall men in the allied air forces, as there were sturdy men and strong men, but you rarely saw a fat man near a combat aircraft. This could partly be ascribed to the wartime diet, partly to the fact that men seldom put on flesh when they face death day by day, and partly to the work of service doctors, who measured height, weight and blood pressure at every opportunity, and a tendency to tubbiness with a brisk instruction to cut down on alcohol and take more exercise. This regime was reinforced by certain air commanders, who liked to see their people wearing singlets, shorts and plimsolls to indulge in callisthenics (PT to the RAF), or taking part in active outdoor games. It was not unknown, when the weather prohibited flying, for an eager-beaver commander to lead his flight crews on a five-mile route march around the field perimeter.

Given the alternative, most men would rather play a ball game than take part in foot drill or callisthenics. Indeed, a love of games was one of the many things that young Americans had in common with their British cousins. That this is no longer entirely true—at least, not of the British—may reflect the view of certain educationalists that competition among children, especially in sport, is really rather bad for them and ought to be discouraged. In the less enlightened 1940s, however, it was generally

agreed that hitting or kicking various types of ball, throwing them or catching them, or running up and down with them, provided harmless pleasure and good exercise for all.

Every permanent RAF station had facilities for Association and Rugby Union football (soccer and rugger) in the winter, and for cricket and tennis in the summer months; many were equipped with gymnasia and squash courts. Even on the less salubrious wartime-built bases (and they were the majority), attempts were often made to level out a field for the footballers and another for the cricketers. On many USAAF bases, similar provision for the enjoyment of ball games was made, and the Special Services were tasked with making the appropriate equipment readily available.

Walking past a station sports field in the afternoon, provided that the sound of aero

accurate he has been previously. There are always clouds and cloud layers to contend with.

Now back to the locker room. The new men sometimes have trouble deciding how much to put on, but after a few missions a man soon figures how he can maintain a certain amount of comfort with his minimum of clothing. Too many clothes cause discomfort, too few cause trouble in the opposite extreme. Going from normal temperatures to the low thermometer settings that prevail at altitude in a matter of minutes necessitates some close figuring in the wardrobe department.

Flying gear was worn

far left: A gunner's heated 'blue bunny suit'; left: A B-17G of the 100th Bomb Group, *Humpty Dumpty*.

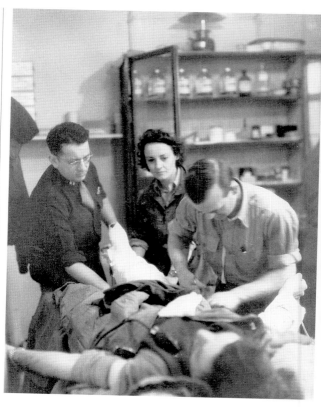

engines did not drown all else, it was sometimes possible to hear the mellow whack of bat on ball, or the solid thump of a big kick down the ground. Murmurs of "Well played, sir", "Good shot", and the sound of three or four people clapping, quietly and politely, would suggest that a game of cricket was in progress; more vociferous acclaim would indicate a game of baseball, softball, or any type of football, American or British.

The occasional spectacle of an American, courageously participating in a cricket match, was only rivalled in its comicality by the sight of an Englishman (especially one who had not played "rounders" as a child) trying his hand at baseball.

Standing at the "wicket" with the bat held high, John Doe from Wyoming tends to ignore any ball which bounces before it reaches him—a ball regarded by cricketers as being "on a length". Receiving a "full toss", he whacks it high into the outfield, hurls down the bat and sets off briskly in the direction of the position known as "cover point". The ball is returned by a fielder to the "wicket keeper" who calmly removes a "bail" from the "stumps". The umpire raises a finger, signifying "Out". Baffled, Doe returns to the pavilion, and the next "batsman" takes his place. "I told you, Yank," says the team captain sternly, "we run between the wickets, not around the field."

"Yeah, I guess I forgot." As well he might: the laws of cricket (never known as "rules") are labyrinthine in their complexity.

Doe's batting side are eventually "all out" and, after the ritual of consuming tea and buns, they take the field. In due course, Doe is called upon to bowl. Here, he thinks, is the chance he has been waiting for. Was he not star pitcher for his high school team? He winds up and hurls down a ball which whistles past the batsman's chest. The umpire lifts a hand and intones "No ball".

"Whaddya mean—No ball? That was strike one in my book."

The umpire shakes his head. "You threw it—that's a no ball."

"I pitched it. What do you want me to do—take it to him on a silver tray?"

"No. You have to bowl it."

Percy Prune's performance on the baseball diamond is equally bizarre. Initially, he requires to know where the "stumps" are. Informed that they do not feature in the ball game, he takes his normal stance with the bat tapping on the plate and, receiving what to him is a "full toss", prods the ball away and, carrying the bat, trots towards the pitcher's mound. He is surprised and dismayed to be instantly thrown out at first base. Later, stationed in right field, he invariably tosses the ball in to the catcher or the pitcher, despite the urgent cries of the basemen. Given a chance to take the pitcher's place, Prune lobs his cunning "leg breaks" on what he thinks of as "a length", only to have each ruled as a "ball", which utterly confounds him.

The fact was that both John Doe and Percy Prune were best suited, by training and experience, to the sports they knew and understood. To expect either, unprepared, to play the other's game was to deal in unreality. As well, put Doe's crew in a British heavy bomber and send them to a distant target in the middle of the night; as well, commit Prune's crew to a daylight mission in a Flying Fortress, maintaining close formation all the way. Each did it his way—the way that he knew best—and together they did it round the clock. It has been said of team games that they are warfare in miniature, and so a useful form of training for the main event. But games have certain rules or regulations, and there were no rules in the European skies. Up there, Doe and Prune, each doing it his way, flying by his own rules, were complementary and equally effective.

"I had pneumonia and spent three weeks in a hospital run by Americans. I got one vitamin a day; they were rationed. No medicine other than rest." - Calvin Swaffer, pilot, 303rd Bomb Group

"Should an enemy flying bomb appear to be about to descend, it would be advisable to retire to the shelters."
- note on the score card, Harrow School cricket match, 1944

piecemeal according to personal taste and crew position. Usually the Lanc's heating system blew warm upon the wireless operator, roasted the bomb aimer and left the navigator to freeze. So most of the navigators were wearing the whole gear, from leather Irvin jackets to silk under-socks. So were the rear gunners. Most W.Op. A.G.s on the other hand had only the mandatory helmet, boots and Mae West over the same working blue and white roll-neck sweater that they had worn at supper.
—from *Bomber* by Len Deighton

left: Wounded B-17 crew members are treated after a raid on a target in Germany in 1944.

Roger Armstrong was a B-17 radio-gunner and a member of the 91st Bomb Group, based at Bassingbourn, near Cambridge, England. Here he recalls one of his most memorable missions.

"I felt a tug on my shoulder, and before I could open my eyes and come out of the wonderful dream I was having, someone tugged again. He put his mouth close to my ear and shone a flashlight in my face. I realized I was not in Sioux Falls, necking with a beautiful brunette at Sherman Park. I was in the 401st Squadron barracks at Bassingbourn, looking at the duty corporal. 'Breakfast at 0300,' he said, 'briefing at 0400', stations at 0515.' And he was gone.

I shouldn't have been surprised. The day before, on October 14th 1944, we had dropped 'nickels' on Cologne; among them were copies of *The Stars and Stripes* printed in German, with a message to the Luftwaffe from General Doolittle, calling them a bunch of cowards and challenging them to a battle over Cologne the next day. Hilmer Beicker, our flight engineer, was born of German parents in Houston, Texas, and he had read the whole thing out to us over the intercom. We had all pitied the crews who would be going on the next day's mission after an insult like that.

While brushing my teeth, I admired the clean, yellow tiling in our latrine, and I thought how lucky we were to be stationed at a permanent base built by the Royal Air Force in 1938. The latrines were never crowded and we had central heating, so no battles with pot-bellied stoves like we had in basic training.

As I dressed quickly in a suntan shirt and old olive drab pants, I couldn't help feeling fear, deep inside. I was ashamed to admit that I was afraid, but I found in later years that you weren't normal unless you had that feeling. It was really dark when I went outside. I tested the temperature, and put on my fur-collared B-10 jacket. My bike was in a rack outside the door, but the light batteries were dead so I had to steer with one hand, with a flashlight in the other, as I rode to the combat mess hall.

All the combat crews ate at the combat mess

QUALIFIED QUAIL

Finally, loaded down with equipment, we pile into the trucks to go to the dispersals. Silence settles in and serious faces, each one a mask for thoughts of the job ahead and the details of the mission, stare out at the disappearing perimeter track. It is generally grey dawn by then. At the ship, the gunners, engineer and radio opertor have checked things over. The officers each go over their specialties. The pilot gives last minute instructions and information on bail-outs and evasive action for

below left and centre: Radio-gunner Roger A. Armstrong.

the area being flown over.

From then on it is a case of clock-watching, for take-offs have to be made on the second. Every man is keeping it to himself, but he is thinking and praying that this one will come off all right. Sort of wishing it were over but pushing that thought back in his mind. Contents himself with checking, checking, studying everything carefully, checking. If something is not quite right, but cannot be fixed at this late date, he curses and figures out his alternative, swearing he will get the son of a bitch who neglected that when he gets back. Generally, he is so glad to return that he will just mention the item to the guilty party with a laugh.

so the Air Force could control the types of food we ate. Nothing was fed to us on mission days that would cause gas in the stomach or the intestinal tract, because the gas would expand as your plane climbed to altitude. No one like the powdered eggs, especially when there were green spots on them. There was a large grill outside the serving line where we could fry eggs to our taste. We purchased our own eggs from the farmer whose back yard was right behind the hardstand of our B-17. When the pilot or the crew chief ran the engines up, the prop wash struck the chicken coops and the feathers really flew. We could never figure out how those hens could lay with all that going on. When the farmer was out of hen eggs, we would buy his duck eggs out of desperation, to avoid those horrible green and yellow powdered eggs.

After breakfast, we drifted over to the briefing building, the only Quonset hut on the base.

Time drags along until suddenly, the throttles are steadily pushed forward and the runway is flowing underneath. Air speed builds up until the pilot shouts 'Wheels!' and the mission is really on. Invariably, there is a tussle with prop wash and some nervous moments until altitude is gained. Then the whole crew silently sighs and settles down to the relief of getting on with the job.

Tuesday, 15 August 1944 Flew with an awfully green crew today. It was their first flight over England, so found myself navigating, setting up the bomb run, directing, instructing in all the positions. Surprised myself with what I knew.

Pilot Keith Newhouse survived his tour of duty with the Eighth Air Force, thirty-three combat missions, and returned safely to his wife, Jean, in Chicago.

Yes, quaint and curious war is!/ You shoot a fellow down/You'd treat, if met where any bar is,/Or help to half-a-crown.
–Thomas Hardy

clockwise from top left: B-17 radio gunner, tail gunner, waist gunner, B-17 bombardier, B-24 command pilot.

It was a king-size hut because it had to seat thirty-six or thirty-seven crews. There was a mission map of the British Isles and the Continent on a large board set on the stage, with a curtain hung over it. I sat down with Hilmer and the rest of my crew: the pilot, John J. Askins, came from Oakland, California; the copilot, Randall H. Archer, from Chester, West Virginia; the navigator, Anthony Delaporta, from Philadelphia, Pennsylvania; the bombardier, Paul W. Collier, from Hamilton, Texas; the waist gunner/armorer, Ralph Azevedo, from Mill Valley, California; the ball turret gunner, Robert N. Webb, Jr., from Dyer, Tennessee; and the tail gunner, Roy E. Loyless, from Houston, Texas. I noted the time was just 0400. Right on cue, one of the Headquarters officers barked, 'Tenshut.' Colonel Terry walked in at a brisk pace, stepped onto the stage, and said, 'At ease, gentlemen.' He gave us a pep talk and turned the briefing over to the S-2 Intelligence Officer.

The S-2 walked over to the map, carrying his pool stick, and pulled the curtain up, ever so slowly, as if he savoured every moment of the anxiety he was causing in his audience. The red yarn indicated we were going to Cologne, and the reaction was a moan, which gradually crescendoed. The target was the marshaling yards, and we were to disrupt the supplies of armour, artillery, and troops to Aachen, where our soldiers were fighting. There were pieces of red plastic on the map which represented the areas of heavy flak. It bothered us that the S-2 officer would sometimes shift those pieces around, as though he wasn't sure of where the concentrations were. We all knew they were around the large cities; the problem was that no one knew how much mobile flak had been moved into the target area on flatbed train cars.

The weather officer said that the cloud over England was about 19,000 feet thick but not too bad over the Continent. The operations officer gave a time hack so we could set our watches to Greenwich Mean Time, and then we were dismissed. On the way out, we had to pass the three chaplains. Now, I didn't particularly want to be reminded that I might soon meet my Maker, so as we passed I looked the other way. When we got into the fresh air I realized how warm a room could get when the men in there all became concerned about what fate might hold for them that day.

There were other briefings for the pilot, copilot, navigator, bombardier, and me. I reported to the communications building to pick up the codes of the day, the verification codes that were sent when messages were transmitted or received. The communications officer gave me an aluminum briefcase containing the codes, along with log sheets and pencils for recording my messages while on the mission. the codes were printed on rice paper so you could eat them if you were shot down. The officer mentioned that the Germans broke most of our codes within twelve hours. I was also given the colors of the day for the Very lights, which we fired when passing over a convoy or a naval vessel so they wouldn't mistake us for a German plane.

In the equipment room, we collected our Mae Wests, parachutes and harness, oxygen masks, headsets and throat mikes, goggles, gabardine coveralls, heated suits, leather helmets and steel helmets with earflaps that covered your headset. There were heated felt inserts to go inside the sheepskin and leather flying boots, and silk gloves to wear inside the heated leather gloves. We stowed the gear in our equipment bags, and then we picked up the escape kits, which contained a silk map, a

From our very first sighting of the bombers we could see Jerry fighters reeling and diving onto the mass formation. It was a picture that only the devil could have enjoyed. Planes were rent by fiery explosions; white blossoms of parachutes could be seen here and there as the victims of the air battle drifted to earth. We threw ourselves into the melee in a desperate attempt to stem the slaughter of the Fortresses.
– from *The Look of Eagles* by John T. Godfrey

Germany must collapse before this programme which is more than half completed already has proceded much further . . . We can wreck Berlin from end to end, if the USAAF will come in on it. It will cost between 400-500 aircraft It will cost Germany the war.
–Sir Arthur Harris, C-in-C, RAF Bomber Command, to Winston Churchill, November 3 1943

far left: 8AF Staff Sergeant Clarence Johnson, a B-24 Liberator gunner; left: The 8AF shoulder patch; centre: The badge of an aero engine worker of World War Two; top: The emblem of Yuma Army Air Field, the base where Roger Armstrong trained to become a gunner.

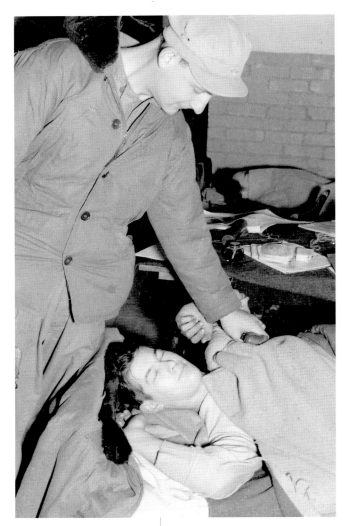

razor, high-energy candy, a plastic bottle, water purification tablets, and translation sheets in Flemish, Dutch, French, and German.

They had taken photos of us when we arrived at the base, which you were to give to the Resistance if you got shot down, so they could make you an identity document. I never took my photos along (a chief German interrogator told me recently that they could tell your bomb group by the civilian coat you were wearing the day they took your photo). We didn't take the .45-caliber Colt automatics along, either, because S-2 had found the possession of a gun had give the Germans an excuse to shoot you.

It was a five-minute ride in a six-by-six truck from the hangar to the dispersal area where our B-17, *The Qualified Quail*, was parked. We all had our own thoughts and everyone was quiet on the way. It was a gray, depressing morning, and the overcast was down to 100 or 150 feet. The driver stopped in front of our plane. It carried the markings of the 'triangle A' on the tail and our squadron letter 'K.' The wing tips, tail plane, and stabilizer were painted red, which indicated we were in the 1st Combat Wing. The markings helped the group to assemble and then to find our Wing. We all looked in the bomb bay to see what kind of bombs we were carrying: if you carried delayed-action bombs, you had to take off anyway, even if the weather changed, and drop them in the North Sea. We had a full load of 250-pound bombs and two clusters of M-17 incendiaries on the top shackles.

I put my heated suit on over my coveralls, and this was a mistake, because as soon as I climbed into the plane to check out the radio room, I always got the call of nature. As usual, I found a semisecluded spot to take care of that. At the same time I could hear Beicker

This intensive on-the-job training was giving the new pilots a good look at some of the air war's highlights. Flak, the armour-piercing fire from anti-aircraft guns on the ground was ever present; at altitude its innocuous appearance as soft and colorful, fluffy puffballs belied its lethal impact. Frequently Axis and Allied airplanes could be seen crashing or exploding in midair, then spiraling or plunging to earth. They'd pray all airmen would have a chance to escape, and then they'd see those who broke free tumble from their disabled craft, some softly drifting earthward like pale, silken blossoms, and others, nipped in the bud, plummeting unopened.
–from *Donald's Story* by Sandra D. Merrill

far left: An early wake-up call for an 8AF crew member scheduled to fly this day; left centre: Air crew dressing for a mission; left: Leaving the crew room for the aircraft; below far left: The goggles of an American air crew member; left: B-24 gunners.

I've been wondering if you ever received my Air Medal. It says here on a little piece of paper: "Awards and Decorations—an Oak Leaf Cluster is awarded for wear with the Air Medal previously awarded to the following named Officer, Organization as indicated, Army Air Forces, United States Army. Eugene R. Fletcher 2nd Lt." The citation was the same as with the Air Medal. You know, meritorious achievement, courage, coolness, skill, and all that malarky which makes good propaganda. Of course, they forget to tell how many MPs it takes to get me aboard my ship before takeoff time. It isn't bad, though, so don't worry about me. The crew really makes a good team and we're always looking out for one another.
– from *Fletcher's Gang*
by Eugene Fletcher

Does the road wind uphill all the way?/Yes, to the very end./Will the day's journey take the whole long day?/From morn to night, my friend.
–*Uphill*
by Christina Rossetti

Originally, the Fortresses used to fly against the enemy with only nine men aboard; one gunner operated both waist positions. It wasn't long before the Air Force found that wouldn't work. Battle-wise German fighter pilots—and the boys will tell you that no one on earth, including Mr Boeing himself, knows more about how to attack a Fortress than the German fighter pilots—used to hang around the fringe of a B-17 formation and wait for their chance. From one side, one or two of their Luftwaffe friends would start a beam attack on a Fort. Immediately the waiting Nazis would see the muzzle of the waist gun on their side point sharply to the sky, indicating that the waist gunner had dropped the heavy end of that gun to pick up the gun on the other side for a shot at the attacker. That was the crafty Jerries' cue. When they saw that waist gun pop into the air, they flipped over and bored head-on in a beam attack from their side, pouring in cannon and machine-gun fire without any opposition from the waist gunner who still was busy on the other side.

from *Air Gunner*
by Sgt. Bud Hutton and
Sgt. Andy Rooney

left: Captain Howard Slaton, pilot, and the crew of the B-24 *Arise My Love and Come With Me.*

throwing up. He said, 'I don't know why, but once I enter the waist door and smell the interior of the plane, I get sick at my stomach.' I told him what it did to me and not to worry about it. It was that smell–of oil, gas, canvas flak suits, and ammunition boxes.

In the radio room, I checked the spare chest-type chute pack, the walk-around oxygen bottle, and the four-by-four piece of armour plating the crew chief had found for me. My radios and rack of frequency ranges were all in place, and so was the frequency meter, in case I needed to check the accuracy of what a dial on the receiver read.

John and Randy, with Beicker and the crew chief, checked the exterior and interior of the plane, while the gunners checked their guns and ammunition. When the engines were started, I heard them cough and splutter before they started to run. We put on our headsets and checked the intercom, and the John ran the engines up while the ground crew stood by with fire extinguishers. The plane vibrated and became very noisy. I heard the sound of the brakes being released as John moved onto the taxiway and fell in behind the ship we were to follow in the line for takeoff. I turned on my radios and the IFF. I would monitor the Division frequency during the mission; the IFF would send a continuous code while we were over friendly territory so the coastal defences wouldn't shoot at us.

The lead squadron took off at 0600, and by 0622 all twelve were airborne. John turned onto the runway and ran the engines up while he held the brakes on. The plane kind of jerked into a rolling start as he released them. Runway 25 was 6,000 feet long, but it seemed he was never going to lift that heavy load off as we gathered speed. Then the plane broke

The inexperienced crews bombed short, so we used to put our markers right at the far end of the target. People had a tendency, when they saw all the flak and searchlights, to drop their bombs quickly and get the hell out of it–so that raids always tended to creep back.
–from *The Bombing of Nuremberg* by James Campbell

above: A fine image of the interior of a B-17 bomber showing the two waist-gunner positions and the suspended ball turret.

The Americans thought little of the idea of area bombing. Their diplomats, business men and journalists had, of course, still been in Germany during the most ineffective phase of its application in 1940 and 1941. They believed that precision attacks upon key targets,, such as those envisaged by the British at the outset of the war, were the key to effective strategic bombing. They therefore resolved to operate in daylight. Since they had no fighters to go the distance, they put powerful armament into the Fortresses and Liberators and devised formation tactics designed to make the most of massive firepower. They expected their bombers to fight their way to and back from their targets.
–from *The Bombing Offensive Against Germany* by Noble Frankland

Once on the runway, with three or four aircraft ahead of him waiting to take off, McGovern set the brakes and revved up the engines. Rounds went through the checklist with him. When that was complete and the plane in front had started down the runway, McGovern released the brakes. Beside him, he could hear Rounds praying. "Every takeoff I made in World War II was an adventure," McGovern later admitted. A B-24 did not take off like a fighter. It started rolling slowly, only reluctantly picking up speed. He felt "this thing is never going to get enough speed to get off the ground—there's just no way I'm going to make it."
–from *Wild Blue* by Stephen E. Ambrose

loose from the pull of gravity and we were airborne. I noticed I had held myself stiff while we were moving down that runway, but now I relaxed. Watching out of the radio room window by my desk, I saw we were higher than the village church steeple, then suddenly we were in the overcast and flying blind.

John had to fly at a given speed and rate of climb for so many minutes, then turn right, still climbing, and turn again so we were making one big square around the Bassingbourn Buncher beacon. It was quite nerve-wracking in the overcast. It was so thick, I could barely see the left wing tip. A voice on the intercom said, 'Submarine at nine o'clock level.' It was Azevedo, the right waist gunner. No one answered. The plane bounced around and we knew it was from the prop wash of another B-17 out there somewhere.

Randy's voice came over the intercom: 'Copilot to crew, we are passing through 10,000 feet, so oxygen masks on, please.' A few minutes later he said, 'Oxygen check,' and we answered to our names from tail to nose: 'Loyless okay,' Azevedo okay,' 'Webb okay,' and finally 'Collier okay.'

We broke out of the overcast for a few minutes, and saw twenty or thirty B-17s around us. The third squadron from the 91st was just below us. Then, we were climbing back into the cloud, still making squares over the base Buncher. Finally it began to look a little lighter and we popped out of the mess. We were to fly high squadron of the group, and the group was to lead the 1st Combat Wing, with one wing ahead of us. Collier saw the lead squadron forming up and we located our element leader of the high squadron. It was still hazy, but with just sufficient visibility to get the group formed, and we set course for Clacton at

That morning on takeoff the airplane exhibited a tendency to settle back to the runway immediately after becoming airborne. This was not a dangerous condition but just something to know and be prepared to cope with. Her flying characteristics had changed since our last flight. This was not unusual, for no two airplanes fly alike. At the end of the flight I pronounced her combat ready, and the ground crew called her back into service.
–from *Fletcher's Gang*
by Eugene Fletcher

Settled in the bomber cockpit with its myriad of instruments, switches, controls, and gear, the airplane commander and the division air commander run through the long check lists, the air commander reading the list while the bomber commander physically touches each control and carefully observes each item of the long list. At the ten positions in the bomber, crewmen are running through similar check lists, assuring themselves as far as humanly possible that all systems are functioning. The airplane commander establishes communication over the interphone and requests a status report from each position.
–from *Heritage of Valor*
by Budd J. Peaslee

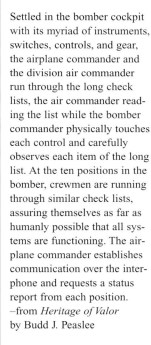

top left: A large hut at Deenethorpe, the 401st Bomb Group base; top right: A 100th BG bomber, *Mason and Dixon*; left: The old tower at Deenethorpe.

I was 100 yards on his tail. The B-17 fired, took desperate avoiding action. The only thing that existed in the whole world was this American bomber, fighting for its life, and me. My cannons blazed away. Pieces of metal flew off. Smoke poured from the engines. They jettisoned the entire bomb load. One tank in the wings had caught fire. The crew was bailing out. Trautloft's voice cryed over the radio, "Achtung, Adolf, Mustangs! I'm beating it—guns jammed." And then, with the first bursts from four Mustangs—I sobered up. There was no mistake about the B-17; she was finished, but I was not. I simply fled. Diving with open throttle I tried to escape the pursuing Mustangs, which were firing wildly. Direction east, toward Berlin. The tracer bullets came closer and closer.
–from *The First and The Last* by Adolf Galland

right: Some 8AF daylight raids began in darkness.

20,000 feet. The 381st and 398th Bomb Groups had taken off after us, and our group leader did a series of 'S' turns to let them catch up and form the combat wing.

We left Clacton two minutes early at an altitude of 21,000 feet. The winds over the Channel were greater than briefed, and John told Tony, the navigator, that the whole wing was doing another S turn because we were catching up on the wing ahead of us. We were at 27,000 feet when we arrived at point 2 on the route to Cologne, still two minutes early but with everyone spaced at normal intervals. Over the bomber channel, I heard the weather ship, *Buckeye Blue*, report that the route weather was good but that contrails were forming at the bombers' altitude. Then *Buckeye Red* said that Cologne was overcast and that the PFF [Pathfinder] ships would be needed to locate and zero in on the target with radar.

Out over the Channel, just before we reached the Continent, the gunners had test-fired their guns. They had charged their guns before we reached high altitude, because the barrels shrank at low temperature, and if you didn't have a shell in it, the gun probably wouldn't fire.

As we flew toward Cologne, Tony called John and said" 'We're running parallel to the front lines, that's why we can see flak up ahead.' I thought, why aren't we flying on the Allied side, instead of over the German lines? Meantime, I was copying a message for the wing commander in the lead ship from the 1st Air Division. There were about a dozen German ground operators jamming the frequency, but Division was sending the Morse on a modulated tone that sounded like a big truck horn honking. You soon got used to that tone, and the jamming didn't really bother you.

We had put our flak suits on as we entered

German territory, and I snapped the chest pack or the right ring of my harness. It left an area vulnerable, but I felt the chute would absorb low-velocity flak or even a bullet fired at long range. Suddenly the plane rose and fell four or five times. There was flak below us, not doing any damage but it was worrying me. I concentrated on copying some of the German code, because the busier you were, the less you thought about getting hit, but they were just holding their keys down or tapping out a series of 'V's. I lost interest and got back to trying to get rid of the ache in my chest, thinking about the curtains of flak we would be going through at Cologne.

The wing commander started a series of S turns to throw the German gunners off, and John told us what was happening. We all felt John was the best pilot in the group, and he was also a good communicator. He always advised us on what was going on. We in turn watched out from our positions and told him if we noticed any mechanical or structural problem with the plane.

I listened in on the group voice channel and heard the pilot of the lead PFF ship in the low squadron say, 'We have lost our bombing radar.' The lead command ship said, 'Drop on our smoke bombs at the target.'

We were getting both tracking flak and box barrage flak as we flew past Cologne to the south and picked up our IP [Initial Point], where we started our run in to the target. The plane was really bouncing up and down, and I moved my piece of armour plating across the radio room to the chaff chute. We were carrying seven cartons of chaff bundles, which were held together by paper strips until they were pushed through the chute and hit the slipstream. Our group would create thousands of false blips on the enemy's radar screens to help the groups behind us, the way the group ahead was helping us. On the right side of the ship, I

Thousands of Amreican airmen straggled through the cold damp atmosphere into the many combat mess halls at 0500 that Thursday morning. Breakfast in the combat messes was quite logically considered the most important meal of the day. To fight a war at 25,000 feet a man must be in the peak of condition. He should be well fed on selected non-gas-generating foods. There could be little worse than a key crewman doubled over with indigestion or vomiting into his oxygen mask as the fighters attacked. Basic to the combat mess were the barnyard fresh eggs that were the envy of the officers and men of the ground crews. They could look forward each day to the hated and maligned powdered eggs that had been shipped in from faraway America. Occasionally a groundman might develop a private source of fresh eggs for which he would pay the equivalent of a half dollar apiece to some understanding bootlegging farmer. These eggs he would reverently carry to the mess hall and induce some friendly cook to do a job on them, always "sunny side up" or "over easy" but never scrambled. To scramble fresh eggs would be sacrilegious and besides, they would then look like powdered eggs.
–from *Heritage of Valor* by Budd J. Peaslee

The Americans had been flying daylight raids from England since mid-1942, supporting the night attacks on Occupied Europe by R.A.F. Bomber Command. Commencing in November 1943, each Eighth Air Force Heavy Bombardment Group doubled its operational strength from thirty-six bombers to seventy-two. From small beginnings in 1942, the Eighth Air Force, by mid-October 1943, had grown to twenty-one bomb groups and nine fighter groups. Barely eight months later, in early June 1944, the Eighth had more than doubled its air strength to forty-one bomb groups and fourteen fighter groups. This mighty force was quite capable of putting nearly 3,000 combat aircraft into action at any one time and very often did so.
–from *The Münster Raid* by Ian Hawkins

right: A superb photograph of an 8AF bombing mission at the moment of the drop. These are B-17s of the 96th Bomb Group with vapour trailing from their engines. They are flying in a combat box formation and encountering significant 88mm flak.

built up a flak shack of chaff cartons on my armour plating. Webb was too large to wear his flak helmet in the ball turret, so he loaned it to me. I pulled my own helmet down over my eyes, placed Webb's over my reproductive organs, and started throwing chaff.

Suddenly the radio room lit up bright red, and the plexiglass roof window blew inward in a thousand pieces with a number of shell fragments. Then another shell exploded just above the nose. We went into a dive, leveled out and eased back into the formation. What had happened was that a piece of flak had come through the windshield and struck John on the right shoulder of his flak suit, turning him in a clockwise direction and making him chop all four engines with his right hand, which was holding the throttles. Randy had pushed the throttles forward and flown us back into position.

Hilmer Beicker came out of the top turret and saw John struggling to turn himself forward. His seat belt was so tight he was having a tough time, so Beicker went to help him. At that moment, Randy reached for his flak helmet and was just putting it on when another piece of flak came through the window and struck him on the head. Beicker stopped him from falling on the yoke, and grabbed the first aid kit. Randy came to and shook his head as Beicker was wiping the blood out of his eyes. It turned out that the flak had only grazed his forehead.

Beicker took a look at the instruments, looked around the flight deck and went back to the top turret. There was a hole in the plexiglass and a chunk out of the housing; otherwise the turret was in good shape.

I was just throwing a bundle of chaff out when another close burst, which I heard, sent three pieces through the skin of the plane four or five inches from my head. If I had been

"Bombardier to Pilot, we're on the bomb run." That meant the aircraft had to be level and steady for the bomb drop. At this point the bombardier in the lead aircraft took charge. The other bombardiers watched his bomb bay and the moment they saw the first bomb fall from the lead ship they released their loads. On the bomb run the lead bombardier was in control of the ship through the Norden Bomb Sight. It connected into the automatic pilot. When the moving indices of the sight lined up properly, the bombs were released. The Norden Sight computed air speed, altitude, wind drift, and all other factors that could influence the accuracy of the bomb strike. –from *Combat Crew* by John Comer

reaching for another bundle, my head would have taken all three fragments. The holes peeled outward, so the fragments had come right through the ship. I looked around: the right side of my liaison set had a hole the size of your fist in it.

Another burst hit us, and a piece of flak struck my left glove, ripping the leather open from my wrist to the end of my thumb. I felt the blood get warm on my hand, and visualized the thumb–shot off inside the glove. I didn't want to take the glove off, but I knew I had to because of the bleeding. I was relieved when I saw that the thumb was still attached to my hand. I dumped some sulfa out of the first aid kit on two cuts and put a bandage on. This had kind of held my attention, and I realized that John had been calling on the intercom: 'Pilot to radio, pilot to radio . . .'

I answered: 'Radio to pilot.'

Pilot to radio–Azevedo is down in the waist. See what's wrong.'

I grabbed my walk-around oxygen bottle and took off for the waist. Azevedo was lying on his back. I saw him blink, so I knew he was alive. When I squatted down beside him, it was obvious he had been hit in the right thigh. Having checked that his mask was securely connected to the right waist oxygen supply, I disconnected my walk-around bottle and plugged into the left waist hose. I took my Boy Scout knife and cut the leg of his pants open. The hole was the size of a silver dollar. It was bleeding but not pumping blood, so I assumed the fragment had missed the femoral artery.

When I took my gloves off, my fingers stiffened up so they wouldn't function properly. I had to keep putting the gloves on to warm up. It got so bad I called the pilot and told him I needed help. By this time I was feeling a little

drunk and I kind of plopped down beside Azevedo on my behind. He kept pointing at the ceiling, and I looked up and saw that the oxygen line I was plugged into had been sliced in two. I thought, although the flak had eased off, they were still trying to get me, one way or another. I plugged back into the walk-around bottle and after a few deep breaths of pure oxygen I felt normal. It wasn't as good as feeling half-drunk.

Beicker arrived to help, and between the two of us we got a pressure bandage on Azevedo's wound, but the temperature at our altitude did more to stop the bleeding. The copilot called for an oxygen check, and the first on his list didn't answer, so I crawled on back to the tail, lugging the walk-around bottle. I got to Loyless on my hands and knees. His eyes were as big as saucers and he was holding the cord to his mike, which a piece of flak had cut in two, three or four inches from his throat. I plugged into his jack box and told Randy what had happened.

Back at the waist, Beicker had found that the piece of flak had come out at the back of Azevedo's thigh. We started all over stopping the blood at that point and putting sulfa on the wound. Then we bandaged him up and put a couple of blankets round his legs. To talk to Beicker I had to take my mask off, yell in his ear, and put the mask back on quick. I yelled, 'Maybe we should give him a shot of morphine–he could be going into shock.' Beicker held his cupped hand behind my ear: 'I think we should. You give it to him.'

My medical knowledge was confined to what I had picked up in the Boy Scouts, *Reader's Digest*, and a Red Cross class at Creighton University in the Aviation Cadet program. I yelled back, 'I've never given a shot before.

far left: A 390th BG mission interrogation; left: Radioman Roger Armstrong's bomber *Qualified Quail*; below: B-17Gs of the 390th Bomb Group attacking Marienburg, Germany.

A 20 mm cannon shell penetrated the right side of his plane, exploded under the pilot, damaging the electrical system and radio compartment, killing the radio operator, who bled to death after both legs were cut off just above the knees. Another 20 mm shell entered the left side of the nose, tearing out a section of the plexiglass about two feet square; it also tore away the left gun installation and injured the bombardier in the head and shoulder. A third 20 mm shell penetrated the right wing, went on into the fuselage and shattered the hydraulic system; releasing the fluid into the cockpit. A fourth 20 mm shell crashed through the cabin roof, and cut the cables to one side of the rudder. A fifth 20 mm shell hit the Number 3 engine, destroying all engine controls. The engine caught fire and lost its power—luckily, the fire later died out.
–from *First of the Many* by Captain John R. McCrary and David E. Scherman

The stresses of an Eighth Air Force bombing mission are evident in the faces of this B-17 crew just back from their day-trip to Germany.

Maybe you should do it: you know all about engines and stuff like that.'

Beicker's eyes looked kind of funny. 'So what? You know all about radios. And you showed me a Red Cross card one time where it said you had qualified for first aid.' Azevedo was lying there and he could hear my side of the conversation in his headset. He kept trying to get our attention, and finally he said, 'You guys aren't giving me any dope.' I said, 'Look, Azzie, you haven't got much say in this matter.' He said, 'Neither one of you guys knows anything about medicine. And when we got our shots at Sioux City, Beicker fainted when the first needle went into his arm.'

That was true; they gave him three more shots while he was on the floor. Anyway, I was about to lose my voice from yelling. I took the morphine out of the first aid kit. It looked like a small tube of toothpaste with a needle in the end. I warmed it under my heated suit and aimed the needle at the muscle a few inches from the front hole in his thigh. At first I pushed real easy and it didn't go in. I looked up at Beicker. He looked away. I shoved hard and it slid into the thigh. I squeezed the tube, and in a few minutes Azevedo had drifted off to sleep.

I looked out of the window and saw we were still in flak. The plane shook and a burst over the nose knocked the bombardier off his seat. Later, I saw the dent in his helmet, and a lump on his head to match. He crawled back to the bombsight and I heard him say, 'Bomb bay doors are opening, follow the PDI.' that was the pilot direction indicator on the instrument panel.

The group's bombs were dropped from 27,000 feet at 0928. The clouds had cleared and we were able to see our bombs striking the marshaling yards. John had feathered the numbers one and three engines while we were working

. . . the P-51 Mustang, an aircraft with perhaps the strangest history of any in the Second World War, but certainly one of the most important ever produced in the history of military aviation. It achieved what had long been regarded as a technical impossibility, that is, the range of a heavy bomber and the performance of an interceptor fighter. It was the instrument which released the potential of the strategic air offensive.
–from *The Bombing Offensive Against Germany* by Noble Frankland

top: The B-17 *Little Miss Mischief* after her fiery belly landing at Bassingbourn; right: B-24 crewmen just back from a trip to a target city; far right: The devastated ruins of Bremen, Germany in 1945.

Because the Lancaster could carry double the average load of its American counterparts, the British delivered the heavier weight of bombs on a typical mission, 660 tons compared with 388 for Spaatz's aircraft. [Reichs Armaments Minister Albert] Speer considered the night raids far more dangerous than daytime strikes, "since heavier bombs are used and an extraordinary accuracy in attacking the target is reported." Thanks to the navigation and bombing aids devised by British science, Bomber Command had struck with greater precision than Harris had anticipated.
–from *The Men Who Bombed The Reich*
by Bernard C. Nalty and Carl Berger

We judge ourselves by what we feel capable of doing, while others judge us by what we have already done.
–Henry Wadsworth Longfellow

top left: The ruined tower of St Nicolai church in Hamburg; top right: The old Orderly Room at Grafton Underwood; right: The crew of *Buckeye Belle*, a 384th Bomb Group B-17G at their Grafton Underwood base.

on Azevedo. Other planes near us also had engines feathered. John got number one engine started again and we were able to stay with the formation. Several bombers from the lead and low squadrons were straggling behind. On the fighter channel, I heard the lead ship ask for 'little friends' to assist the damaged planes.

There was cloud at our altitude when we reached the Channel, and the group let down to get under it. This helped the stragglers to keep up with the formation. The fighter protection was excellent. At 1143 we crossed the English coast at Clacton, and the wing broke up with each group heading back to its own base, pretty well strung out and flying loose.

I went back every ten minutes to see if Azevedo was okay. I took his pulse to see if maybe he had died, but his heart was beating and his skin was warm. I took his mask off when we were at low altitude. John called me to the flight deck as we approached Bassingbourn, and asked me to load the Very pistol with red/red flares to show he had injuries aboard. Looking out through the broken window I saw a number of planes also flying flares. On the final approach, the tail and ball gunners took their positions in the radio room, and the navigator and bombardier came out of the nose.

The ambulances were lined up on the left of runway 25. As we touched down, one raced along the grass beside the runway, and when we turned off and stopped near the control tower the medics were ready to come aboard and remove Azevedo. Instead of taking him to the base hospital they took him to Wimpole Hall, which was set up to treat the more serious injuries. I was kind of glad they took him there. It had been the home of Rudyard Kipling, who was a favorite in my family. My father used to quote Kipling's poems in his

sermons at Sioux Falls.

We left *The Qualified Quail* by the tower with a number of other badly damaged B-17s, and a truck took us to the interrogation building. We were escorted to a table where the S-2 officer poured double shots of scotch into coffee cups. He wanted to know what we all saw on the mission and asked about our injuries.

Randy was sitting next to me; he had rolled up his jacket sleeve and was pushing at something just under the skin of his arm. It was a metal splinter almost four inches long. He had worked it almost out when the S-2 asked what he was doing. Randy said, 'I felt my arm itch. I just found a piece of flak in it.' He pulled it out all the way and put it in his pocket. The S-2 saw the nicks on his forehead and asked if he wanted to see the flight surgeon. Randy said no, he had a date. I did too. I said I had treated my cut hand in the plane. John didn't mention the bruise on his shoulder; he told me later it was sore for three weeks.

After interrogation we took a look at *The Qualified Quail*. After finding two hundred holes we got tired of counting. John, Beicker, and the crew chief were looking at something under the right wing. As I walked up, John said, 'Our main spar was almost shot in two. If I had known about it, I wouldn't have banked so steep, and I would have taken it easier coming in for landing.' It turned out that of thirty-six B-17s of the 91st Bomb Group, sixteen sustained minor damage and twenty had major damage.

We had an excellent lunch of steak and potatoes, with ice cream for dessert. I took a shower and went into Royston where I met my date. We did some pub-crawling, and next morning I slept in as we didn't fly a mission. Two days later, they sent us back to Cologne."
– Roger A. Armstrong

As soon as Gibson's Lancaster came within range of the flak guns, George Deering in the front turret opened up on the towers. The flak seemed accurate but it failed to hit the aircraft. The powerful retaining spring opened as the bomb release button was activated and the backwards spinning bomb fell away at 00.28 am, rotating at 500 rpm. Relieved of the weight, the Lanc lurched upwards, Gibson continuing the movement as he sped up and over the dam wall. The bomb bounced three times and appeared to slam into the parapet dead on target between the two towers. Hutchinson fired a red Very flare over the dam as a signal to the others that they had dropped. Passing over the dam, Gibson's rear gunner, Trevor-Roper, began to fire on the gun towers.
–from *The Men Who Breached The Dams*
by Alan Cooper

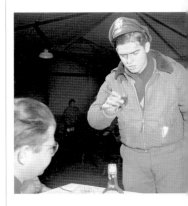

above: A well-earned mission whisky.

LOCAL HEROES

I got another letter from August. ". . . how are you doing," she wrote. ". . . I got sort of lonesome for you so I thought I'd drop you a line and let you know how much I'm missing you . . . do you know . . . I've been writing you every day and how often do you write me—once a week . . . Oh God, how I wish you were on your way flying home to me who has my arms outstretched waiting for you to enter them." She was really winding up. Right about then I would have given plenty for some of that who-has-my-arms-outstretched . . .
"Please hurry home, will

In a city or a major country town, the sudden arrival of two thousand men in uniform would cause no great stir: they would be readily absorbed into the multitude. But in the villages and hamlets of truly rural eastern England, where everybody knew the name, way of business and social status of everybody else, where one more heiffer in a herd of cattle, or one new pair of underpants on the washing-line, would not pass unnoticed, such an influx was a matter of some consequence. It was, the natives recognized, a corollary of war. Churchill had told them that it would be no fun, and he was absolutely right: the sound of the aircraft kept the kids awake at night, furthermore they frightened horses and put the hens off lay. Also, the airmen were around and among them everywhere—extrovert and boisterous, filling the buses, crowding the pubs and cafés, forever chasing girls.

At least, the natives told themselves, these

young officers and sergeants—ranks, incidentally, which most of them looked far too young to hold—at least they were doing something about attacking Jerry, which was more than could be said for most of the military. And they weren't such bad lads, once you got to know them: really quite pleasant, when they hadn't drunk too much. Why, three or four of them were in church on Sunday morning, and one lad brought two tins of ham for little Billy's birthday treat.

In their own good time, the stolid country people accepted the invasion, just as their forefathers had accepted the assaults of man and nature through the centuries. In their quiet way, they—or most of them— came to take the strangers to their hearts.

That was what Albert Tyler found, when he joined the 379th Bomb Group at Kimbolton as a flight engineer and top turret gunner. "I liked Kimbolton," he said, "I liked the little village-the way it was laid out, the people. They were all just very friendly. One of them in a pub said 'Sergeant, when you want a good roast beef dinner, you just come right on up.' It was a delightful, wonderful dinner that those people fixed."

Richard Stamp was barely eight years old when the Lancaster crews started operating from the new-built airfield near his father's land. In the early evenings, he saw the skies of Lincolnshire full of enormous aircraft, climbing in their hundreds; he saw the bombs stacked in pallets on the grass beside the road. "They came and fetched them," he said, "when they were wanted for a raid. Of course, we got to know some of the aircrews. They used to walk around the farm, and Mother gave them supper. They were fine chaps, but they were never here for long. They'd go on a few raids and that would be the end of them. I remember Mother crying when they didn't come back—

she thought they were so young for that to happen to them. You'd get attached to them, and it was for such a short time."

Certainly, the farming men of the eastern counties had a unique experience of the bomber war. They got to understand, better than most civilians, the essential fragility of aircraft, and how surely they conformed with the law propounded by Sir Isaac Newton. They realized that take-offs and landings could go wrong, for they saw the evidence. When an engine failed on take-off or during an overshoot below the aircraft's safety speed, the only way that plane could go was down, and the result was often a most unpleasant mess. Many an old farming man, or more probably his son, can point to a furrow in a barley field or a crater in a meadow where some unlucky pilot made his final landing.

When Don Maffett was assigned to the 452nd Bomb Group at Deopham Green in February 1944, the base was barely fit for human habitation. "The mud and stuff was terrific, but things improved as time went on, and eventually we had excellent facilities for officers and men. The closest village was Attleborough, and we often had the opportunity of getting in there. It was farming country, very colorful, and we enjoyed meeting the people who lived around the base. Occasionally, they would have us to their homes, and they were most interesting people."

One British pilot realized from the start the absolute necessity of establishing a local pied-à-terre—a pub, farmhouse or homestead—somewhere he and his crew could find a haven from the uniform drabness of the billet, the NAAFI and the mess. While still at OTU in the early spring of 1943, training on the two-engined Vickers Wellington, he discovered such a place and wrote a letter home: ". . . The

phone rings in the flight office: there's a gale-force crosswind and night flying is cancelled. Nobody knows whether to be disappointed or relieved, so we just make a lot of noise, and a procession of bicycles hurries through the darkness to the mess. Chaps change into uniform and go to the movies or the dance or to meet their girls. The very strong-willed (like me) sit down and write a letter. Later, I'll cycle with the wireless op. and the gunner to a little pub about three miles away, where the landlady is good to us. We won't go in the bar, but sit in her big kitchen and chat till closing time. The landlady's daughter will bring beer from time to time, and the local postmistress, Miss Spooner, will come in and play the latest dance tunes on the piano. There'll be fried bread and eggs for supper (they keep chickens) , and we'll go back to bed at about 11.30."

Aircraftwoman First Class Phyllis Beck, known in the WAAF as Pip, was a pretty brunette, nineteen years of age, and one of the first half-dozen of her sex to operate the R.T. in a bomber base control tower. While serving at a training field in Oxfordshire in September 1944, she had a free afternoon before her night shift in the watch office. "It wasn't an afternoon to waste," she wrote. "Mollie, Di and I meandered along country lanes, spellbound by the mellow gold of the autumn sun, and we found blackberries in the hedges. Elderberries hung in dark, shining clusters and wild rose hips glowed red. Michaelmas daisies and early chrysanthemums bloomed in the gardens we passed, as well as late roses. On the outskirts of a village about two miles from Barford we came to a thatched cottage, with a most enticing orchard. The trees were heavy with rosy-red apples and purple plums. We knocked on the door, intending to see if we could buy

you? . . . frankly, if I'd only known I'd feel like this about you . . . I would have appreciated you lots more than I did . . . but that's the way things go . . . you don't appreciate anything until it is out of your reach and then you want it worse than before . . .I swear things are different now. I realize lots of things I didn't before . . . one is how fine and decent you are . . .you're a person that anyone would be proud to claim as their own . . ."

I figured she had probably been hitting the sparkling burgundy again.

It was a funny letter, but the hell of it was, it was sort of sad too. She was a gay little girl when I knew her. Nothing mattered. And now all the boys were gone and she was building airplanes and going straight home nights and being a good little girl.

She said she was, anyway, and maybe she was. She always believed something when she said it. But when I knew her nothing she said ever came true.

But it was nice to get the letter. It picked me up a little.

–from *Serenade to the Big Bird* by Bert Stiles

left: American airmen often entertained local British children at parties on the airfields. It was another way of thanking the British for their hospitality and of enjoying the pleasant companionship of kids, something they were otherwise denied for the duration.

some. An elderly man answered, and invited us into the orchard, where he filled two paper bags with apples and plucked a basketful of plums. He would accept no money and told us to come back for more whenever we wanted to."

When the first German Chancellor, Otto von Bismarck, was asked what, in his opinion, was the most important fact of the 20th century, he replied: "That the people of Great Britain and North America speak the same language". Certainly, many airmen from the USA had a sense of kinship with the British islanders as bombardier Larry Bird said: "I have a very warm feeling for Great Britain., I guess one reason is that most of my ancestors came from over there, and most were prepared to some extent for what might await them when they landed there. American war correspondents, based in London, had filed a series of dramatic reports throughout the blitz and after. This one appeared in Time magazine on September 9th 1940:
"In the early days Britain was fighting for Poland, freedom, prestige, and other academic matters. Last week Britons were fighting for hedgerows, chimney pots, foggy fens, swift foxes and horses with heart, the Derby, cabbage and boiled potatoes, squabbles in the House of Commons and in every man's kitchen— things that grow and flourish and are loved in Britain. They were fighting for His Majesty George VI, King and Emperor by the Grace of God. They were fighting for their past, and for the right to make a new Britain. Upon that there was national resolve . . . Their feeling was not bravado. Nor was it always realistic, but great courage is seldom born of the practice of meticulously weighing facts . . . Britain's determination, which even the German press noted last week with 'the admiration that the strong may grant his foe', was not necessarily an accurate

The first preoccupation of most of the new officers was to remove the wire stiffener from their peaked caps. The best course of action then, some maintained, was to fill the cap with beer, when the crown could be moulded easily, and in drying, would set nicely. There was an unwritten custom that officer air crew bent their peaked caps into a shape which, consciously or otherwise, resembled that worn by the Luftwaffe. It differentiated them from mere admin officers and those in other ground trades, who did not fly. Authority turned a blind eye to this particular breach of the dress regulations.
–from *Yesterday's Gone* by N.J. Crisp

left: An officer of the 379th Bomb Group leading a group of English children in games at an outdoor 'kiddies party' on the base at Kimbolton in Cambridgeshire on October 2nd 1943.

. . . the way we were set up in Bombardment in those days, we flew to an Initial Point somewhere near the target area. Then—and only then—did we turn and make our run to the AP or Aiming Point (target itself). The Initial Point varied, but usually it was far enough away to allow us to make a turn— Swing the whole formation around and get leveled out pretty well. The IP might be all the way from fifteen to thirty miles away from the AP. I kept mulling this over, all the time we were getting set at Grafton Underwood and shaping up to fly our first mission. Of course there were a million other things confronting me as well. But hot and bitter, burning in my mind all the time, was the thought: "What are we going to do about the bombing?" Always in the end there was only one answer to be found. It was apparent that we would have to go straight in on the target. It was also apparent that we would have to fly a much longer bomb run. There just weren't any two ways about it. You couldn't swing evasively all over the sky without throwing your bombs all over the lot too.
Next big problem which loomed, was: "So we'll have all our airplanes shot down. that's really too much attrition in any war. No equipment or personnel left for the next mission." If we could believe what other people told us, we'd all get pulverized by the enemy ground-to-air fire. No percentage in that. I prayed there must be an answer lurking around somewhere, but I hadn't found it yet. I didn't say anything to anyone else about this straight-and-level idea—the notion of dispensing utterly

reflection of the military situation . . . In France, only a week before Paris fell, a wave of desperate optimism swept the country, electrifying even the indifferent French workers. The rest of the world might wonder whether Adolf Hitler would parade one day soon from Piccadilly, up Regent Street and across to Hyde Park—and down to the gates of Buckingham Palace. But there was no question in the minds of British men and women. They boast the world's greatest poet and the world's greatest confidence. With both they said last week: 'This England never did, nor never shall, lie at the proud foot of a conqueror!' "

When Ira Eakin set foot in England, it was as no conqueror but as a friend and ally. Eakin was an Army Air Force crew chief, and his arrival followed that of his namesake, Brigadier General Ira Eaker, who had recently established his headquarters at High Wycombe in Buckinghamshire and embarked upon the task— the long and heavy task—which, with American resourcefulness and energy, and due British help, was to transform his tiny bomber force into "The Mighty Eighth".

"When we were first over there," said Eakin, "it was at a place called Watford, and we were sleeping in tents. Don Carpenter and me, we'd been on the damn boat for nineteen days, and we just sacked out. We'd just got to sleeping real good when the sirens went off. Ole Carp said 'The hell with them, I'm not getting up.' And I said 'I'm not either.' So we just laid there, and then they started on our side of London—boom, boom, BOOM, getting louder and louder, coming right towards us. Man, we got outa that tent and laid up against a wall that was there. Right outside of the gate near where we were under that wall, a big red two-storey bus went by,

going north. Them Germans cut loose with a parachute mine and it came down right in front of that bus, and it started coming south—backwards. There was an air raid shelter about a quarter of a mile off, and I didn't hit the ground more than twenty times till I was in that shelter."

"Next morning," Eakin continued, "was when I understood what a bad situation those people were in for food supplies. They had a tent for a mess hall, and I felt kind of ashamed of myself after I saw what those people had to live on. I walked in there for breakfast, and they laid a slab of dark bread on a tray and a glob of marmalade, and big scoop of mutton stew, and a cup of hot tea. The bread looked like it had chips of sawdust in it. I said 'Goddam, I don't know whether I can eat this or not,' But I was pretty hungry, and I did all right with the tea and the sawdust bread and marmalade, but when that mutton stew hit the skillet, well . . . I guess it wasn't that bad. We went out into the street later, and for two city blocks there was nothing standing where that mine had hit."

The New Zealander Hector Bolitho, a writer in civil life, held a wartime post at the Air Ministry in the Strand. Observing the citizens throughout the nights of bombing, he recognized that they had great powers of recovery. "Cynics may suggest," he wrote, "this comes from insensibility. Others will contend that it comes from stubborn courage. It is not easy to judge . . . Are the English so fierce in their courage that no disaster can reduce their spirit, or are they so certain of their insular destiny that the rest of the democratic world is there to attend upon their pride?"

There is bound to be a streak of eccentricity in a race of people who are prepared to inhabit places with such names as Donkey Town,

Maggot's End and Foulbog, and there has to be an element of grit in being ready to acknowledge Goonball, Giggleswick or Crackpot as your home. As a writer in The Sunday Times has pointed out, it must take a certain courage to admit to membership of the Nasty Working Men's Club or the Ugley Mother's Union, institutions in two Essex towns, where the comic possibilities were clearly demonstrated by a local paper's headline: NASTY MAN WEDS UGLEY WOMAN. In comparison, residents of Piddle, Steeple Bumpstead or Pratt's Bottom, need feel no embarrassment.

It would be foolish to pretend that, in World War Two, every single member of the British civil population was a hero or a heroine; few were required to be, or had the opportunity. Many were in danger, some very often, and of them the great majority, to their lasting credit, responded courageously. What was more, they retained their sense of humour, and that wasn't always easy, when they had to board their windows up because the glass was shattered, when they had to make their way to work through streets piled high with rubble and no bus could run, when they passed shops with signs that read NO SWEETS, NO CIGARETTES and NO RAZOR BLADES; worse, to pass by the pubs that had NO BEER. For most people the war called for stamina and grit, not for heroism; it called for putting up with shortages and hardships, not for feats of daring. Often, it came down to doing your best with limited resources, and sticking to your purpose.

Of course, it can't be said that everybody did that—at least not all the time. There were some who were ready to excuse their own shortcomings or a shoddy piece of work with the stock expression "Well there's a war on." That was

easy to say, and hard to contradict. There were others who looked upon the war as a golden opportunity to feather their own nests—the men for whom the British coined the term "spiv". Shrewd and unscrupulous, spivs thrived on scarcity, battened on the honest and made a mockery of rationing. They could always be relied on for a side of bacon, a pound or two of sugar, a tankful of petrol or a pair of nylon stockings—at a price. They knew where to lay their hands on a bottle of Scotch whisky, a book of clothing coupons or a fillet steak. A naive young American, with money in his pockets and unaccustomed to the rules, was an easy target for that kind of rogue. Other nations had their Quislings, their fifth column and collaborators; even the United States briefly had the German Bund. Britain's traitors were of a different order but, unwittingly or not, they were working for the Nazis just the same. Happily, the vast bulk of the people were neither idlers nor spivs: they played their part, large or small, to the best of their ability, and they helped to win the war.

"In the whole world there is no power strong enough to penetrate a country whose people are determined not to be invaded." - Napoleon

"The V-1s are alarming; there is something so inexorable and impersonal about them. One hears the horrible crescendo of their approach and waits, heart in mouth, for the sudden silence which heralds their fall; one has to fling oneself down and 'wait for it'. Then the crash, and the feeling of relief—until the next comes grinding along. Alerts are constant, day and night. Life is certainly full of excitement."
- Margaret Currie, London housewife, 1944.

with evasive action. It wasn't the right time yet to mention such a revolutionary concept. What we did have to do was to get together some semblance of a workable formation, the first day the weather lets us fly.

There must be a master formation, a combination of formations, which would present a maximum opportunity for perfect bombing results, and still constitute itself as an aggregation in which the maximum defensive effort could be maintained. In other words, destructive firepower of our 50-caliber machine-guns, firing from their different position on the planes, and from those airplanes' different positions in the formation, would constitute an effective deterrent against enemy fighter attack.
–from *Mission with LeMay* by General Curtis E. LeMay with MacKinlay Kantor

The rain slanted under the wing on a raw northeast wind. Of Cambridgeshire we had only an impression screened through the deluge— somber flatness, and mud; mud oozing up over the edge of the asphalt circle where we were parked; mud in the tread of the jeep, which rolled away on twin tracks of ocher, leaving us marooned; a vast plain, or lake, of mud stretching off toward a cluster of barely visible buildings.
–from *The War Lover* by John Hersey

I'LL BE DOWN AT THE CLUB

I have been laughing, I have been carousing,/Drinking late, sitting late,/ with my bosom cronies—/All, are gone, the old familar faces.
–*The Old Familiar Faces*
by Charles Lamb

There was a pre-war convention in officers' clubs and messes that certain topics of discussion were tabu; to speak of sex, for example, was not the thing to do, neither of religion, politics nor "shop". An enthusiastic young flier was likely to be told "I say, old boy, do close the hangar doors", and a casual reference to a romantic liaison could bring a stern reproof: "One never mentions a lady's name in the mess, young fellow."

As the days of World War II stretched into months, those restrictions were gradually relaxed. The way of life was changing, and social inhibitions were less rigid than before; furthermore, the peacetime cadre of regular officers was heavily outnumbered by volunteers from civil life and the reserves—young men with emergency commissions, who knew little and cared less about the mores of Cranwell or West Point. They had enlisted to fly and fight for what they knew as democracy, for the western way of life, not to learn an arcane social code. For them, the club or the mess was somewhere to relax, to let their hair down, maybe tell a story, sing a song. Failing all diversions, they might sit in a corner and write a letter home. As for talking shop, if 2nd Lieutenant John Doe or Pilot Officer Percy Prune believed that he had found a way to get more miles per gallon from his aircraft engines, how to keep warm at altitude or improve his gunners' field of vision, he wanted everyone to know. Let the oldsters frown: if they didn't like it, they knew what they could do.

There could be similar small frictions in the sergeants' mess. Some of the old-timers, who had earned their ranks the hard way, through many years of service (and undetected crime), were not entirely tickled to find their lofty status instantly acquired by beardless boys, still wet behind the ears and with air force experience countable in weeks—just because they had acquired a flying badge. But when it became clear that the youngsters' future prospects of a long and happy life were rather less than bright, the feelings of resentment tended to abate. Amicable relations, or at least *modi vivendi*, eventually ensued, there was always bound to be a certain gulf between the men who flew the warplanes and the men who didn't.

There was also the matter of the volunteers' appearance. Some of them, the regulars admitted, seemed to make some sort of effort, but there were others whose style was really quite regrettable. For example, the first thing they did with a new service cap was to remove the stiffener and try to make it look as though it had been trampled by a herd of elephants; under their jackets they wore brightly coloured scarves and turtle-neck sweaters (invariably unwashed); their fleece-lined boots were never polished and their slacks were seldom pressed; they had a tendency to cultivate ridiculous moustaches and to let their hair grow longer than could be considered seemly. What on earth was wrong with a regulation crew-cut or "short back and sides"?

But as the months grew into years, the cheerful iconoclasm of the volunteers had its effect upon the older members—perhaps it revived the spirits of their salad days. At least one Group Captain was known to ride a motor-cycle along the mess corridors and around the ante-room; another's party trick, learned while serving in Iraq, circa 1927, was to eat a wine glass, stem and all. Other senior officers, having downed a tot or two of the right stuff, were inspired to lead the newer fellows in the good old air force songs. Colonels, Wing Commanders and Group

Captains, even Brigadiers, could be seen mounting pyramids of furniture to decorate the mess ceilings with the names of squadron targets, while yet more acrobatic colleagues, enthusiastically supported, made their mark with sooty footprints up the walls. Less active members soon learned to eschew the practice of reclining in an armchair after breakfast with the daily paper, in case one of the naughty younger officers, with a lighted match, approached on hands and knees to set the Times ablaze; they also came to know that, to avoid a "hot foot", it was best to take the post-lunch snooze in some secluded place.

When a mess mate died in action, such of his belongings as, it was conjectured, no next-of-kin would be likely to require, were sometimes sold off at an auction solemnly conducted by the squadron adjutant—usually the only officer sufficiently sober to undertake the task—and the proceeds either sent back to his folks or devoted to some worthy local cause.

On the newly-built USAAF bases in East Anglia, the provision of leisure and welfare facilities was not high on the list of priorities, and some units had to get along with the bare essentials for a while. Armourer Sam Burchell, for example, could recall no club premises for the enlisted men of the 448th Bomb Group at Seething in Norfolk. "There was a place where we could go and drink beer. It was a Nissen hut—not an elaborate place. Sometimes the Red Cross truck would come around with doughnuts and stuff like that. Of course, there were a lot more officers on an air base than there would be on an army base, and there was an officers' club where they had dances on occasion, but I never saw the inside of that."

During 1940 and 1941, the American Red Cross sent millions of dollars worth of welfare

We got up in time for supper and afterwards ran in the rain to the king-sized Nissen hut they called the officers' club. Club? It was a slop-house. Once, later on, when I was low on things to do, I counted forty-seven stuffed armchairs, covered with cracked brown leather, which looked as if they'd been scavenged from a bankrupt old folks' home. A plywood bar stood at one end, and some low round oaken tables were scattered among the heavy chairs.

A big iron stove in the middle of the room had a sign over it saying not to spit on it, but that notice worked like a fresh-paint sign; newcomers couldn't resist doing it once to see their spittle bounce, and they understood the reason for the sign when they took a whiff of their own personal steam. Oof!
–from *The War Lover*
by John Hersey

left: An appealing mural on a wall at the 446th Bomb Group B-24 base at Flixton, near Bungay in Suffolk.

Buzz did not wrestle with the ship. as some men seem to do, and I think I did, for I am a shorty and also was much impressed with the law of gravity. He handled all that airplane with his finger tips, and his movements were gradual, and the ship's smooth. He was a powerful figure, an impressive organization of flesh and cloth and leather and fur and rubber, yet he handled the plane not with power but rather with tender, sad care. His fingers adjusting the trim through a button on the automatic pilot were as sensitive, as plastic, and as modest in relation to the whole man as the knob itself in relation to the tremendous strength of the cables and stress of the wings of the plane. He held the wheel the way he'd hold a martini glass and a butt when he thought he was snowing a dame.
–from *The War Lover* by John Hersey

right: The interior of the officers' club at Ridgewell, home to the 381st BG on December 30 1944.

items and medical materials across the Atlantic to the British people, so it was only right and proper that the British NAAFI (Navy, Army and Air Force Institute) should provide the USAAF with canteen facilities until the Red Cross could arrive upon the scene to meet the need. This the NAAFI did to the best of its ability, but every American serviceman was glad when an ARC Aeroclub opened for business on his base. A typical establishment, such as the one at Grafton Underwood, was run by three young ladies of the ARC with twenty local helpers, and provided a lounge, a library, a snack bar, a card room and a room for pool and ping-pong.

It was the Special Services Officer's task to combat the threat of boredom and homesickness by organizing movies, stage shows and dances on the base. Even a phonograph (or gramophone) could help: "The English appreciate good swing," one pilot wrote, "so the records available are generally excellent. Higginbotham, Basie and all the Chicago men are represented."

The dispensation of alcohol in the Officers' Club at Grafton Underwood was governed by a set of coloured lamps which stood like traffic lights behind the bar. The colours reflected the current combat status of the Group: when no mission was expected an amber light indicated that liquor was available and could be consumed, a red light meant that an alert had been received and the bar would close at eight o'clock, and a green light shone when a mission was cancelled on account of weather. Then, as pilot Lawrence Drew of the 384th Bomb Group remembered: "There would be some kind of party, and the bar was open just as long as we stayed. They would break out a late breakfast for us—toasted cheese sandwiches, kippers, and goodies like that."

The fact that it [air power] was important [in explaining the Allied victory in World War Two] was not in doubt. General air strategy was not the same as an independent strategy, and throughout the war the Allies emphasized the complementarity and interdependence of air power with the army and the navy. The achievement of air supremacy on its own was no guarantee of victory, but combined with the efforts of the other services its contribution was substantial. This was particularly true of bombing. If there was doubt about the ability of bombers to carry out an autonomous strategy to any effect, there was no doubt that bombing made a major contribution to the winning of the key campaigns at sea and on land. To the end Eisenhower insisted that the bombers had an 'overriding priority of co-ordination with the ground force offensive operations'. In this capacity air power, pursued as a mixture of strategically dependent objectives, both eliminated the enemy air force as a threat, and exercised air power against enemy ground forces and supplies. These functions of air power were two sides of the same coin. Only those powers that adopted a general air strategy were able to fulfil both functions successfully, and thus to reap all the benefits that air power, in the circumstances of the Second World War, could bestow.
–from *The Air War 1939-1945* by R.J. Overy

Podington in Bedfordshire was one of the bases originally intended for the RAF's embryo Pathfinder Force, but in 1942 it was reassigned for occupation by the Eighth. The 92nd Bomb Group, alliteratively known as "Fame's Favored Few", moved in on August 8th—the first group to fly to the UK from the USA non-stop. One of the pilots was Ray Wild. "The barracks were Quonset huts," he said, "maybe twenty feet wide and thirty feet long. They put up club buildings for the officers, the NCOs and the enlisted men. There were separate clubs for the flying officers and the ground officers, connected by a long canopy. There were always a lot of fights going on in the gravel agitators' club."

In comparison with Podington and all the other wartime bases the officers' mess at Bassingbourn was positively sumptuous in furnishings and style. It was known by the USAAF as "the best country club in the ETO". The fact that it lay only forty miles from London made it singularly vulnerable to visits from high- ranking officers and other VIPs, for whom it provided facilities of an order suited to their rank. It was built in the days when Britain's Air Ministry appeared to have been keener on competing with the War Office in building splendid messes than in buying the modern warplanes that their airmen would so soon and so desperately need. Came the war, and while the RAF bomber crews went up against the Luftwaffe in obsolescent Fairey Battles, Bristol Blenheims and Handley-Page Hampdens, at least it could be said that the messes were as good as any occupied by Hermann Goering's men.

Horsham St. Faith was another peace-time RAF base and, although a number of additional temporary buildings were erected to accommodate the USAAF, the officers' club was a well-established structure. "It had a huge fireplace," said navigator Charles J. Bosshardt of the 458th Bomb Group, "with a game room, a bar and a whole lot of booze. I spent days on end with nothing to do but play games such as ping-pong, blackjack and checkers, with now and then being called for a mission. There was a party on my 22nd birthday, but no girls were present. I danced with Dick Cruse of Ypsilanti, Michigan. He had a cigar in his mouth and burned my cheek with it."

Pilot Calvin A. Swaffer of the 303rd Bomb Group recalled the club at Molesworth. "We had movies in there, and played crap games and poker. It was easy to lose a lot of money when you weren't familiar with the English currency. You figured a pound note as a dollar, when in fact it was equal to about $2.40 at that time. The first meal I had there, there was this dish of chocolate-covered peanuts on the table. I got me a handful and tossed half a dozen into my mouth. They had a terrible acid flavor, and I ran to the latrine to spit them out. They weren't peanuts—they were vitamin pills."

Keith Newhouse of the 467th Bomb Group, whose diary provides an admirable record of a bomber pilot's life and times, made these notes at Rackheath: "The officers' club is merely a smoking and card room with some cider and beer. A fifth of Scotch is opened per night, first come, first served. We've been playing poker until we see aces in front of our eyes. I really went down a few evenings ago, but I've won back to almost even. Today perhaps I can get back on the credit side."

"Some of the more interesting programs we hear at the club come from Germany," Newhouse continued. "Right now we have a string ensemble, with guitar and accordion, doing a wonderful job of cheering us up. Lord Haw-Haw keeps us amused twice an evening also."

Another wartime diarist was RAF bomb-aimer Campbell Muirhead of No. 12 Squadron. He took a less tolerant view than Newhouse of the traitor William Joyce, who broadcast daily propaganda programmes for the Nazis, and who owed the lordly sobriquet to his fruity accent. "Listened to him telling me what a swine I was to be dropping bombs on innocent civilians. Jesus wept! That nation was all behind Hitler when he was winning: there's nothing innocent about them. They're getting what they deserve. Twiddled the dial and listened to some station featuring Glenn Miller: he played 'Perfidia' (with those immaculate Modernaires), then Ray Eberle singing 'At Last'. But that bugger Joyce. They say they'll hang him after the war, and he deserves it—for that nasal, grating voice as much as for what he says. I do hope they catch him, but I'm pretty certain that they won't." [Muirhead need not have worried: Joyce was caught and duly hanged].

There was no television and, ipso facto, no video machines. People went to movies, to dances and the theatre; they listened to records and the radio. Jazz had come to stay and, in Britain, there were several imitations of the American originals, but the big sound of the moment was the smooth, rhythmic music known as swing, played by bands such as those led by Artie Shaw, Benny Goodman, Tommy Dorsey and Glenn Miller.

Some of their recordings—*Stardust*, for example, *Take the A Train* and *Frenesi*, will always be remembered by the men and women who lived through those times, but dance tunes are ephemeral and tastes in music change. With one exception, records of the big swing bands are seldom heard today. The exception is the music

of the Miller band, which has come to be identified with the 1940s, as evocative of wartime as the sound of sirens and the roar of heavy bombers, as the voice of Roosevelt or Churchill on the radio, or of an air-raid warden shouting "Put that light out!" When the producer of a movie or a television programme wants to conjure up the aura of those days, he will have the sound man dub in the opening bars of *Moonlight Serenade* or *American Patrol*.

Of course, Glenn Miller's melodies were pleasant, the arrangements excellent, the musicianship superb and the vocals stylish, but so were those of Goodman, Shaw and Dorsey; it does not explain the enduring place that Miller holds in the veterans' affection. That requires a further look. Known throughout America in the 1930s as a trombonist and composer, Miller had risen to the top of his profession, leading his own orchestra, when the war began in Europe. He enlisted in the USAAF in 1942 and, as Captain Miller, formed what would become the best and most famous of all service bands. In June 1944, with Lieutenant Don Haynes as manager, Miller took the Army Air Force Band to England, and for the next six months they played anywhere and everywhere to entertain the troops. A typical week's work, in those early days, consisted of five or six live concerts and eight radio broadcasts or recording sessions.

"Why do robins sing in December,
Long before the Springtime is due?
And even though it's snowing, violets are growing,
I know why and so do you.

- from *Sun Valley Serenade*,
Mack Gordon and Harry Warren

Sometimes gentle, sometimes capricious, sometimes awful, never the same for two moments together; almost human in its passsions, almost spiritual in its tenderness, almose Divine in its infinity.
–from *The Sky*
by John Ruskin

Give us the strength to encounter that which is to come, / That we may be brave in peril, constant in tribulation, / temperate in wrath, and in all changes of fortune, and down to the gates of death, loyal and loving one to another.
–Robert Louis Stevenson

MOONLIGHT SERENADE

Major Alton Glenn Miller climbed into a C-64 Norseman aircraft at the Twinwood Farm airfield near Bedford, England at 1:15 p.m. on 15 December 1944. The cloud base was low and the visibility poor. He and two other American air force officers were headed for Paris to prepare the way for a series of concerts by Miller's Army Air Force Band. In minutes the aeroplane disappeared into the overcast. No trace has ever been found of it or its occupants.

Major Miller assembled a musical organization that was recognized as one of America's greatest morale factors during the Second World War. During its service in the European Theatre of Operations, the band appeared in more than 300 concerts, often in bleak, cold hangars on the remote airfields of the Eighth Air Force in England. These appearances were attended by more than 600,000 airmen and military personnel. Additionally, the band made more than 500 live and transcribed radio broadcasts to many thousands of other personnel. Perhaps the finest tribute to the contribution made by Glenn Miller and his musicians came from General Jimmy Doolittle, Commander, Eighth Air Force, who said: "Next to a letter from home, the Glenn Miller Army Air Force Band was the greatest morale builder we had in the E.T.O."

From the diary of Lieutenant Don W. Haynes, public relations officer and manager of the Glenn Miller U.S. Army Air Force Band, and one of Miller's closest friends:

19 June 1944   After one week of processing for overseas duty, beaucoup shots, inoculations and what not, sixty-one enlisted men, with 2nd Lieutenant Don W. Haynes in charge, Captain Alton G. Miller left yesterday via Air Transport Command for London. We departed New Haven at 0830. Arrived Camp Kilmer at 1500. More processing started immediately, and more needles. Carbine rifles and warmer uniforms were issued to the men. Lectures and films, and more needles. We were confined to the base. No telephones. We were allowed to write letters but could not disclose where we were. For a return address, we were told to write: "Somewhere on the East Coast." The mail, of course, was censored.

29 June 1944   Trucks and a staff car transported us to the billet for the band at 25 Sloane Court. We were to learn that 90 per cent of the buzz bombs came directly over this section of London, better known as "Buzz Bomb Alley." Glenn had been meeting with SHAEF brass about moving the AAF band out of London. SHAEF was fearful that we'd be doing a

We took off at nine thirty at thirty-second intervals and assembled over the base, and our group flew to Thurleigh and made a big turn to the left and fell in behind the Thurleigh group, a thousand feet higher, and together the two groups rounded out the full circle and headed for King's Lynn, whence we were to leave the coast of England; two more groups joined up on the way. We left King's Lynn exactly at zero hour, at about ten thousand feet, and we steadily clicked up over the Wash to twice that high.
–from *The War Lover* by John Hersey

right: Major Alton Glenn Miller, who assembled and led the fabulous U.S. Army Air Force Band.

broadcast and a buzz bomb would make a direct hit on the studio, which would, of course, let the enemy know they had the range on the center of London, as they were monitoring all broadcasts out of London. We left SHAEF headquarters, Glenn, Col. David Niven, Paul Dudley and I, and were driven 52 miles north of London to Bedford, to look over facilities in an abandoned pottery factory that might be converted into a broadcasting studio. We then headed for the American Red Cross Club, which was within walking distance of the "studio." A most charming and accommodating British woman, Mrs Bowes-Lyon presided over the officer's club and dormitory and assured us that Glenn and I could be accommodated there, and our contingent of sixty-one enlisted men could be put up at the EM's Red Cross facility on Ashburnham Road, a mile or so away on the other side of town. We had dinner at the Club through the kindness of Mrs Bowes-Lyon, whom we later learned is the sister of the Queen. Back to London and Glenn seemed greatly relieved that we had secured a studio and billets for the men, and could get them out of Buzz Bomb Alley. His main concern was for them and felt a personal responsibility for each and every one of them, as it was he who had pulled strings through top brass in Washington to get the outfit overseas, not being content with just broadcasting to entice young men to join the Air Force, and playing Bond and Recruiting Drives in the U.S.A. His desire was, as he put it, "To bring a bit of music and entertainment to the guys who were sluggin' it out for all of us in the front-line trenches."

It doesn't get dark here until 2330 during the summer. Glenn had taken a two-room suite at the Mount Royal Hotel, which was located just two blocks from Marble Arch. However, he had used it only to bathe, shave and change clothes, though he had spent five nights in London prior to meeting us in Gourock . . . the reason? Buzz Bombs! Rather than trying to sleep there, and running to the basement of the hotel every time an alert sounded, he had slept on a cot in a deep cellar of the British Broadcasting Corporation along with other personnel in that area. He had told us that we could set our watches at 2345 by the first alert of the night as, invariably, the Nazis launched their first buzz bomb at that time. Sure enough, at 2345, fifteen minutes after darkness had closed in, the mournful wail of the sirens sounded, which meant that a bomb was heading across the channel from a launch site on the French coast. Less than three minutes later we could hear the motor noise of the flying bomb. An officer at SHAEF had told us that buzz bombs were destroying homes, apartments and other buildings in London and Greater London at the rate of 1,200 every 24 hours, and this had been going on for three months. Glenn told me that the day after he arrived in London a direct hit was scored on a marketplace, killing more than 500 men, women and children. It was not compulsory to seek safety in a shelter and many people disregarded the alerts. As a consequence thousands were killed.

5 July 1944   I took a weapons carrier and a driver from a nearby AAF Service Command Base and went into SHAEF headquarters in London. Picked up a sack of mail and, while having lunch with the transportation officer, he casually mentioned that a buzz bomb had dropped into Sloane Court at 0800 Monday morning, the day after we had moved the boys out of there. After finishing my business at

We failed to hit our primary for some unknown reason, so we headed for the last resort target. I thought the lead bombardier was making for a small town with a fair-sized marshalling yard. He wasn't. About time for "bombs away," he closed the doors. The same thing happened at an average-sized town north of Frankfurt with a beautiful railroad yard, waiting to be creamed. But the joker closed the doors. We ended up bringing our 10 500-pound G.P. bombs back to the base. I never thought I would see the day when we would bring back a full load from the middle of Germany. There was positively no excuse for not dropping them someplace.
–from *Fletcher's Gang* by Eugene Fletcher

At sixteen thousand I took off my helmet. There was a puddle of drool in my oxygen mask. I rubbed my face but it felt like a piece of fish. The candy bar tasted wonderful.
–from *Serenade to the Big Bird* by Bert Stiles

All aircrew were volunteers, and could not be ordered to fly. However, those who changed their minds were deemed to have shown 'Lack of Moral Fibre'. LMF was a nagging, continual problem for Bomber Command both during operational training and on the squadrons. –from *Yesterday's Gone* by N.J. Crisp

above: In tribute to Major Miller, a bust of him graces the facade of the Corn Exchange in Bedford where his Band of the AAF played on its tour of England in the war.

SHAEF, my curiosity got the better of me and I had the driver take back by way of Sloane Court. The entire section for four square blocks was roped off, so we parked and walked the remaining distance. We stood in front of what had been 25 Sloane Court. The entire front of the building was blown in and the place was a shambles. The bomb had dropped about 75 feet from the entrance to the building directly in back of an Army truck which had just picked up 25 MPs from their barracks down the street. There were no survivors. In addition, 88 others had already been dug out of the ruins of the buildings on Sloane Court, with others still unaccounted for. While viewing this damage, an alert sounded and as we heard the approaching buzz bomb coming we ran for an archway in a building still standing a half block away. The flying bomb passed almost overhead at an altitude of not more than 300 feet. The motor stopped and we saw it dip earthward but veer off to the left. We threw ourselves on the pavement and opened our mouths, a precaution which sometimes saves ear drums. The bomb exploded, the earth shook and debris filled the air. We remained on the ground for several minutes with arms folded over our heads, face down. Shattered glass and debris in the air soon subsided, but when we got up and brushed ourselves off it was practically dark at four o'clock in the afternoon! The dust and dirt in the air caused the transformation from daylight to dusk. This one was too close for comfort, having hit less than two blocks away. We ran over to the stricken area amid ambulance sirens and screaming people. Only two ambulances had arrived at the scene from nearby stations so we helped lift two badly injured old men onto stretchers. Within ten minutes there were a dozen or more ambulances, and impro

vised ambulances, carrying dead and injured out of the partially bombed out tenements . . . one stretcher with a woman badly bleeding from the head and neck, with a seven or eight-year-old little girl running alongside the stretcher hanging onto her hand and crying aloud from fright. It soon became apparent we were not needed there. We returned to our weapons carrier five blocks away and back to Bedford with an eye-witness story we wouldn't forget for the rest of our lives. Glenn's insistence on getting the boys out of Sloane Court had paid off, and when I related what had happened there less than 24 hours after we had moved them to Bedford, he didn't seem too surprised and intimated that he had had a feeling about that place–an intuition. Then he said, "Haynsie, the Miller luck has been terrific. I don't want to be around when it changes."

9 July 1944 First broadcast over the AEF Network and the BBC out of improvised studio "8-H." In a matter of 24 hours Glenn Miller's American Band of the Supreme Allied Command was the talk of the British Isles. Newpapers heralded its greatness, musicians in London found out where we were stationed, and as petrol was very scarce, they took the train from London to Bedford to see and hear the band rehearse or watch a broadcast from 8-H. We soon learned that British bandleaders were refusing to precede or follow us on the BBC, that they suffered by comparison with this star-studded outfit from the U.S.A.

25 July 1944 Three C-47s picked us up at Twinwood Farm for an appearance at an Air Transport Base in Newbury, shortly before noon. Played to approximately 4,500 at this base, had dinner here, and, unable to return by air to Twinwood due to bad weather, buses took the men back to Bedford. Dudley, Glenn and I were driven into London by staff car. We had nine buzz bomb alerts during the night, but we slept at the Mount Royal, regardless. The Miller luck continued.

29 July 1944   Took the entire unit to Pinetree near High Wycombe by bus. The staff car was in the Motor Pool for repairs, so Glenn and I went in a jeep. Pinetree was the headquarters of the 8th Air Force and USTAFF, the nerve center of the bombing raids being planned here, and General Jimmy Doolittle's headquarters. Played a late afternoon concert outside to the entire complement of this base. The band was set up on "crash trucks" for elevation and many of the British General Staff attended. After the concert General Doolittle climbed up on the crash truck, shook Captain Miller's hand and then spoke to the crowd, "Next to a letter from home, Captain Miller, your organization is the greatest morale builder in the ETO." Glenn and I were driven to General Doolittle's "castle" for dinner. Seven generals and ten full colonels made it their home (away from home). Spent the night here. After breakfast, we drove to 8th Air Force Headquarters with Generals Doolittle and Anderson and from their offices over to the "Mole Hole", a fortress of concrete chiseled out of the side of a hill, impervious to even a direct hit by bombs or shells, and down below the surface of the ground more than a hundred feet. Tight security here. Glenn and I were vouched for by Doolittle and shown around. Having been sworn to secrecy about what we saw here, I am prevented from elaborating further.

2 August 1944   Over to Kimbolton, another B-17 base, this afternoon for an outside concert to 4,500. Same reaction as always. These guys are so hungry for entertainment and they love this band. At every appearance, it never fails, a dozen or more GIs come up to Glenn and the boys and say, "Last time I heard the band was at Hershey Park, Pennsylvania," or "Glen Island Casino," or "the Palladium in Hollywood."

16 August 1944   The band had been transported via trucks and we met them at Bentley-Priory. We set the band up on a huge veranda overlooking a lawn in front of the beautiful mansion which had originally been built by Lord Nelson for Lady Hamilton. It is now being used as a hospital for the injured being brought over from the battle fronts in France. Those who could not be brought out on the lawn, were hanging out of the windows. The band was playing their first tune, "In The Mood," when a buzz bomb appeared. The band kept playing (but much softer) as Glenn wanted to be sure he could hear its motor cut out, but it didn't and in less than thirty seconds it was out of sight. Back to Bedford via trucks and staff car.

23 August 1944   We took trucks and the staff car and played a hangar at Podington, a B-17 base, at three o'clock in the afternoon. 5,000 eager GIs crowded in and devoured every beat. Six B-17s from Framlingham picked us up at 4:30 and flew us to their base a hundred miles away near the east coast. This base was celebrating its 100th mission over Germany. After a very good dinner in the combat mess we played for a dance in a hangar that had been cleaned out and decorated with straw, hay, trees, and everything else they could lay their hands on. English girls were permitted on the base, and some brought their mothers, to get a good meal. Forty kegs of beer were brought in, as well as 10,000 doughnuts, and there was plenty of the hard stuff in evidence from the private stock of men who had been saving up for this party. After the dance, the C.O. gave a

We were like old men. It seemed like the sun had gone out of the world. I looked in the mirror and a haggard mask of a face stared back at me. The eyes were bright. And the veins were cleanly etched in the whites, and the pupils were distended. We were all like that.

"I'm gonna get grounded," Sam said. "They're trying to kill us off."

We'd been in the group twelve days. The first four days we did nothing. The next eight we flew.

Grant had a thin face anyway, but by then it was like an axe. Bird was impossible to get along with. Neither of them could sleep.

I could sleep. Or maybe it was a form of death. I would stretch out in my sack and feel my muscles give way completely. There was no pleasure in it. They just went flat and lifeless. And then my nerve endings would die for a while, until Porada came to wake us up.

"Breakfast at two. Briefing at three."

He was always nice about it. Quiet and easy and insistent. I would lie there and the glare of the light would smash back into my mind.

Somewhere in the Reich today. Somewhere in that doomed land. There was a movie named *Each Dawn I die*. It was like that.

After I got my clothes on, and out into the night, it was better. I'd stand still and look away at the stars and ask Lady Luck to bring me back home. Just ask her. Just hoped she'd stay with me another day. One day at a time.

–from *Serenade to the Big Bird* by Bert Stiles

'A storm . . . a hurricane . . . a sea of fire.' Everything experienced in the Battle of Hamburg before this time had been seen in other bombed cities, although not often on the same scale. But what coffee-factory foreman Hermann Kröger saw, in his little corner of Hammerbrook, was a small part of a completely new and most horrific result of aerial bombing. This 'storm of fire' later became the subject of intense scientific study and it was concluded that not even the most severe natural fires, such as forest fires, ever reached the intensity of the occurrence experienced in eastern Hamburg during the early hours of Wednesday, 28 July 1943. The German word *'Feuersturm'* was immediately coined and brought into use to describe this phenomenon; that word was recorded in the main log of events being kept by the Hamburg Fire Department a little over one hour after the storm started. The English word 'firestorm' is a simple and adequate translation.
–from *The Battle of Hamburg* by Martin Middlebrook

Music should strike fire from the heart of man, and bring tears from the eyes of woman.
–Ludwig von Beethoven

party for the band at the Officer's Club, where fourteen quarts of Scotch were set up on the tables when we walked in. The C.O., a young full colonel, asked Glenn and I if we'd like to attend a briefing at 2:30 a.m., which we most certainly accepted. At 2:30, after two hours sleep, the C.Q. awakened us and took us over to the briefing room. Coffee and doughnuts removed some of the cob-webs and we sat down amongst the crews of 39 B-17s assembled in this rather large room with maps from floor to ceiling. The weather officer got up and with the aid of notes, gave a 20-minute briefing on the weather they would encounter on the bombing mission today, a complete description of the cloud layers at the various altitudes, and over the target, as well as temperatures (all below zero). He was followed by the strategic bombing officer, who gave the time they would start their take-offs, the time they would rendezvous with other bombing groups, and where and at what altitude, the exact time they would head across the channel, and where their fighter escort would join them, and at what altitude and precise time. He then unveiled a map showing the target area itself, and when he did, several of the crew members groaned audibly. A pilot seated next to me had been making notes all during the briefing and turned to me, "This is a tough one, heavily guarded by anti-aircraft gun emplacements. We lost four ships out of our group the last time we bombed this one." The target for the day was Schweinfurt where, I later learned, was located the largest ball-bearing plants in the world, and now was turning out Messerschmitt fighter planes for the German war effort. The strategic bombing officer was pointing out on the map where heavy anti-aircraft fire might be expected, especially over the target area.

The exact time they were to "go in" for their bombing run and where the bombs were to be dropped was given in great detail. It was apparent that these missions were on the planning boards for many days. After the briefing instructions were completed there followed a question and answer period with pilots, navigators and bombardiers asking the questions and the briefing officers answering each in detail. At four o'clock the briefing ended with a countdown to set their watches to the second. And after a last swallow of coffee, the crews filed out of the briefing room and into waiting trucks and jeeps which took them out to the flight line and their bomb-laden B-17s. Glenn and I were very impressed with the thoroughness and precision of the entire briefing. We thanked the colonel for allowing us to witness it and Glenn and I walked back to our billet, thinking about those guys in the briefing and wondering how many of them might never attend another briefing. Back to bed and up at nine o'clock. After a nice breakfast of fresh eggs and bacon, toast and coffee, we were flown back to Thurleigh, arriving there at noon. Then back to studio 8-H for a 2:30 p.m. broadcast and another at 8:00 p.m. A very eventful 24 hours.

15 October 1944   I received a call from SHAEF that Glenn was to report to Headquarters first thing in the morning. Important, the colonel said. Spent a quiet night at the Mount Royal. Over to SHAEF for breakfast and then to Headquarters where we learned that General "Beetle" Smith had ordered Glenn to report to his HQ in Versailles immediately. Orders were cut for Major Alton G. Miller to proceed via SHAEF shuttle to Paris and thence to Versailles. I saw him off, both of us wondering what General Smith, Eisenhower's Chief of

Staff, could have in mind. Four days later Glenn called from London and asked If I would drive in and pick him up, which I did. He described entering the office of General Smith's Secretary-Aide, a WAC lieutenant, in the Palais de Chaillot, Versailles, made himself known, and ten minutes later was motioned through the general's door. With shoulders back and gut sucked in, he walked to within a few feet of the General's desk. Smith was studying a paper which lay flat on his desk and had not yet looked up at Glenn, but finally raised his head and looked directly at him with a stern, unsmiling face. Glenn was standing with heels together and brought his arm up in salute, the General answering same with a cursory movement of his right arm in the general direction of his head and said, "Sit down, Major Miller." Glenn sat down in the nearest chair to the left of the General, and before he could cross his legs, the General said, "Major Miller, how would you like to take command of the United States Army Band?" Glenn answered, "I wouldn't like that, sir," to which Smith answered rather gruffly, "Why not?" Glenn said, "They don't play my kind of music, sir", to which the General, not at all happy, replied, "That's all, Major Miller. You may go." Glenn hadn't been seated more than thirty seconds and the interview was already over. He got to his feet, saluted (the salute not being returned as the General had already returned his attention to the papers on his desk), and departed in a hurry. It seems that the Army Band (now in the ETO) was a favorite pastime of General Marshall, who happened to be General of all Generals and was running our participation in World War II from the Pentagon in Washington, and who was very unhappy with the showing of the Army Band

in competition with the bands of our Allies. He had voiced his displeasure to someone in the Pentagon who told him that there was a fellow named Glenn Miller in the ETO who headed an outfit that was the talk of everyone who came within hearing distance of it and who just might be the guy to streamline the Army Band, if anyone could. General Marshall passed the word on to General Smith, who had located Miller and summoned him to his headquarters for "the shortest interview on record." We were to hear no more of Glenn taking over the Army Band as the General must have been impressed with Glenn's precise, straight-forward answers, and rather than command him to take over something that he wouldn't be happy doing, no doubt felt it best to let well enough alone. We continued our broadcasting and recording schedule.

4 November 1944 Glenn and I returned to Bedford for broadcasts afternoon and evening, with a hot poker game at the Officer's Club until the wee hours. Came out eight pounds to the good. Glenn couldn't draw any good cards (unusual for him), so he dropped about eighteen pounds. Driving in from the Officer's Club to the ARC Club, Glenn was in a very pensive mood and talked like I had never heard him express himself before.

"Don, I have a strong feeling that I'll never see Helen and Stevie again. I know that sounds odd, but I've had that feeling for some time now. You know the Miller luck has been phenomenal for the last five years, and I don't want to be around when it changes." Whether the fact that he had lost in the poker game had brought this on or not, I don't know, because he nearly always won in poker, with the dice, picking hit tunes. Everything that he touched seemed to have a gold or silver lining. This

. . . I was attempting to spot enemy fighters, which seemed to be attacking from all directions. The nose of a B-24H was never made for sightseeing in any form. We had two small side windows sort of low so you could only glimpse a few things— mostly our wing men—to the side. The nose turret offered the nose gunner an excellent view from the front but, when he was in the turret, I couldn't see anything because his body blocked the view. The only place where I could look out and see anything was the astrodome—a small Plexiglas bubble above me. Around and below the rim of the bubble was a heavy steel flange about three inches wide. It was the mounting ring for a Navigator's astro-compass— a gadget most of us never used except in training. Now, if you poked your head up in the astrodome, you had a three-hundred-sixty-degree view of the world above our airplane and that's where the enemy fighters were. There was only one problem. We were issued regular Army tin helmets, just like the infantry troops wore, along with flak jackets to protect us. We wore the helmet perched on top of our regular leather helmet when we were under attack. The "pot" sat on top of our earphones and, when I would try to look out, the pot hit the top of the astrodome and wouldn't let my eyes get above its rim, effectively eliminating my view entirely. So, I took the pot off. I was doing great work calling out the fighters to the gunners when there was a loud "clang" right beside my left ear. I ducked, pulling my head in like a turtle. Just then, John shouted over the radio, "Eephus, put your god-damned helmet on!"

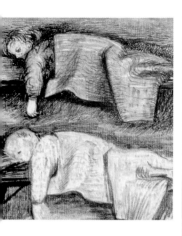

(Eephus was a nickname I picked up over there.) I did just that, and that was the end of my observing.
–from *50 Mission Crush* by Lt. Col. Donald R. Currier USAF (Ret.)

top: At the height of the band's tour of English venues, the Germans sent V-1 flying bombs across the Channel. This drawing by Henry Moore shows English kids sleeping in a tube station of the London Underground.

was a different Glenn Miller than I had known before. He was never one to believe, or give in to intuitions or superstitions. I had noticed that he was quite nervous and jumpy the past few weeks, and often, while walking in the blackout from a restaurant to the hotel, his walking pace was such that to keep up with him, you'd find yourself walking at a very fast clip, like he was in a hurry and had many things to do and not enough time in which to do them. This nervous energy, coupled with British-cooked unappetizing food, had taken quite a few pounds off Glenn, as well, and since our arrival in the British Isles, he had had several bad sinus attacks which hadn't done him any good either. His military gabardine blouses, which we had tailored at Saks Fifth Avenue, didn't fit him now. Glenn and I sat in front of the fireplace at the Red Cross Officer's Club until we got drowsy, then showered and went to bed.

18 November 1944   Glenn returned from Paris and Versailles. Raining like it would never stop when I drove into London to pick him up. On the way back to Bedford, Glenn outlined a proposed movement to Paris for a six-week period on or about the 15th of December so that the band could entertain the frontline troops on leave in the Paris area and in hospitals. We gave the proposal to the band and told them it was up to them to make the decision in that it meant we would have to record six weeks of programs (102 shows) in addition to keeping up the regular schedule. They unanimously favoured doing just that . . . to get to Paris.

22 November 1944   Glenn and I had a conference phone call with the BBC and General Barker (in Versailles) and our trip to Paris is now definite for a six-weeker. General Barker suggested that I come to Paris and make

arrangements for billets, transportation, mess facilities, etc for the band.

23 November 1944   Thanksgiving Day dinner at the Grosvenor House (Junior Officer's Mess) and very good, too. Turkey with all the trimmings. My orders came through to leave for Paris tomorrow morning, but put it off one more day, until Saturday. Our cigarette rations were cut off today!

14 December 1944   Had lunch with Colonel Baessell at the Officer's Club and he said he was going to Paris tomorrow and asked if I would like to join him. Told him I was taking the band over on Saturday and that Glenn was leaving today if the weather cleared. The Colonel said nothing was flying out of the UK today because of the bad weather and suggested that we call Glenn in London and have him fly over to Paris tomorrow with he and Flying Officer Morgan. We called Glenn and, sure enough, he was grounded and had little hope of getting out tomorrow as there had been no SHAEF shuttle to Paris for the past five days and he was outranked even if flying weather prevailed tomorrow. So, he welcomed the Colonel's invitation and asked me to drive in and get him. Left for London right after lunch, arriving at the Mount Royal at four o'clock. Glenn was all packed and ready, so back to Bedford we went in time for dinner with Colonel Baessell at the Officer's Club. After a few hands of poker with the Colonel, Major Koch, and Warrant Officer Earlywine, Glenn and I left for the ARC Officer's Club to get a good night's sleep, as the Colonel would be calling early, as soon as he got weather clearance. Glenn and I sat in front of the fireplace at the club until 3:30 a.m. He was in a talking mood, and though he had said earlier that he wanted to get a good night's sleep, he seemed restless and not at all tired, so we sat and talked, and planned. We talked about the post-war band, taxes, etc, and came to the conclusion that we would work not more than six months a year. The other six months we'd play golf, buy a trailer and go up into the Northwest and do some salmon fishing on the Columbia River, raise oranges at "Tuxedo Junction," Glenn's ranch in Monrovia, California, do an occasional recording date and, the balance of the time left, we'd just loaf! And, of course, devote some time to our families (Glenn and Helen had adopted one youngster from the Cradle in Evanston and had their request in for a girl, and Polly and I had requested a boy from the Cradle, but had postponed the adoptions while I was in the Service.) It was Glenn's plan to deed a piece of his Tuxedo Junction ranch to Polly and myself, and we'd build a home there, and Glenn and I would be partners in a post-war band, he having reiterated several times that, with taxes as they are, one can net only so much money, and in view of the fact that he already had a nest-egg socked away, he wanted me to be set up the same way financially. We even discussed who would be in the post-war band, and our first engagement after getting out of uniform was to be for Bob Weitman at the Paramount Theater in New York. These were the plans we discussed into the wee small hours of that cold, rainy December 14th.

15 Decmber 1944   I was awakened by a phone call from Colonel Baessell at nine a.m. The weather was still bad, couldn't get clearance this morning but it showed signs of clearing by early afternoon, so he suggested that Glenn and I come out to the club for lunch and bring Glenn's luggage, because if the weather cleared, they'd go to Paris this afternoon.

Glenn was awake when I returned from the lobby telephone and, though I had intended climbing back into the sack for a few winks, he wanted to get up, so we got up, dressed and after first getting an egg a piece out of the footlocker, we went out to the dining room and into the kitchen where they boiled our eggs, and we ordered waffles and tea. Neither of us could go those powdered eggs, so I made a deal with a farmer a few miles outside of Bedford, for one dozen eggs a week in return for a carton of Chesterfield cigarettes. Consequently, six days a week we had one egg a piece and the seventh day we just had a waffle. This was really a sub rosa deal as rationing in Great Britain was very strict and even the farmers had to account for everything they raised, hatched or conceived. However, this particular farmer was a part-time conductor on the railroad and I struck up an acquaintance with him going from Bedford to London one day when the Wolesley was laid up in the Motor Pool. It seems he had entered a smaller production from his hens than they were able to produce and as a result, had a few extra eggs. Glenn and I had a few boys in the band who didn't smoke, so we had been trading our chocolate bars for their cigarette rations, and had some extra cigarettes with which to make the trade for the eggs. It worked out very well for all concerned. We read the morning papers and loafed around the lounge for a couple of hours. Glenn rechecked his bag and we went by the EM's billet and found everything in readiness for our move to Paris the next day. Then out to 8th Air Force headquarters and the Officer's Club. Colonel Baessell was packing his bag when we entered his room. The Colonel said he had just talked with Flying Officer Morgan at Station 595, a base 100

top: The office of the wireless operator in the control tower at Twinwood Farm, the RAF field from which Miller and two other USAAF officers took off for Paris on their final flight.

We set our course from the southern tip of the Möhne Lake, which was already fast emptying itself—we could see that even now—and flew on in the clear light of the early morning towards the south-east. We flew on over little towns tucked away in the valleys underneath the Ruhr Mountains. Little places, these, the Exeters and Baths of Germany; they seemed quiet and undisturbed and picturesque as they lay sleeping there on the morning of May 17th. The thought crossed my mind of the amazing mentality of German airmen, who went out of their way to bomb such defenceless districts. At the same time a bomb or two on board would not have been out of place to wake them up as a reprisal.
–from *Enemy Coast Ahead* by Guy gibson V.C.

miles to the north. Morgan said the weather was improving and he would know shortly after noon whether or not he'd get clearance for the flight to Paris. While at lunch, the Colonel was called to the phone. He returned smiling and said that Morgan had just received clearance and would pick them up at Twinwood Farm within the hour. Major Bill Koch and Warrant Officer Earlywine strolled out to the staff car with the Colonel, Glenn and myself. Glenn and the Colonel closed the door and I drove to General Goodrich's chateau, which was in the general direction of Twinwood Farm, as the Colonel wished to see the bed-ridden General for any last minute instructions. General Goodrich was being returned to the States in the coming week, having suffered a severe heart ailment and Colonel Baessell was to arrange for his trip by ship on his return from Paris Sunday. Glenn and I sat in the staff car while the Colonel ran in to the General's chateau, and it started to rain again . . . dark clouds, the low-hanging variety, were now much in evidence and Glenn expressed doubt that F.O. Morgan would be able to even find Twinwood Farm to pick them up. Ten minutes later we drove up to the Flying Control tower at Twinwood, shut off the motor and sat in the car awaiting the arrival of F.O. Morgan. The hard rain had now leveled off to a steady drizzle and, looking skyward, the ceiling was not more than 200 feet. I also began to doubt that Morgan could locate the field. He was now overdue, and we sat smoking and talking for more than half an hour. Then the Colonel bundled his trenchcoat up around his neck and got out of the car. He climbed the ladder leading up to the control tower. Ten minutes later he came back down and told us that Morgan had taken off in a C-64 fifty-five minutes ago and was

due here any minute. Glenn, visibly nervous, couldn't sit in the staff car any longer, opened the door and got out. He peered skyward and his glasses quickly became blurred from the drizzle. He was wiping them off with his handkerchief when the Colonel and I decided that the smoke-filled air in the car was getting pretty "ripe", so we got out and joined Glenn on the concrete strip. Glenn said, "Morgan will never find this field. Even the birds are grounded today." He might have been right. There wasn't a bird in sight, nor was there anyone or anything in sight. Then we heard a steady drone of an airplane motor. It seemed to be in a northerly direction and it was getting louder when the Colonel said, "That's Morgan, alright." The engine noise was getting louder now and it sounded like the plane was directly over the field and not too high. We couldn't see it. The cloud layer couldn't have been more than 200 feet. Now the motor noise was diminishing as the plane was apparently past the field and heading south. "What'd I tell you, Colonel, in this muck he can't even find the field. He's missed it," said Glenn. "Don't bet on it, Glenn," said the Colonel. "Morgan's a helluva pilot. He flew thirty-two missions in B-24s and he's used to weather like this. My money says he'll be on this airstrip within ten minutes." As the Colonel talked, the sound of the motor over the far end of the field indicated the plane was in a turn, and a couple of minutes later it came through the heavy overcast directly over the center of the field. We climbed back into the staff car and drove out to the end of the airstrip and Morgan taxied back down the strip and turned alongside the car. Leaving the motor running, he opened the door of the small nine-place cabin job and greeted us with a wave. "Hi. Sorry I'm late. Ran into some heavy squalls, but the weather is supposed to be clearing over the Continent." The Colonel handed his bag to Morgan and went back to the car for the case of empty champagn bottles he was taking to Paris. Bottles are scarce in France and unless you have the empties, they won't sell anyone a case of champagne to take out. I shook hands with Morgan and tossed Glenn's B-4 bag through the open cabin door. Glenn and the Colonel climbed aboard. The Colonel seated himself in the co-pilot's seat and Glenn sat in a bucket seat directly back of the Colonel, facing the side of the ship. Morgan climbed into the pilot's seat and, as they all fastened their seat belts I waved goodbye and said, "Happy landings and good luck. I'll see you in Paris tomorrow." Glenn replied, "thanks, Haynsie, we may need it." I closed the door, secured the catch and stepped back from the plane to get away from the prop wash as Morgan waved and revved-up the motor. He released the brakes and they started down the runway gaining speed and were soon airborne. In less than a minute they climbed into the overcast and out of sight. I got back in the staff car and drove back to Bedford and the ARC Officer's Club. It was 1:45 p.m. when they took off and they should arrive at Orly Field, Paris, in two and a half to three hours. The Canadian-built C-64 in which they were flying has a cruising speed of 125 to 140 miles per hour. I had lunch at the club and then kept a dental appointment. Back to the EM's billet to find everything set for our move to Paris early tomorrow morning. Ate with the boys and then back to the club to read for an hour before packing my bag. Up at 0545 and after a fast breakfast we boarded the bus for Bovingdon airdrome outside London. Still raining and plenty damp and cold. Two hours later we arrived at Bovingdon. All planes

grounded. We were told that if the weather didn't clear by noon, we wouldn't get off until tomorrow. Drank coffee and ate doughnuts until 12:30. Then, not getting a clearance, we returned to Bedford and hugged the fireplace until dinner.

17 December 1944 Up at 6:00 a.m. into the buses and arrived at Bovingdon at 08:30. Same deal as yesterday and the Flight Control Officer told me there hadn't been a plane take off for the Continent in the past six days! We had to hang around the base and shortly before noon we boarded the buses back to Bedford. But I arranged for the three C-47s to pick us up at Twinwood Farm IF the weather cleared tomorrow. Flight Control is to call me in the morning. So, Monday . . .

18 December 1944 At ten a.m. the Flight Control Officer at Bovingdon called me and said the planes were taking off as he spoke and would pick us up in forty-five minutes for the move to Paris. We loaded the buses and went out to Twinwood Farm and as we drove onto the airdrome three C-47s were circling the field for a landing.

Beautiful day with sun peaking in and out of the clouds and no rain! First nice day in a week. Loaded the equipment and men onto the planes and we took off for Paris at 11:25. Fifty-five minutes later we passed over the White Cliffs of Dover and out over the English Channel, passing over the French coast at 12:50. Landed at Orly Field at 1:45. Though a coded message had been sent by Bovingdon Flight Control that we were en route and to have transportation waiting at the field. There was none there when I checked in at the Transportation Desk. I checked Friday's arrivals and found that Glenn's plane had not landed there. I called the Transportation Officer at Seine Base Section and found that

"These Fortresses are wonderful aircraft—perfectly maneuverable, steady as a battleship and incredibly efficient. We thank you in America for these bombers." The Royal Air Force pilot completed reading the neatly typewritten notes on the table before him. He looked up at the lights over the studio door in the offices of BBC. The red light went out. "We off the air?" he asked the studio technician. His companion nodded.

The pilot gestured with distaste toward the typewritten sheet from which he had read his broadcast. "Of all the bloody rot . . ."
—from *Flying Forts*
by Martin Caidin

Wagner's music is better than it sounds.
—Bill Nye

. . . he gave me the nod, and I pressed the starter button for number one, and I could hear the whine of the inertia starter in the wing. I unlocked the primer and set it to number one and pumped up a solid charge of fuel. Buzz was counting off the seconds, and he nodded again—still yammering about those murderers in Wing—and I flipped the switch to mesh and craned and saw the momentary burst of blue smoke sweep out into the prop wash as number one caught and we heard the roar and felt the shaking of all that energy. We went to work on number two.
–from *The War Lover*
by John Hersey

Glenn had not contacted him about confirming the arrangements I had made re the buses meeting us at Orly Field. I called Major May at SHAEF in Versailles. He hasn't seen or heard from Glenn and didn't know he was coming over a day ahead of our scheduled arrival. In fact, he said he had been expecting me since last Friday and thought that Glenn and the band would follow on Saturday, but knew that bad weather had grounded *all* flights out of the United Kingdom the past week. I told him that Colonel Baessell and Glenn had left Twinwood Farm in a C-64 last Friday at 1345. Another voice on the phone said, "Where did they get clearance from? This is General Barker speaking." I told him that Flying Officer Morgan had gotten clearance at Station 595 and had picked up Colonel Baessell and Major Miller at Twinwood. General Barker then told me to see that the boys were billeted properly in Paris and for me to pick up a staff car and driver and get out to SHAEF at Versailles as soon as possible, that he and Major May would do some checking and they'd be waiting for me, that perhaps they were forced down at another field and hadn't reported in. It was very apparent that the General was quite gruff and displeased. So, I told him I'd see him at Versailles on or about 1800. I got on the phone and tried to locate Colonel Baessell (he was quite well known in Paris, having made frequent trips over here, plus the fact that this was a man who left an indelible impression wherever he went. He was loud and boisterous, and enjoyed life to the fullest). I first called the concierge at the Ritz Hotel, where he often left messages. But the concierge said he hadn't seen the Colonel since his trip over here in November. The Maitre D' at the Raphael told me the same thing. The billeting officer at Seine Base Section said neither Major Miller or

Colonel Baessell had checked in there. My last call was to Lt. Jereski at Special Services and when he told me that he had not heard from Glenn, I was convinced that they had not arrived in Paris. Out to SHAEF shortly after 1800. General Barker and Major May had been busy since I had talked with them from Orly Field, calling bases on the Continent as well as bases on the English coast. They found one rather startling fact. A single motor ship had been charted out of the UK from a southerly point headed over the Channel in the general direction of Paris but was not reported as flying over the French coast. They had also learned that no anti-aircraft guns had been fired from any coastal point between the hours of 1400 and 1800. General Barker had placed a call to General Goodrich at my suggestion, as I felt certain Colonel Baessell would have contacted General Goodrich had he encountered any trouble, as the Colonel was due back on Sunday (yesterday). While we were talking and exploring the possibilities of what might have happened, the cross-channel call to General Goodrich came through. General Barker motioned for me to pick up the phone on Major May's desk. After General Barker had inquired as to Goodrich's condition, he asked if Colonel Baessell was there and with that Goodrich let out a blast to the effect that Baessell flew to Paris on Friday and was due back yesterday, and the so-and-so hadn't returned and he hadn't heard from him. Barker than brought Goodrich up to date on what was going on and told him I was on the extension, so I augmented what Barker had already told him.

He was furious when I told him they had flown a C-64, which he said had no de-icing equipment and icing conditions had been prevalent at Twinwood and over the Channel. Goodrich expressed great disappointment with F.O. Morgan (his personal pilot) for flying a C-64 over the Channel in that kind of weather. General Goodrich said he'd have a search started as of daybreak tomorrow, but that it appeared to him that they had iced up and gone into the Channel. He knew how close Glenn and I were and he assured me that he'd leave no stone unturned to find out what happened, that there was a possibility they had been forced down in some remote spot and had not been able to get to a communications centre to report their whereabouts. General Barker hung up the phone and said to me, "It looks very bad, Lieutenant. I'm afraid Major Miller has had it!"

19 December 1944   Called Major May several times during the morning. Nothing new. Reports did come in but revealed nothing new, and as each hour passed it became more apparent that General Goodrich's assumption that the plane had no doubt iced-up and gone into the Channel was the logical explanation. Four full days have elapsed since I saw them off at Twinwood Farm and not a trace of that plane since it went out over the English coast headed south for France. The narrow corridor from the coast of England to the French coast was ninety miles, all over water. German-held positions along the French coast prevented going the short route, the route the Channel swimmers take.

20 December 1944   Called Major May at SHAEF first thing, but he has received no word that would give us any encouragement, and said that he and General Barker have all but given up any hope of finding Miller, Baessell and Morgan alive, if they are found at all. He said that we might as well prepare ourselves for the worst and that if no trace is found or reported today, he must turn in a Casualty Report tomorrow morning . . . which means that Helen Miller will receive a telegram tomorrow afternoon from the War Department that her husband is "Missing in flight as of 15 December 1944." There is no way I can get word to Polly in New York City to get out to Tenafly to be with Helen and my only hope is that she is already there.

28 December 1944   Spent the entire day at SHAEF making depositions on Glenn's departure from Twinwood Farm. Took our mail to the billet and when Sergeant Sanderson sorted it he found a delayed cable for me from Helen Miller. She reported everyone at home Okay and felt confident Glenn would show up. Here we were concerned about her and she sends a cable to bolster *our* morale.

9 July 1945   One year ago today we set up shop in Bedford, England. Played Nuremburg Stadium today to 40,000 screaming and cheering GIs. This same stadium was the scene of many of Adolf Hitler's gatherings. where he displayed the strength of the Nazi Party amid banner-waving crowds of sympathizers.

11 August 1945   Dropped anchor off Staten Island at 7:30 p.m. Anchored there all night and at 0630 the morning of 12 August we steamed slowly past the Statue of Liberty and up the Hudson River. Docked at Pier 84. Called Polly and stopped off to see her at our apartment for an hour, then out to Tenafly to see Helen. Should have mentioned the reception we got coming up the Hudson . . . tenders and harbor boats blowing their whistles, with signs "Welcome Home Glenn Miller AAF Band" and "Well Done Miller Band. Welcome Home." It was good to be home again, but we had returned minus one, Major Glenn Miller.

at left and below: Four views of RAF Twinwood Farm as it appeared in recent years.

The ships, waiting to fall in line, were like old friends. *Final Than Dinah, Hoor's Dream, Chug Bug, Howzat Again, Round Trip Ticket, Baggy Maggie, Expendable VI, She Can't Help It, Flak Sack, Eager Virgin, Big Bum Bird, Miss Take, Friggon Falcon, Ten Naughty Boys, Heavenly Hooker, Rats Wouldn't Stay, Torch Carrier, Betty Grable, Alabama Whammer, Lady Be Good . . .* –from *The War Lover* by John Hersey

**I THINK I'M
IN LOVE**

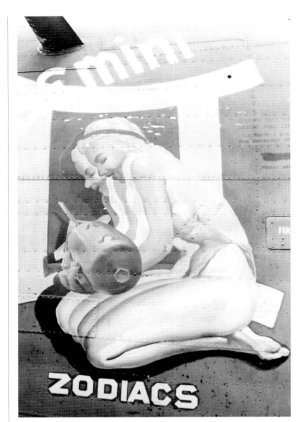

top left: Another of
the Philip Brinkman
Zodiac nose art
series for B-24s of
the Sudbury-based
486th Bomb Group;
top right: Beautiful
Delectable Doris, a
B-24 of the 389th
BG at Hethel near
Norwich; right: An
American Red Cross
girl welcomes these
air crewmen back
from a daylight mis-
sion to Germany.

In the 1940s, Britain suffered from a multiplicity of shortages: of food and fabric, petrol and chemicals, sugar, soap and sunshine, to name but a few. There was never any scarcity of girls. There were millions of them around, in the WRNS, the ATS, the WAAF and the Air Transport Auxiliary, in the WVS, the Land Army and Civil Defense, the Ambulance Service and the Auxiliary Fire Service, in the NAAFI and the Red Cross, in telephone exchanges, factories (they made up 44 per cent of the work force in the aircraft plants) and hospitals, "British Restaurants", offices and shops, or simply helping mother keep the home fires burning.

Many tens of thousands of Britain's servicemen were fighting overseas, and there would have been a marked imbalance of the sexes in East Anglia and Lincolnshire if the home-based RAF had not been reinforced by the arrival of the US Army Air Force.

Every American assigned for service in the ETO was provided with a US War Department pamphlet, in which he was advised that, in Britain, a lot of girls wore uniform, and that they were doing a man's job— including transportation, anti-aircraft gunnery, communications, radio and radar. "There is not a *single record* in this war," ran the text, "of any British woman in uniformed service quitting her post or failing in her duty under fire. Now you understand why British soldiers respect the women in uniform. They have won the right to the utmost respect. When you see a girl in khaki or air force blue with a bit of ribbon on her tunic—remember she didn't get it for knitting more socks than anyone else in Ipswich."

It was only natural that any pretty girl, and many not so pretty, living on an air base or in the vicinity, was likely to find herself the object of some young man's devotion, not to mention his respect, on more than one occasion, and any normal soldier or airman (and normalcy was general) was sure to be enraptured by a female face or figure late or soon. In the heightened atmosphere, certain inhibitions could go by the board, and happy, brief liaisons frequently occurred, some of which developed into serious relationships. To put it another way, a guy and a girl might fall in love.

Most girls in the services found the situation perfectly agreeable, and took pains to look their best at all times—especially on those glad occasions when they received an invitation to the movies, to a party or a dance. WAAF R.T. Operator Pip Beck described how she prepared for a function in the sergeant's mess at Waddington near Lincoln, in 1941: "Our 'best blues' were pressed and buttons polished until they shone like silver. Shoes gleamed; shirts and collars were freshly laundered, and stockings clean, although they were indisputably lisle, not silk. We washed and set our hair, combing it down just a little longer than was permissible, so that it curled on our collars and below our ears. I enjoyed the sensation of shaking my head and feeling my hair swing softly, loose from the ribbon I usually wore. I put on lipstick and eye shadow, and blended a spot of make-up on my cheeks. Then the last touch—a dab of perfume—the ubiquitous 'Evening in Paris'. Half the WAAF section must have wafted into the dance wearing it. We were ready . . ."

There were many girls, of course, who had no thought of romance when they joined the services. They enlisted for patriotic motives, because they felt it was their duty, and they greatly resented being known as "aircrew comforts", or "females, officers, for the use of". One such girl revealed her feelings to Pip

Lovers in peace-time / With fifty years to live, / Have time to tease and quarrel And question what to give; But lovers in war-time Better understand. The fullness of living, / With death close at hand.
–from *The White Cliffs* by Alice Duer Miller

Dear Boys of the R.A.F., I have just seen that the R.A.F. flyers have a life-saving jacket they call a "Mae West," because it bulges in all the right places. Well, I consider it a swell honour to have such great guys wrapped up in you, know what I mean? Yes, it's kind of a nice thought to be flying all over with brave men . . . even if I'm only there by proxy in the form of a life-saving jacket, or a life-saving jacket in my form. I always thought that the best way to hold a man was in your arms—but I guess when you're up in the air a plane is safer. You've got to keep everything under control. Yeah, the jacket idea is all right, and I can't imagine anything better than to bring you boys of the R.A.F. soft and happy landings. But what I'd like to know about that life-saving jacket is—has it got dangerous curves and soft, shapely shoulders? You've

Beck: "It really is too bad the way the WAAF aren't taken seriously. So many people seem to consider we're here for one purpose only—to get a man! I joined up with very deep feelings about what I was doing, and they had nothing to do with men."

Other girls, with feelings no less patriotic but rather more ambivalent, found the proximity of a thousand men entirely to their liking, and to fancy one or two of them, or maybe half a dozen, was enjoyable and natural. Dating was not difficult, kisses and cuddles were happily exchanged; the only problem was that kissing and cuddling were liable to escalate in fervour and in scale.

top: The Bell pub at Spilsby hosted the Lancaster crews of Nos 44 and 207 Squadrons; right: The Petwood Hotel, the unofficial headquarters of No 617 'Dambusters' Squadron, based at Woodhall Spa; far right: The Woodman Inn was the watering hole for the Yanks of the Nuthampstead-based 55th Fighter Group and 398th Bomb Group.

I THINK I'M IN LOVE

Sometimes, through carelessness or ignorance, precautions were forgotten, nature took its course and pregnancy ensued. One WAAF remembered that, of six girls in her barrack room, five were in "the family way" (to use a local term). To this, the official attitude was strict: when the condition was discovered, or could no longer be concealed, that young woman was immediately awarded her discharge from the service. The prospective father might or might not step forward to do "the decent thing", the expectant mother might or might not expect him to; occasionally, she was not entirely certain who he was.

Guys, like girls, come in different shapes and sizes, and it was the tall, dark, handsome type who tended to attract the prettiest of girls (and maybe always will); regular, homely looking guys could have their successes, and even short, balding, ugly guys, given a modicum of personality and charm, could obtain their share. A love-sick airman who lacked all these attributes, physical and social, had to fall back on the barter system: so much candy for so many kisses, so many cigarette packs for so many cuddles, so many pairs of nylons for whatever they might fetch . . .

If she played her cards right, a WAAF could sometimes get to fly as a passenger with a bomber crew, maybe on an air test or a practice

heard of Helen of Troy, the dame with the face that launched a thousand ships . . . why not a shape that will stop a thousand tanks? If I do get in the dictionary—where you say you want to put me—how will they describe me? As a warm and clinging life-saving garment worn by aviators? Or an aviator's jacket that supplies the woman's touoch while the boys are flying around nights? I've been in Who's Who, and I know what's what, but it'll be the first time I ever made the dictionary.
Sin-sationally,
Mae West

mission. Unofficially and rarely, a female civilian working on the base might be taken for a flight. To the crew it was no hardship, and really rather fun, for her to fly along with them; for the girl, it was adventure of the highest order, to be remembered and recounted evermore. Navigator David Oliver remembers one such happening in his time at Wickenby: "The skipper had a delightful girl friend, whom we took up on a practice bombing detail, she borrowing the rear gunner's battle dress. She was thrilled to bits, blissfully ignorant of a very near miss over the range, until excitement got the better of her and she vomited violently over my navigation table, where I had stationed her for the landing. That took some explaining back at base. Shortly afterwards, I received my handkerchief back, washed and highly scented. And guess what—the skipper married her when we were tour-expired."

There were men who took the view that the middle of a war was not the time for romance: some feared that dalliance might blunt their sense of purpose, that the diversion might impair their will to fly and fight. Others eschewed it for purely moral reasons. "With us," a British pilot said, "it was a case of here today and gone tomorrow. It wouldn't have been fair to the girl." Another RAF man, not quite so high-minded, put it this way: "I cut girls out entirely while I was on the squadron. I didn't want to be dreaming of some little darling when a Ju-88 was creeping up behind me."

It could not be said that those who took these monkish attitudes were in a majority: there were some who adopted an opposite position, and never ceased in their pursuit of sensual delight. They went along with old Khayyam

Roll me over, in the clover,
Roll me over, lay me down,
And do it again.
–from a popular song
of World War Two

far left: Airmen of the Eighth Air Force celebrate American Independence Day jitterbugging at a Red Cross dance; left: Another dance, organized by the members of the 359th Squadron, 303rd Bomb Group at Molesworth in Cambridgeshire, March 22 1945.

when he advised: "Take the cash in hand and waive the rest. Oh, the brave music of a distant drum!" But most fliers were content to let nature take its course: they did not search for romance but, if it should beckon, they wouldn't run away and hide.

There was, however, a certain sort of girl of whom it was best to stay well clear—the sort who, by some quirk of destiny, turned out to be a *femme fatale* in every sense. The names, ranks and numbers of her successive boy friends inevitably featured in the lists of killed or missing. In due course, the dread word "jinx" would get around, and the ill-starred damsel would find herself condemned to walk alone.

There was the case of a darkly beautiful WAAF crew-bus driver at a bomber base in Lincolnshire, who enthralled in turn two gunners and a wireless operator; none of them survived to enjoy her favours long. When she transferred her affections to a civilian in the Clerk of Works department, he promptly contrived to kill himself while riding a motorcycle. A young sergeant pilot, newly posted in, was instantly attracted and arranged a date. His intentions were frustrated by his crew, who connived to lock him in the map room at the time of the appointment. "Jinx, my arse," complained the pilot, when eventually released. "She's just had bad luck."

"Yeah," said his rear gunner, "and we don't want it rubbing off on us."

Most relationships worked out rather better; they brought a lot of happiness and did little harm. They might vary in duration from a one-night stand (there are British citizens, now in middle age, who owe their existence to the briefest of liaisons) to "going steady". But attend a meeting of an old bomb group or

bomber squadron, move among the veterans, and there will be at least one couple who will tell you how it happened: Sal was working at the Red Cross Aeroclub when Joe was flying from Alconbury, or Pete met Betty at a dance in Lincoln when he was based at Waddington. They fell in love when death was all around them, and they love each other still.

"The majority of English girls were very good dancers. They had learned all the latest dance steps, and were addicted, as we were, to the American big bands."
- Roger Armstrong, radio operator, 91st Bomb Group

"Three miles from the airfield, there was a hostel for fifty Land Army girls, and for a while we were the only crew who knew about it. Wonderful. A fellow in the crew married one of them, eventually."
-Jim Barfoot, mid-upper gunner, No. 7 Squadron

top far left: *D-Day Doll*, A B-17G of the 447th BG at Rattlesden, Suffolk; top centre: Lovely Libra, another of the Brinkman Zodiac creations at Sudbury, far left: Lt. Col. Dave Schilling taxiing out in his P-47 to escort bombers of the Eighth Air Force; above: One panel of a huge mural in the former mess hall at Horham, Suffolk.

AT THE MOVIES The drama of the Second World War in the air has frequently been recreated in motion pictures, some more successfully than others. Probably the finest of these efforts was *Twelve O'Clock High!* Here are some stills from it and from others of the genre.

far left: Robert Wagner and Steve McQueen in a scene from *The War Lover*, a 1962 release; left: Robert Shaw and Richard Todd in *The Dambusters*.

right: Wagner and McQueen in their B-17, *The Body*; below centre: A still from Command Decision with John Hodiak and Clark Gable; all other stills: Arguably the best of the films about World War Two was *Twelve O'Clock High!*, which featured Gregory Peck, Dean Jagger, Gary Merrill and Hugh Marlowe. Written by Eighth Air Force veterans Beirne Lay Jr. and Sy Bartlett, the story is largely based on events at an 8AF base in England when the group commander was sacked for "over-identification with his men". He is replaced by the no-nonsense Frank Savage, who is initially despised by his crews, but in time wins them over and gives the group the pride and respect it deserves. In the process, Savage, like his predecessor, falls prey to the same failing. When asked by Twentieth

Century Fox producer Bud Lighton, to boil the plot idea down to four or five words, Lay and Bartlett pondered the request for a few weeks and came up with: the disintegration of Savage. The film was beautifully made and is as durable and relevent today as when it was first released in 1949. So powerfully effective is the dialogue that the film has been used for years by business in a range of organizational and motivational training. Many of the events portrayed in *Twelve O'Clock High!* actually occurred in the groups of Eighth Bomber Command during the air war against Nazi Germany.

left and above: Near the end of the film, Savage is about to board a B-17 to lead another raid into Germany, when he suffers a debilitating breakdown. Hugh Marlowe, as Col. Ben Gately, takes over for Savage, to successfully lead the group on the mission.

RIGHT IN THE OLD PUCKER STRING

Our B-17 was totaled. Not only was it full of holes, but the impact of hitting the ditch had bent the fuselage and there were big wrinkles in the skin just back of the radio room. It would be scrapped for parts. It was fifteen minutes or so before a truck got there to take us back to the base. We stood there looking at our crippled B-17, walking around it and commenting on the holes, jagged tears in the aluminum. Although we didn't say it, I know we were all thinking the same thing: how did we manage to destroy an airplane and not a single one of us get hurt?
–from *Countdown!*
by Fred Koger

right: Göering's Nightmare, a 303rd Bomb Group B-17G after a belly-landing at Molesworth in July 1944.

Missing names on the roster, vacant places in the mess-room, empty beds in quarters—all were likely to evoke what the poet called intimations of mortality; in a newer idiom, they could get you right in the old puckerstring. This was the feeling experienced by pilot Robert White of the 390th Bomb Group when he returned to Framlingham from the Merseburg mission of November 30th 1944. Twenty-eight B-17s had failed to return, including seven from the 390th. White found his barrack block totally deserted—except, that is, for a group of men who were collecting the kit of missing fliers for shipping to the States. "It gave me a sinking feeling in the pit of my stomach," said White. "I wanted to find me a barrel of whiskey, crawl inside it and get plastered for a week—so I could put the whole thing out of mind."

There came a point in every man's tour of missions, USAAF or RAF, when he realized he was following a hazardous career. Some, like Charles Bosshardt, sensed it from the start. "On the first mission, you were frightened to death, of course. I wore my flak vest and helmet, and I took several extra flak jackets to line the floor of the B-24." Other men flew on unconcerned for quite a while, but they all got the message late or soon. Few let it worry them, they just grew a little older overnight. Co-pilot Bill Ganz of the 398th Bomb Group didn't get it until his tenth mission,. "Believe it or not," he said, "I didn't realize you could get killed. You saw the flak, you saw airplanes veering off—but even over Pölitz when we were hit by the fighters, I didn't have the fear. Then a couple planes in our formation were just blown up in pieces. There was that box of black, and we had to fly on through it. From then on I was frightened."

Rear gunner Paul Sink of the 493rd received

O God, assist our side: at least, avoid assisting the enemy and leave the rest to me.
–Prince Leopold of Anhalt-Dessau

top: A giant flak tower remaining in Hamburg long after the end of the war; right: A key weapon in the defence of Germany during the massive attacks of the RAF and the USAAF, the highly effective Focke-Wulf Fw 190 fighter; far right: The station armoury at RAF Marston Moor in Yorkshire.

the message over Munich on February 25th 1945. "That was the first time I saw an aircraft shot down. People were blown out of the aircraft. Some of them had parachutes, some of them didn't. This was when I realized no one was playing games."

The late Sir Douglas Bader, one of Britain's best known fighter leaders, who, despite the loss of both legs in a pre-war flying accident, was constantly in action from the first days of the war until he bailed out over France in 1941 and became a POW, was a man whose nerve and courage were a legend in the RAF. Many years later, he was asked about his feelings when he went into combat with the 109s. "It felt as though a hand had gripped my heart," he replied. "If that's what fear is, then I was afraid."

Nobody will ever know how many airmen prayed when they recognized their peril: some would pray instinctively, some would never think of it. Ball turret gunner Ken Stone of the 381st Bomb Group was one man who admitted that he did—at least on one occasion. "It was the second time I saw the fighters. I was afraid that would be it, and I prayed. I was often scared, but I never got so bad I couldn't function. I always had a clear mind—I was just scared to death. Also, I wanted to get home."

Soon after radio operator Roger Armstrong joined the 91st Bomb Group at Bassingbourn, he and a crew-mate were on their way to breakfast while the group's bombers were assembling in formation high above their heads. "We had never seen so many B-17s together," Armstrong said. "Suddenly we saw a small black cloud and then heard an explosion. Two planes had collided in mid-air. Three dots fell from the planes and white parachutes appeared. Our eyes were glued to them when we saw three black streams of smoke, and the

As they watched it the bomber seemed to swell up very gently with a soft *whoomp* that was audible far across the sky. It became a ball of burning petrol, oil and pyrotechnic compounds. The yellow datum marker, which should have marked the approach to Krefeld, burned brightly as it fell away, leaving thin trails of sparks. The fireball changed from red to light pink as its rising temperature enabled it to devour new substances from hydraulic fluid and human fat to engine components of manganese, vanadium, and copper. Finally even the airframe burned. Ten tons of magnesium alloy flared with a strange greenish blue light. It lit up the countryside beneath it like a slow flash of lightning and was gone. For a moment a cloud of dust illuminated by the searchlights floated in the sky and then even that disappeared.

–from *Bomber*
by Len Deighton

right: The smashed cockpit of an Eighth Air Force B-24 Liberator bomber.

You're here to do a special job, you're here as a crack squadron, you're here to carry out a raid on Germany which, I am told, will have startling results. Some say it may even cut short the duration of the war. What the target is I can't tell you. Nor can I tell you where it is. All I can tell you is that you will have to practice low flying all day and all night until you know how to do it with your eyes shut. If I tell you to fly to a tree in the middle of England, then I will want you to bomb that tree. If I tell you to fly through a hangar, then you will have to go through that hangar, even though your wing-tips might hit either side. Discipline is absolutely essential.
–from *Enemy Coast Ahead* by Guy Gibson V.C.

dots became falling bodies that struck the ground a few miles west of the field. We both had a sick feeling in our stomachs. From then on, I realized that this was deadly business, and not some exciting adventure on a movie screen from which you could walk out and back to a normal life. After that, I developed a sick feeling whenever I saw that our crew was down to fly. For years I thought I was the only one with that reaction, but I learned later that you weren't normal unless you felt fear."

All these airmen, in their different ways, came to terms with fear, and didn't let it stop them doing what they had to do. Most of them realized that, in their situation, to be afraid was natural. In fact, as Armstrong found, any other reaction could be regarded as abnormal. Fear, for a combat man, provided it didn't actually make his hands shake, was a preferable condition to complacency or apathy.

One Lancaster pilot, who flew thirty missions at a time when the odds against survival were four to one at best, was always slightly worried if he did not feel afraid. "I tried to imagine a flak gunner down there, or a fighter sneaking up behind us. That kept me on the ball." He feared both flak and fighters, but believed he could evade them if he and his gunners stayed alert and concentrated. Searchlights, on the other hand, filled him with alarm. "To see those long, white fingers groping for you—that gave me the creeps. I'd watched a lot of aircraft being caught in searchlight cones, twisting and turning, before the guns or a fighter clobbered them. It was not a pretty sight. I'd do anything—anything short of a snap roll or a loop—to stay out of searchlights."

With a healthy respect, then, for what the enemy could do, a capable crew and a serviceable aircraft, there was only one thing more the combat flier needed to make it through a tour, and that was to be lucky. The best of men could die, and the best of crews go down, if Lady Luck, in all her fickleness and unpredictability, wasn't riding with them. There are many stories about the small events which made the crucial difference between staying alive and dying; men attributed their survival in those crucial moments to their guardian angel, to the mascot in their pocket, and sometimes to their God. Frank Nelson tended to favour the latter explanation. "I was sitting in the turret", he said, "looking at my map and at the coastline coming up. I wanted to hit our corridor very exact. I leaned forward to get a better look, and it sounded like somebody shot a forty-five right in my ear. I straightened up, and there were two holes in that turret—a piece of flak had gone all the way through, right where my head had been. I'm not a strictly religious man, but I believe in God. There was some reason why I leaned forward other than just looking at the coastline."

At night, the anti-aircraft gunfire appeared in the sky as a pattern of flashes, yellow, white or orange depending on proximity and the atmospheric density; in daylight, it was sometimes possible to see a shell climbing towards you before it exploded in a cloud of dirty smoke with, if it were near enough, a vivid scarlet center. "Over Berlin," said Larry Bird of the 493rd, "I saw an 88mm shell come up, and it just sat there for maybe two or three seconds from the time it stopped rising until it started dropping, just sort of hanging in the air, suspended. As it started dropping it exploded. Yeah, you could see them once in a while."

"There was barrage flak," Bird continued, "which they just threw up and hoped you ran into it, and tracking flak, where they put one in front of you and one behind you, and the next

Lambert was following the classic manoeuvre of the corkscrew and chanting its litany as he went, to warn the crew: diving port, climbing port, roll, climbing starboard, diving starboard, roll, diving port, climbing port . . . a corkscrew can be executed in such a leisurely fashion that it occupies ten miles of air space (some pilots corkscrewed like this the whole journey) or it can be the brutal wing-wrenching, back-breaking manoeuvre that Lambert now put into effect.
–from *Bomber*
by Len Deighton

below: The derelict control tower at RAF Wymeswold in Leicestershire.

one got you. On April 4th 1945, when we went to Kiel, I heard one go off behind us, which was very close. I yelled 'turn, turn.' and I don't know whether the pilot or the co-pilot turned, but one or the other racked the plane up in a ninety degree bank and we peeled off the formation. That third shell went off right where we would have been."

Writing in his diary, Keith Newhouse noted the experience like this: "Flak has a terrible fascination. There is a five-ball burst, and the black smoke rolls out like a plume dancing in a heavy wind. Then it is caught by the slipstream and disappears. If it is close enough to hear it is a rather subdued 'poof'. The pieces sound like hail on the plane."

Navigator W.W. Ford of the 92nd had a simi- lar sensation: "You have a funny feeling when you see it. You look out there and it's fascinating because it comes up like a little armless dwarf—there's a round puff and usually two strings that come out of the bottom like legs. Then shortly after it sounds like somebody is throwing gravel all over the airplane. You know that it can hurt you very badly but you watch it. You're fascinated by it, kind of like watching a snake."

On returning to Podington from a later mission, the tail gunner of Ford's airplane was removing his guns from the turret to load onto the ordnance wagon when he noticed a hole about the size of his fist in the fabric of the control surface. "A piece of flak had gone through," said Ford, "just forward of his line of

sight. He went white and started shaking. He was home, he wasn't hurt, but he took a look at that hole and he just fell apart."

RAF pilot Alan Forman feared fire more than anything. Early in the war, he had witnessed the crash of a Wellington and seen the rear gunner burning in his turret. The sight and the smell of that were to stay with him through forty years of flying. "We didn't have self-sealing fuel tanks to start with," he said "and they were always likely to catch fire if they were hit. When I think of McIndoe's guinea pigs' at East Grinstead—chaps who had been burned—I would have preferred to die than walk around like that. But that's just my attitude, it's an individual thing."

Anthony Verrier, author of *The Bomber Offensive*, wrote that "Bomber crews, individually and collectively, were fatalists on the whole; you 'bought it' or you didn't. Although the better than average commanders could argue the dangers of this attitude, and endeavour to train and lead their crews into exercising some choice—even the limited but essential one of keeping alert and ensuring that all crew members could size up and communicate to each other a combat situation, quickly and clearly—repeated operations and the physical, mental and emotional toll of each made it hard to get across." For the daylight offensive crews the strain was maybe greatest of all; there was nothing to do at all but try to stick in formation; "From the day you first get in a B-17 they say formation flying is the secret. They tell you over and over. Keep those planes tucked in and you'll come home.' But nearly 80,000 young men did not, or did so wounded."

For the night bomber crews, Verrier decided, it was a different matter. They could not defend themselves with covering fire, like the B-17s

and B-24s. It was every crew for themselves, he wrote, "And here one comes close to the explanation of what kept men flying. The crew was everything; the individual, very little."

In the late afternoon of Sunday, July 25th 1943, the Eighth Air Force's 1st Bomb Wing attacked the port of Hamburg. The 303rd Bomb Group led the wing, and Dave Shelhamer's B-17 was in the second element of the group's low squadron. "As we started the bomb run," he said, "the flak came up very thick, and the fighters were hitting us through it. Immediately after bomb release, a 20 mill cannon shell shattered the tail gunner's left arm, knocked out the gun on his left-hand side and pierced his oxygen hose. Another shell came in the nose and exploded in the ammunition box for the navigator's gun. Coates got some pieces in his left thigh, but stayed on his feet and at the gun. Next, a shell came into Garrett's ball turret and exploded between the side plate and the left gun, which was lucky for him. He wasn't hurt, but he climbed out very dazed. In the meantime, the tail gunner had got out of his turret as far as the tail wheel and passed out cold. Garrett got back to him with a portable oxygen bottle and brought him round OK. A cannon shell hit the prop on No. 2 engine and spattered on the plexiglass beside my head, but the engine kept running."

The fighters continued their attacks until the formation was over the North Sea. Their ferocious onslaught had cost the 1st Bomb Wing fifteen B-17s. Shelhamer's aircraft was not in good shape as he approached the English coast. "No airspeed indicator, no brakes, the right tyre was flat and we were low on gas. When we landed at Coltishall, just south of the Wash, the bombardier called out the airspeed from his indicator in the

Charlie pointed his guns at the stars. The night sky above was full of them, twinkling away. He found them a huge comfort. There was usually something to look at in the darkness: the changing light and and shade of the sky, the passing clouds, the detail on the ground far below. It was when he could see *nothing*— just total blackness all around the turret—that he felt most alone. The stars were like friends, cheering him on. He knew there were billions of them and that their light took years to reach Earth so that what he was seeing wasn't really there any more, but that didn't worry him. And he knew there were other galaxies you couldn't see at all because they were even further away. Other worlds maybe.
–from *The Crew*
by Margaret Mayhew

By now we had flown around them enough for them to know we were their little friends. Usually we never flew close to Fortresses because they had a bad habit of shooting at anything that came in their range; their fear of enemy fighters caused them to be trigger-happy when any small plane appeared. Slowly, ever so slowly, I joined in formation with the Fortress.
– from *The Look of Eagles*
by John T. Godfrey

right: 401st Bomb Group B-17 gunner John Hurd at his Deenethorpe base and, far right: in his Stalag 17B prisoner of war identification photo; below: The aftermath of a B-17 crash and explosion at the 305th Bomb Group base near Chelveston, England.

 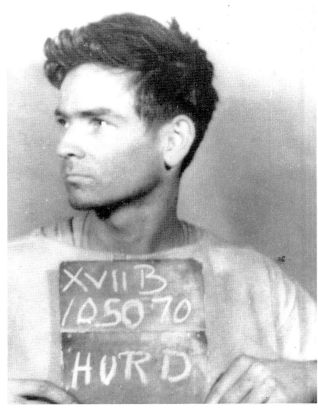

nose. An ambulance came out to the ship and took Coates and the tail gunner to the hospital. That was my ninth mission and it could only have been rougher if we had actually gone down."

Heavy, medium or light, no one who flew an aircraft through a flak barrage was likely to forget it. "You could hear that 'whoomf'," said Ray Wild, "and it moved the plane. That was a near miss, within fifty feet. And you could hear the shrapnel, like pebbles on a tin roof." Or, as a Lancaster bomb-aimer described it, like being in a greenhouse in a storm of hail.

The thousand white-hot fragments of an 88 millimetre shell, if they exploded within a hundred yards, could penetrate the skin of an aircraft with only the slightest loss of force. They could go on to sever cables, hydraulic lines and oil pipes, to puncture fuel tanks, reservoirs and tyres, and to detonate explosives. As a secondary effect, they could slice off heads and limbs, and afflict the human body in other nasty ways. It was the thought of such traumas that caused combat men to flinch—to duck behind the fabric of an aircraft, however insubstantial, when the flak was bursting close enough to harm, it made you wind the seat down on the Berlin bomb runs, although the skin of the cabin was as fragile as the plexiglass, it caused radio man David Lustig to slam the plywood door shut when he looked down through the bomb-bay and saw the fireworks show below; it was why navigator Frank Nelson preferred the phantom security of his compartment to what he called "the glasshouse" in the nose.

In 1942, Colonel Malcolm C. Grow, chief surgeon of the Eighth Air Force, put his mind to the matter of combat crew protection, and much research was undertaken, with the Wilkinson Sword Company of London foremost in the field. By the autumn of 1943, most bomber crewmen of the USAAF were wearing some form of helmet and light-weight body armour. There was a small loss in pay-load, a decrease in the numbers of killed and wounded, and a big boost in morale.

Pilot Robert White watched, with some amusement, the use made by his navigator of the new equipment. "He dropped his desk down to where it was lower than coffee-table height. He put a sheet of armour plate on the floor, then he put on his flak suit over his parachute. He sat there on the floor, Indian-style, and all you could see was these pieces of flak suit with a helmet on top. Every now and then a hand would reach out . . . one of the crew drew a cartoon for *Stars and Stripes* showing our fearless navigator under combat conditions."

The idea of crew protection, however, found little favour in the corridors of Whitehall. To the British service chiefs, helmets were for soldiers and armour was for battleships, fighting vehicles and tanks. Chaps in heavy bombers must be content with what they had—one steel sheet behind the first pilot's seat and a fire-proof door between the cabin and the fuselage. It was only when the RAF heavies began to operate in daylight that someone suggested it might not be a bad idea if the fliers wore hard hats; several airmen did that, but seldom on their heads—they seemed to be more concerned with protecting other parts.

"There may be danger in the deed, but there is honour too."
- W.E. Aytoun

"No man has learned anything rightly until he knows that every day is Doomsday."
- Emerson

Halifax and Lancaster crews were prone to rejoice when a few squadrons of Stirlings formed part of the bomber stream. Flying several thousand feet below them, the Stirlings served to attract more of the shit from anti-aircraft guns. Anyone who completed a tour of ops on Stirlings was a rare specimen, and the chances were that he was not only remarkably skilful but had access to so much luck as to be practically immortal.
–from *Yesterday's Gone* by N.J. Crisp

TIME OUT

right: Coombe House, a WWII 'rest home' run by girls of the American Red Cross for the airmen of the Eighth Air Force; below: A field of bluebells on the grounds of Coombe House, Shaftesbury; far right: One of the most popular songs of the war years.

For the English airman "leave" usually meant time at home with his family, but for his American counterpart there could be no such comfort. Off duty, he would spend his time, money and emotion however it suited him . . . at liberty to enjoy himself on a "48." Home leave was something to be looked forward to only after a long tour of duty in England–he would have to try to unwind on occasional three-day passes to London or one of the other "liberty towns."

On base, the American could relax briefly in an officer's club or aero club, where he could read, have a beer or play cards. Informal in furnishings and tone, these clubs were often given names by the fliers who used them; The Auger Inn, for example, at the 353rd Fighter Group's base near Raydon.

Sometimes, if lucky, a Yank would be befriended by a local family, welcomed and fed as one of their own. It was a unique experience for both guest and host. With few exceptions, these Americans had never before been outside their country, some never having crossed the border of their home state. Equally, many of their English hosts had never before met foreigners.

A forty-eight-hour pass was eagerly awaited by the American airman. It meant a time out of war and, often, a trip to London. An American airman takes us along for the ride: "You stood on that train, your feet numb in the drafty corridor, the windows steamed so that even the bleak Suffolk landscape was hidden in the November curtain of cold. There was the jerking, stopping, backing, and starting again. You cursed the heat lever over the seat. It never worked.

But then it was April, a half year later. You left your overcoat in the wooden crate that served as a wall locker, stuffed some shaving articles in your musette bag and hopped the five fifty or the eleven o'clock bus from the gate. You were taking off on a 48 to London. It was spring and you felt eager.

No tickets now at the fourteen-bob-the-round-trip rate. In April '45, you began getting reverse lend-lease travel warrants to any point in the UK. You waited on the platform for the train to pull in from Norwich, buying a *Daily Express*, *Mail*, *Post*, *Sketch* or *Illustrated*. Then you read the signs–THERE'LL ALWAYS BE A MAZAWATTEE TEA–and watched a farmer herd two goats off the Bury train through the passengers. And you looked over the local civilians, the British officers and the scores of American airmen, a few of them with all their gear starting the trip back to the States. Local trains arrive with school kids in shorts and high wool stockings, clutching their books like schoolkids anywhere. Office and shop girls, Scottish officers in kilts, clean-shaven GIs starting on leave and returning ones, unpressed, unshaven and unwell.

There was the morning a few months after D-Day when your train was an hour late and then you saw why. A hospital train steamed in to pick up a score of U.S. wounded, casualties headed for the States. There was no ceremony. No coffee with doughnuts and brave smiles. The wounded just stared right back at those who stared at them, their eyes dull and tired . . .

You sat in the compartment and slept most of the way. That is, you sat when there was a seat. One of the eight that could be crowded into each compartment. Opposite you was a minister who smiled in a kindly, professional way; three gunners from the B-17 field near Bury, invariably sleeping; two civilian women next to you reading a cheaply covered book and holding boxes and babies; a civilian smok-

I had come down with what the MO called a bad case of shakes. He had been watching me for some time. The twitching about my eyes and mouth was now quite noticeable and my hands trembled. It was nothing serious if caught in time. A week's rest away from the base, away from its tense excitement, was what the doctor recommended. If I would like to spend my time in a "flak" home, arrangements would be made. That wasn't for me; most of the boys there were from bomber crews, who suffered more from the shakes than fighter pilots. They were the ones who had nicknamed the rest home.
– from *The Look of Eagles* by John T. Godfrey

Everybody I had met in England was courteous, if not cordial, and everything I'd seen was fascinating. I wondered why a lot of the guys in the Group bitched so much about England and the English.

I lit a cigarette, stepping underneath an arch over a shop doorway before lighting my Zippo. I'd seen other people do this, and I assumed that a naked light would get me an admonition from a bobby. And the bobbies were out in force, sauntering along with their hands clasped behind their backs. Then I met my first Piccadilly Commando. She bumped into me by accident, or so it seemed. She said, "Sorry, ducks," but didn't move away. And I responded with a corny and unoriginal. "Sure is dark, isn't it?" I could make out her fur coat and blond hair, but couldn't tell what she looked like.
–from *Countdown!* by Fred Koger

right: Another of the Eighth Air Force rest homes, Stanbridge Earls; far right: AAF Station 523, Coombe House, Shaftesbury, Dorset in February 1944.

She was pretty. She was built. She was American. So she was the past, and a halfway prayer for the future. I could see her in saddle shoes and a knocked-out sweater and skirt. I could see her sucking on a coke straw, and I could see her all ruffled up after a long ride home in a rumble seat. She was a symbol of something that was always there, in the back of the mind, or out bright in the foreground, a girl with slim brown shoulders, in a sheer white formal with a flower in her hair, dancing through the night.

–from *Serenade To The Big Bird*
by Bert Stiles

ing steadily, his pipe acrid and penetrating, tobacco shreds sprinkled unnoticed on his well-worn coat. You read the signs on the train: IF DANGER SEEMS IMMINENT, LIE ON THE FLOOR, advised the poster next to the watercolour of the cathedral. IT IS DANGEROUS FOR PASSENGERS TO PUT THEIR HEADS OUT OF THE CAR-RIAGE WINDOWS warned a message over the door with the window you opened by working a heavy, leather strap.

Italian POWs were standing and sitting around the freight cars at Brandon, smoking and waving, but mostly just watching and joking with each other. The civilian next to you explained that the land in this area was all under water a long time ago, and that the cathedral was raised on the only high ground in the vicinity. You see planted fields slipping by. CARELESS TALK COSTS LIVES . . .

You reach Cambridge. Only two stops now and you'll be at Liverpool Street Station–London. The train picks up speed through the canals and pastures the other side of Cambridge and finally, you pass the row-houses, each with its vegetable garden facing the railroad track, an air raid shelter in the garden, and each with laundry out on the lines. Ten minutes now . . . You are up on an elevated track banked on both sides with the ruins and debris of bombed-out apartment houses, factories, churches and office build-ings. You know then that you are in London.

Liverpool Street Station . . . 'Tickets please.' The station is noisy with hissing steam from your train, the familiar voice of the girl announcer and the crowds of people heading for the tube. It is unlike any American train station, for there are no hilarious meetings or emotional good-byes. Everyone is intent upon

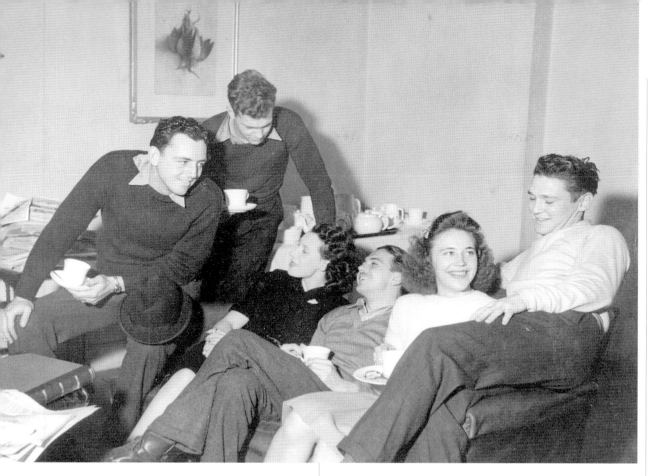

If there's a dish / For which I wish / More frequent than the rest / If there's a food On which I brood / When starving or depressed, / If there's a thing that life can give / Which makes it worth our while to live, / If there's an end / On which I'd spend My last remaining cash, / It's sausage, friend, / It's sausage, It's sausage, friend, and mash.

Sausage and mash, / Sausage and mash, / Hope of the hungry and joy of the just! Sausage and mash, (not haddock or hash), / Done till they bubble and done till they bust! Your truffles are toys, / Your oysters are trash / Contrasted, my boys, / With the homelier joys, / The beauty, the poise, Of sausage and mash.
–from *Sausage and Mash* by A.P. Herbert

his own journey; to the London man or woman the train is not a novelty, it is a God-sent chance to get away to the country for one night of solid sleep away from the bombs, V-1s and V-2s. To the GI arriving, the train is no novelty either. It has been a boring, uncomfortable means of getting to the city where he plans to stay awake . . .

Your pass is almost up. You get to the station at eight o'clock and find a seat. Then you joke with the girl you met or brought along and maybe try a cup of scalding tea in the canteen. You're on the eight twenty. Now you find sleep easy, and you no longer have to keep you uniform pressed or clean. *You* are unshaven and tired, and you smoke and read the London papers . . .

Forty-eights to London were a little different each time you went. You remember some of the sights and sounds, and the flat English countryside divided by trees, hedges and waterways. You will never forget the voice of the girl calling trains at Cambridge and the shafts of light cutting through the steam in Liverpool Street Station."

When the American airman went to London, he sought out many of the sights that he might have visited as a civilian. After Buckingham Palace and St. Paul's cathedral, he went to the Houses of Parliament and Hyde Park. In the evening he drifted over to such welcoming venues as the American Melody Club, The Washington, and the The Nuthouse. There were a few special attractions frequented by the fliers, among them Rainbow Corner, an establishment on Shaftesbury Avenue operated by the American Red Cross. Another was The American Eagle Club in Charing Cross Road. Then there were the ladies of the street known as "Piccadilly Commandoes", who favoured

221

right: A Royal Air Force leave pass issued in October 1943; below right: A detail graffiti from the smoked ceiling of the Eagle pub in Cambridge, England.

Airmen who had survived ditchings said that contact with the water was like driving into a brick wall at forty miles an hour. You stood an excellent chance of being knocked unconscious by the impact—and it was a bad time to be unconscious because as soon as the aircraft stopped smashing and splashing through the water it was desirable to get out. Hurriedly.
–from *Bomb Run*
by Spencer Dunmore

Out of the strain of doing,
Into the peace of the done.
–from *Gone*
by Julia Woodruff

the Yanks with their best attentions.

At dinner time, our man had an alternative to the tired, uninspired, limited fare offered by English restaurants then. The American officer was entitled to dine at a facility known as Willow Run, after the great Michigan auto assembly plant then producing B-24 bombers. Willow Run was located in the Grosvenor House Hotel in Mayfair. There our Yank could always count on having some of the American dishes he missed most, such as steak, pork chops, fried chicken, buttery mashed potatoes, pancakes, and ice cream, treats to temporarily take his mind off the war and the austerity of wartime Britain. These delicious diversions were prepared for him by chefs brought over from some of the best and most appealing restaurants in the America of the 1940s, from the great hotels to the small but distinguished local eateries in the heartland.

Another way to relax on R&R was at the large country houses that had been turned over to the U.S. Army Air Force for use as "rest homes." The Air Force understood the importance of such interludes in restoring war-weary fliers to combat-ready condition. One such facility was Broadlands at Romsey, the country home of Earl Mountbatten. Exhausted and flak-happy types were delivered by B-17s to nearby Stoney Cross airfield for a week away from the battle front. Coombe House, at Shaftesbury, was a rest home run by American Red Cross girls. One of them, Ann Newdick, wrote of her life at Coombe House– "the flak farm," as U.S. airmen called it. "It's January in England, so the morning sun is rare and welcome. Breakfast is bacon and eggs. Apparently the grapevine knew it too because half the house is up for breakfast, 20 or so combat fliers disguised in

sweaters, slacks and sneakers. Plans are afoot for golf, tennis and skeet shooting in the back yard, but the loudest conversation and most uproarious kidding centres around the four who are going to ride to the hounds in a country fox hunt. On a rainy day there's almost as much activity at Coombe House— the badminton court in the ballroom is our chief pride. But nevertheless, the Army calls it a Rest Home. It looks as English as the setting for a Noël Coward play, but even as you approach the house you discover that actors and plot are American. You meet a girl in scuffed saddle shoes and baggy sweater bicycling along a shaded drive with a dozen young men. You'd guess it was a coed's dream of a college house party—not a military post to which men are assigned and where girls are stationed to do a job. We have so much fun that we usually forget its military purpose, and so much the better, because this house party is a successful experiment to bring combat fliers back to the peak of their efficiency.

There are four of us here, American girls sent overseas by the Red Cross. Never in our wildest dreams did we expect such a job. At first we felt almost guilty to be having such a good time. I was talking about what a picnic it was to one of the boys. 'That's the way it should be,' he said with authority. When I looked again I remembered that he was a medical officer who'd been at Coombe for about six weeks. In our conversation, I found out that he was Captain David Wright, Psychiatric Consultant for the Eighth Air Force. He had spent six weeks in careful observation to decide the value of Rest Homes. 'Coombe House and the others like it,' he said, 'represent the best work of pre-

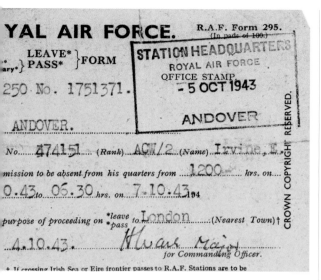

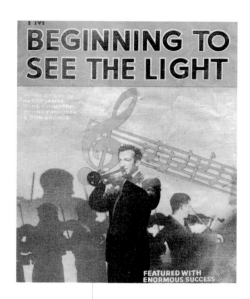

right: H.M. The Queen chatting with the American aircrew of the B-17 *Rose of York*; far right: 8AF aircrew in Piccadilly Circus, London, on a 48-hour pass; below right: Aircrew of the 379th Bomb Group enjoying a Red Cross show at Kimbolton on January 11 1944.

Our two countries, parted long ago by war, were brought together again by war in a unity and understanding such as we had never known. Through long years of endeavour and endurance we shared all things, and though we lost so much we found a lasting friendship. We shall never forget those gallant American soldiers, sailors and airmen who fought with us, some in our own ranks, countless others from our shores. To those who did not return the best memorial is the fellowship of our two countries, which by their valour they created and by their sacrifice they have preserved.
–Prime Minister Winston Churchill

ventative medicine in the ETO. Very definitely, Rest Homes are saving lives–and badly needed airmen–by returning men to combat as more efficient fliers.' A remarkable per cent-age of men who finish their tours have had a chance to be in Rest Homes some time during their combat tour. There isn't any one word to describe the varying states of mind of combat fliers when they are just plain tired. Tired because it's hard work navigating a B-24 or shooting out of the waist window of a Fort. Tired as anyone is after intense mental and muscular strain—intermittent though it is, the lulls in between are not long enough for the flier to get past the let-down stage before he plunges into danger again.

At first the Air Force ran these Rest Homes alone. After two had been established, a large part of the responsibility was transferred to the American Red Cross to make them as un-military as possible. Army Quartermaster out-does itself on food, and 'Cooky' in the kitchen does it to perfection. Fried chicken, steaks, eggs and ice cream are regular items on the menu, all served by pretty waitresses. 'Irish Mike' and Cooky, and all the rest of them are contributions of the Red Cross which disguise the technical and military nature of Coombe House almost beyond recognition, and we four American girls show no obvious solicitude for anyone's morale. We turn down an invitation to play bridge if we want to dance with someone else. Lack of Army demands and freedom from regulations help create the free and easy tempo of the place. The whole feeling is one of such warmth and such sincerity that men come away knowing they have shared an experience of real and genuine living." And this in the midst of war.

Come to Britain! The rooms are so old / And so picturesque that you won't mind the cold. / The bed's over there and the light's over here; Don't put out your boots if you want them this year; The maid has a beard, the cold mutton perspires, / But come to Britain and visit the Shires!
–from *Come to Britain* by A.P. Herbert

VIBRATIONS

Presently he turned off on a side road, propped his bike against a hedge and strode slowly a hundred yards out onto an enormous flat, unobstructed field.

When he halted he was standing at the head of a wide, dilapidated avenue of concrete. which stretched in front of him with gentle undulations for a mile and a half. A herd of cows, nibbling at the tall grass which had grown up through the cracks, helped to camouflage his recollections of the huge runway. He noted the black streaks left by tires, where they had struck the surface, smoking, and nearby, through the weeds which covered it, he could still see the stains left by puddles of grease and black oil on one of the hardstands evenly spaced around the five-mile circumference of the perimeter track, like teeth on a rign gear. And in the background he could make out a forlorn dark green control tower, surmounted by a tattered grey windsock and behind it two empty hangars, a shoe box of a water tank on high stilts and an ugly cluster of squat

right: The now demolished control tower at Polebrook, WWII home of the 351st Bomb Group.

There are certain happenings in life that can neither be classified as undisputed fact nor as total fiction: they seem to lie somewhere in between. We hear from time to time of extraordinary occurrences, any one of which would be dismissed by the majority as a piece of fantasy or, at best, as the product of a hyperactive imagination, but which nonetheless are real enough to those who witness them. The lives of quite ordinary, solid citizens are sometimes touched by inexplicable encounters or events, and these are usually connected with something that happened in the past. It may be that some happenings don't answer to a normal time scale, that they are set in a different dimension and have a different frequency, that they linger on—an everlasting echo of a past event.

Many strange stories emanate from England's eastern counties—the flat lands of East Anglia and Lincolnshire, and the Yorkshire plains, from where the heavy bombers flew. There are stories of a phantom Lancaster that takes off from Elsham Wolds, of the sound of engines in a hangar at North Pickenham, of the voice heard at Tibenham shouting orders through a non-existent Tannoy, of the roar as a pilot checks his engines at full power, rattling the windows in what is now a glider clubhouse, of the growl of heavy aircraft returning in the morning to a long-deserted base. Night travellers have seen a flarepath burning in the meadows where an air base used to be; a group of airmen have been witnessed, walking on a path that was only there in wartime, and passing through a wall that was built in recent years; there have been sounds of conversation in what was once a crew room, of laughter and movement in an empty squash court.

It often seems to be the way with abnormal

sights and sounds that they occur at places where people have died suddenly: historic battlefields, the sites of ancient massacres, gallows grounds—and wartime airfields. Certainly, sudden death was commonplace for the young men from America and the British Commonwealth who flew and fought from England in the bomber war. Sometimes, at these locations, visitors have experienced a feeling of great sadness, even of despair; given the physical and mental associations, this is understandable. It is notable, however, in the weird anthology of airfield apparitions, that not one of them appears to have been malevolent: no greater harm than a frightening has befallen any witness. Well-established phantoms even come to be regarded with some familiarity, if not to say irreverence, and this seems to be the case with Lindholme's phantom air gunner.

The RAF base at Lindholme was built on four hundred acres of South Yorkshire, in the middle of a peat bog known as Hatfield Waste. The airfield opened for business in 1940 and, that August, a squadron based at Lindholme took part in the RAF's first mission to Berlin. By the following July, two Polish squadrons were in residence, operating Wellingtons. Most of the crewmen had escaped from eastern Europe to carry on the fight, leaving their families behind. Their strong purpose was to kill as many Germans (and, when time permitted, to love as many women) as they could.

Returning from an attack upon Cologne, one of the Polish pilots overshot the runway and crash-landed in the bog. None of the crew was ever found. Their Wellington still lies there, occasionally emerging, some say, when the methane gas inside the fuselage expands. The local story goes that, on these occasions, the tail gunner emerges out of Hatfield Waste and

left: The entire ten-man crew of the B-17F, *Jersey Jinx*, catching a lift to the interrogation hut after their mission.

Nissen huts.
Not a soul was visible, nothing moved save the cows, nor was there any sound to break the great quiet. And yet Stovall, standing there solitary against the green landscape, was no longer alone. Nor, to him, was the suit he wore still blue. Rather it was olive drab, with major's leaves on the shoulders, as befitted the adjutant of a heavy-bombardment group.
A gust of wind blew back the tall weeds behind the hardstand nearest him. But suddenly Stovall could no longer see the bent-back weeds through the quick tears that blurred his eyes and slid down the deep lines in his face. He made no move to brush them away. For behind the blur he could see, from within more clearly. On each empty hardstand there sat the ghost of a B-17, its four whirling propellers blasting the tall grass with the gale of its slip stream, its tyres bulging under the weight of tons of bombs and tons of the gasoline needed for a deep penetration.
–from *Twelve O'Clock High!* by Beirne Lay, Jr and Sy Bartlett

right: The runway at RAF Dishforth; far right: A plaque on the house that was the birthplace of Sir Arthur Harris, head of RAF Bomber Command in World War Two.

wanders, apparently at random, around the environs of the base. He has appeared so many times that he has come to be known as "Lindholme Willie".

In 1953, when Lindholme had become the RAF's bombing school, Reg Cliffe, a corporal armourer, completed his duties in the early morning hours and returned to the ordnance office, which was located in a hangar. "I sent one of the men," said Cliffe, "to check that the hangar door was locked. He was older than us, about thirty, an ex-miner from Newcastle and a stable sort of chap. Within minutes he was back, as white as a sheet and trembling like a leaf. He said 'I've seen him', and described a figure in a flying suit with helmet and Mae West. After that nobody ever went to lock the doors alone after dark."

Later that year, an instrument mechanic, working on a Lincoln bomber (the Lancaster's successor) in the middle of the night, saw a shadowed figure approaching the dispersal pan. The mechanic put his head out of the cabin window, and the figure raised a hand in a gesture demonstrating eating. "You want the mess?" the mechanic called, "Officers or Sergeants?" The figure tapped a shoulder, indicating a commissioned rank. The mechanic gave directions, and continued with his work. Next morning he mentioned the incident to his NCO and described the figure's clothing. "That's a Sidcot suit," the sergeant said. "Aircrew haven't worn Sidcots since the war. You've seen Lindholme Willie, my lad."

Since those sightings, the phantom has appeared to many different witnesses, including the CO's wife and a Colonel on an army exercise. Willie also made the columns of the Daily Telegraph: " . . . at dusk in the winter of 1969 a pilot ejected from his jet after take-off

bottom: The old tower at Little Snoring, an RAF Mosquito base in World War Two.

There will be a briefing for a practice mission at eleven hundred this morning. Yes, practice.
I've been sent down here to take over what has come to be known as a hard-luck group. I don't believe in hard luck. So we're going to find out what the trouble is. Maybe part of it's your flying. So we're going back to fundamentals.
But I can tell you now one reason I think you're having hard luck. I saw it in your faces last night. I can see it there now . . . You've been looking at a lot of air lately and you think you ought to have a rest. In short, you're sorry for yourselves.
I haven't much patience with this what-are-we-fighting-for stuff. We're in a war—a shooting war. We've *got* to fight, and some of us have got to die. I'm not trying to tell you not to be afraid. Fear is normal. But stop worrying about it and about yourselves. Stop making plans, forget about going home. Consider yourselves already dead. Once you accept that idea it won't be so tough. If any man here can't buy that, if he rates himself as something special, with a special kind of hide to be saved, then he'd better make up his mind about it right now. I don't want him in this group. I'll be in my office in five minutes. He can see me there.
–from *12 O'Clock High!* by Beirne Lay, Jr. and Sy Bartlett

and landed in the bog. He finally reached the
airfield and peered in through the window of
the lonely caravan occupied by the runway controller. The controller took one look at the
pilot's face, screamed and set off up the runway
faster than an accelerating jet."

It was on a visit to another old bomber station, Holme-on-Spaulding Moor in Yorkshire,
that Edward Garfitt was prompted to write this
piece of verse.

On a long-lost line from a phantom train,
I see a sign on a narrow lane
That looks so odd: 'To the Land of Nod'.
Is it still there as it used to be?
Do old men stare as stupidly
While the young men fly in the hazy sky?
Does a sentry stand at the same guard-post?
Will he raise a hand to the passing ghost
That runs in vain to his blazing plane?
I do not know; and so, by God,
I will not go to the Land of Nod.

In January 1946, a young man named John
Wareing was required, under the terms of the
National Service Act, to undertake a two-year
period of service in the RAF. His initial training was conducted at Kimbolton in
Huntingdonshire, the wartime base of the
379th Bomb Group, USAAF. After a week or
so of "square-bashing", the recruits were considered to be capable of performing guard
duties, and Wareing duly took his turn at the
station gate.

Sometime after midnight he noticed a figure
beside a row of bushes, a hundred yards away.
"I was too shy", he said, "to shout 'Who goes
there', so I waited to see what he would do.
After a few minutes I decided to walk over and

right: Personnel at
ease in a reading
room on an Eighth
Air Force heavy
bomber station in
the English midlands.

232

The war hadn't ended during the night. Every morning that I woke I expected the war to be over. The great gray Nissen huts would have to vanish from the English countryside. The Nissen huts were ugly. They were like great garbage cans cut in half, flung down for men to live in. I am always amazed by the places we live in. But I think it is a way we have of circumventing the fact that we are alive and alive this day, all of us. I spent the morning in the Army talking to the chaplain, Chaplain Ross. He was busy folding up the instruments of his trade for a trip to Ipswich. The chaplain was a nice man. He didn't make the mistake of taking himself too seriously and the men in the Nissen huts would go down to him on Sunday morning just as they go into a pub. To kill time. Which is a phrase I want to analyse one day. All of us were part of that new army of men who never see the people they kill.
–from *Can I Get There by Candlelight*
by Julius Horwitz

top: The High street of Lavenham, near the base of the 487th Bomb Group in the war years; top right: An access panel from an 8AF heavy bomber.

ask what his business was. When I was a few yards away I saw in the moonlight that he was an American officer—I had seen enough in wartime to recognize one. He was in his late twenties, wearing a dark jacket, light-coloured trousers and bright shoulder flashes. He was carrying his peaked cap in his right hand, and his left hand was behind his back. I had a feeling that something wasn't right, and turned back to the guardroom. At the door, I looked back. He had disappeared. I can't say I was frightened. It had seemed quite normal, except for the fact that I knew the Americans had gone a year ago."

That was not Wareing's only strange experience at Kimbolton. Two months later, on a free afternoon near the end of his training, he walked the length of the old main runway to the village at its end. On the way back to his billet, he heard the sound of a bicycle behind him, being pedalled through the snow. He stepped aside. "A uniformed man was riding down the runway—dark, hip-length jacket and light denim trousers. He passed by me, then abruptly turned right towards the hangars. On

the back of his jacket was a blue and white star, and the name 'Campbell' was stencilled on the shoulders. I'm sure it was the same man I had seen before."

Forty years later, passing by Kimbolton, Wareing decided to take a look at his old camp. The feeling he experienced was one shared by many who revisit wartime airfields. "The site that I remembered was now a trading estate, but as I stood there in the rain I became aware that the area was steeped in atmosphere, and that it would always be so."

above: A Nissen hut crew quarters at Hardwick, a B-24 base in Norfolk; left: a .50 calibre machine-gun round found near a hard-stand at Grafton Underwood.

Another phenomenon which featured an American occurred on the airfield at East Kirkby, which lies just to the south of the Lincolnshire Wolds, and was the wartime home of two 5 Group squadrons—Nos. 57 and 630. The aircraft were Lancasters, and the field's radio call sign was "Silksheen".

In 1958, most of the base reverted to the farmland it had been before the war. Down came the hangars, the workshops and the Nissen huts, away went the concrete of the runways and the hardstandings. But Fred and Harold Panton, sons of the farmer who had owned the land pre-war, made it their business to retain the watch tower, and to return it to its wartime state. Their elder brother Chris, a flight engineer, had been killed over Germany (with many other warriors, he lies in the great Allied cemetery at Durnbach in Bavaria). The watch tower was to be the Panton's memorial to Chris and all who flew and died with him.

As the years passed, the watch tower area was found to be frequented by the figure of a tall man wearing a peaked cap, like the one seen at Kimbolton, and a flying jacket. Carrying what seemed to be the remnants of a parachute, the figure was observed to approach the tower, pass through the door and climb to the control room on the second floor. The local belief is that the visitor is a member of a B-17 crew who crashed near the field on December 30th 1944.

Early that morning, as the record shows, thirty-two airplanes of the 92nd Bomb Group left Podington in Bedfordshire to join an attack on a rail bridge at Bulay in western Germany. After forming up and setting course with the 1st Air Division, aircraft 42-97479 had an engine failure. Its mission was aborted, and the load of six 1,000 pound bombs was jettisoned in the waters of the Wash. When a second

The next day, number three engine caught fire during the final approach to landing. A new co-pilot occupied the right-hand seat, a thin young man from New Jersey by the name of Newton. There were frantic moments of opening cowl flaps and closing fuel shut-off valves, feathering and firing the extinguisher. A moment later the aircraft thumped down on the runway. A week later was the Ostend mission. Luksic and Myers were picked off by the fighters. *Boomerang* made it back to Ashley with half the rudder shot away. On touchdown the starboard undercarriage leg collapsed. The wing slapped the runway, bounced, shed its flap and aileron and buckled like a sheet of paper. The aircraft skidded off the runway and spun to a stop in the middle of the field. The surviving crew members hurled themselves out. But there was no fire. *Boomerang* was a write-off, however, her main spar gone.
–from Final Approach by Spencer Dunmore

left: The crew of *We The People*, a B-17F of the 422ns Bomb Squadron, 305th Bomb Group at Chelveston in Northamptonshire.

right: A Maycrete hut at the wartime base of the 453rd Bomb Group, Old Buckenham; bottom: A ruined Nissen hut at Snetterton Heath, the base of the 96th Bomb Group, a B-17 outfit.

I barged into the Crew Room and thought of the one and only time I have ever been into a parrot-house. Never have I seen a crowd of people all in such high spirits at the same time. Confusion, too. Parachutes, harness, flying suits, navigation bags, everything scattered all over the floor as well as the table, without regard for anybody. People were rushing around shouting at the top of their voices; how anybody knew what the others were saying God alone knows. Rations were spread anywhere; people filling their pockets with what they wanted—mostly chewing gum, chocolate and gum-drops as far as I could see—and giving the rest to their navigator to keep in his satchel. I put the stuff in an empty corner, but before I had got my sidcot on most of the rest were gone. I managed to find it eventually and checked it over. Boots, sidcot, helmet, gloves, scarf, harness, 'chute, oxygen tube and rations. Yes, it was all there, but I wasn't going to let it out of my sight again. Lofty came in, towering above everybody else; he wasn't difficult to pick out. He had been dressing in the

TO THE AMERICAN AIRMEN
OF THE '34TH', WHO, IN VALOR,
GAVE THEIR LIVES TO THE VICTORY
THAT MADE REAL THE CHALLENGE
FOR WORLD PEACE AND UNITY

THE 34TH HEAVY BOMBARDMENT GROUP,
A UNIT OF THE UNITED STATES
EIGHTH AIR FORCE
IN WORLD WAR II
APRIL 1944 TO JUNE 1945

left: The handsome memorial to the American airmen of the 34th Bomb Group, a B-24 outfit based at Mendlesham in Suffolk in WWII.

Navigation Office—wiser than I. He kicked me on the bottom and told me to hurry up. He called the rest of the crew and we piled into a lorry standing outside. Percy told me to throw my kit in and jump on, but, thinking I would neve see it again, I hung on to it for dear life. A few people standing on the tarmac smiled and put their thumbs up as we went past. I didn't recognize any of them, but smiled back. The lorry stopped with a jerk.
' "Q" for Queenie, anybody for "Q"?'
–from *Bomber Pilot*
by Group Captain Leonard Cheshire

far left: A flying control officer awaiting the return of his group's B-24s from a raid; left: A crewman of the B-17 *BAD PENNY*, of the 401st Bomb Group at Deenethorpe.

The ugliest of trades have their moments of pleasure. Now, if I were a grave-digger, or even a hangman, there are some people I could work for with a great deal of enjoyment.
–from *Ugly Trades* by Douglas Jerrold

above: An overgrown hardstand at the No 9 Squadron base, Bardney, Lincolnshire; right: English girls pause on their bike ride to watch 8AF mechanics attending to an engine on this B-24 Liberator.

engine failed the pilot headed for East Kirkby—the nearest field—where the Lancasters were being fuelled and bombed up for that night's operation.

Twice the pilot tried to make a landing: twice "Silksheen" sent him around again. On the third approach, the B-17 ran out of sky. The fire was immediate and all-enveloping: no one came out of it alive. The belief persists, however, that one man's spirit continued to exist, and that it was the spirit—the unrequited spirit— of the pilot. It is he, they say, who climbs the watch tower stairs, enters the control room, closes the door and disappears—although there is no other way out of the room. Opinion is that he is seeking the controller who stood on the balcony and fired red flares at him when he was trying to land 42-97479 on that December morning. However that may be, few people at East Kirkby care to enter that control room after dark.

A few years ago, at the entrance to the field, some surviving squadron members erected a memorial to their fallen comrades. The stone bears the numbers of the squadrons and their mottoes (57 Squadron's motto is strangely significant: Corpus non animum muto—I change my body, not my spirit) and a poem composed by W. Scott, a 630 Squadron gunner.

I lie here still beneath the hill,
Abandoned long to nature's will.
My buildings down, my people gone,
My only sounds the wild bird's song.

above: The old main runway at Royal Air Force Kelstern air-base in Lincolnshire.

243

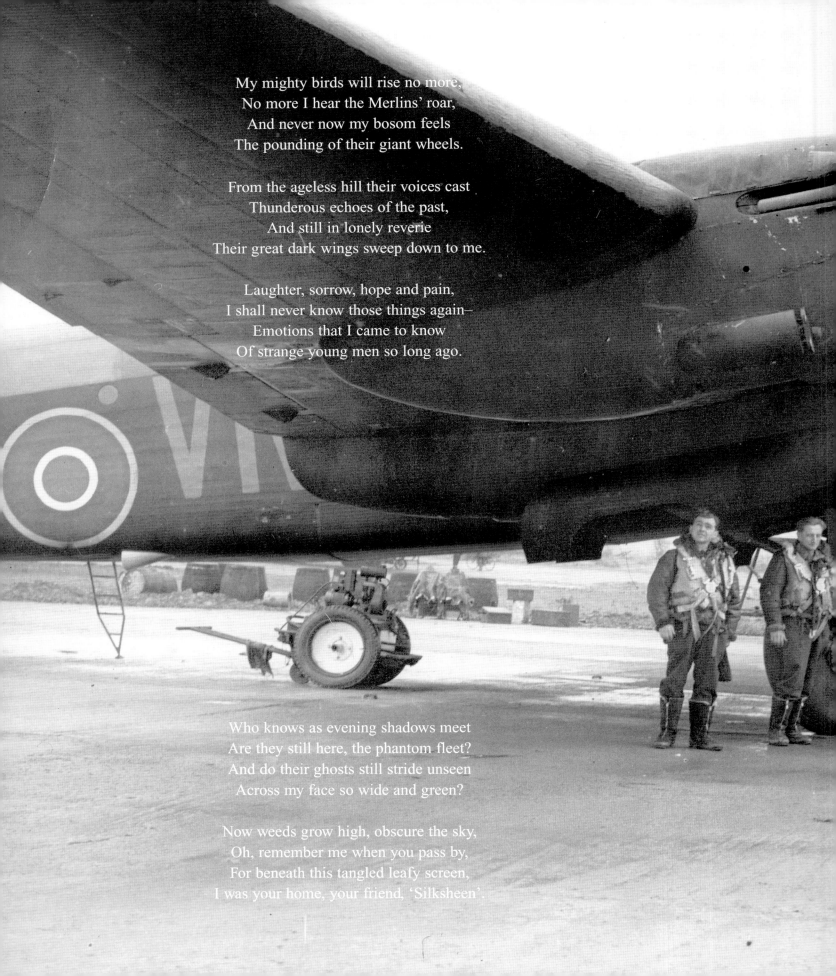

My mighty birds will rise no more,
No more I hear the Merlins' roar,
And never now my bosom feels
The pounding of their giant wheels.

From the ageless hill their voices cast
Thunderous echoes of the past,
And still in lonely reverie
Their great dark wings sweep down to me.

Laughter, sorrow, hope and pain,
I shall never know those things again—
Emotions that I came to know
Of strange young men so long ago.

Who knows as evening shadows meet
Are they still here, the phantom fleet?
And do their ghosts still stride unseen
Across my face so wide and green?

Now weeds grow high, obscure the sky,
Oh, remember me when you pass by,
For beneath this tangled leafy screen,
I was your home, your friend, 'Silksheen'.

below: The Canadian crew of this Halifax bomber.

RETURN TO GRAFTON UNDERWOOD

The time is noon on Friday, May 21st 1993; the place is Grafton Underwood, a village in the county of Northamptonshire, population approximately one hundred. The sun is shining and the air is mild; the hawthorn is in blossom and the ash trees are in leaf. Above the thatched roofs of the old stone cottages, the scattered clouds are almost motionless, bright against the blueness of the sky. A herd of cattle, marshalled by a herdsman and a dairymaid, move slowly down the street en route from their grazing land to the milking shed (it seems they do this twice a day, and bring all traffic to a halt). A car following, pulls up at the gateway to

top: The village of Grafton Underwood in Northamptonshire adjacent to the World War Two base of the 384th Bomb Group; right: General Dale O. Smith at the dedication of a new memorial to the group; far right: A stores hut remaining at the old 384th base.

he village church, and the passenger alights. He is a very tall man, white-haired, with aquiline features and twinkling pale-blue eyes. He is Major General Dale O. Smith, USAF (Retired) and, with many other veterans, he has returned to Grafton Underwood for the first time since, as Lieutenant Colonel Smith, he commanded the 384th Bomb Group when it was based less than half a mile from here, at the height of the battle with the German Air Force in World War II.

Fifty years have passed since the 384th took over the airfield from the 97th who, twelve months earlier, had flown the first bombing mission of the Eighth Air Force's war. In the next two years, the airmen of the group flew over three hundred combat missions in their B-17s, dropped 22,500 tons of bombs, and destroyed 165 enemy aircraft. They won two Distinguished Unit Citations, three Distinguised Service Crosses, fifteen Silver Stars, over a thousand Distinguished Flying Crosses and a host of other honours. To complete the cycle started by the 97th, the 384th dropped the Eighth's last bomb-load on April 25th 1945, in an attack on the Skoda Works at Pilsen, Czechoslovakia.

Now, towering over us, the group's old com

mander takes a long look around. "Oh boy," he says, "isn't this a pretty village? Strictly British, all the way." With the vicar in the lead, we walk along the pathway that runs between the tombstones, and enter the church of St. James the Apostle. The edifice dates from the 12th century, and it would have crumbled long ago if some of the group's survivors, seeing the need for restoration, had not raised the necessary cash. It was they, too, who commissioned the great stained glass window that glows behind the altar, and who made handsome presentations to the Anglican and Roman Catholic churches in nearby Kettering.

With the theme "Coming Home", the Grafton church window shows a B-17 flying across the cliffs of Dover. Above are the national flags of America and Britain, and the crests of the squadrons—the 544th, 545th, and 547th—with the motto inspired by their deputy commander, who was shot down over Hamburg and, from a prison camp, sent a postcard with the message "Keep the show on the road". Below, the inscription reads: "This window is dedicated before God in remembrance of those who gave their lives for freedom during World War II while serving at Grafton Underwood 1942-1945 . . ."

Carefully, the General eases himself back into the car (it wasn't designed for legs as long as his), and we motor to the airfield. The runways have gone, but much of the taxiway remains. In 1944 it gave access to over fifty hardstands for the group's bombers to be dispersed around the field; now it runs through grassland, fields of potatoes, and conifer plantations, fringed by hawthorn, sycamore and birch. The General recalls a spring day in 1944 when fifty-four B-17s took off from here to join the bomber fleet. "And we had no aborts," he says, with justifiable pride. On the north side of the field, on

left: The residents of a Norfolk village adjacent to this American air base wave goodbye to the crew of a B-24 departing for the United States after the end of the European war in the spring of 1945.

far left: The crew of the B-17G *Button Nose* having a last-minute conference on their hardstand before a mission; left: Looking down at some of the 4,200 U.S. heavy bombers that were returned from the German and Japanese air wars following the end of hostilities. This is the storage depot of the Reconstruction Finance Corporation at Walnut Ridge, Arkansas. Here the big planes will be converted into aluminium ingots for peacetime purposes.

the edge of Warkton Common, he points towards a massive pile of logs. It was there, he remembers, that his own aircraft, *Screaming Eagle*, used to stand.

In the south-west corner, at the upwind end of what was runway 240, close to the point where the pilots eased their heavy-laden bombers off the ground, the veterans have erected a handsome granite monument as a memorial to their comrades—1,579 of them—who were lost in action, and to all the others who died of their injuries or in flying accidents. Tomorrow morning, the monument will be the centre-piece for a service of remembrance.

East of the airfield, in Grafton Park Wood, we make a search for the operations block, where they held the secret briefings, collated the intelligence, and maintained communications. It was the group's nerve centre, and the General has a hankering to see it once again. We drive for half a mile along a narrow track until we are deep among the trees: branches and foliage scrape against the bodywork, and the going is rough. Suddenly, the General says "Let's turn left", and we take the path he indicates as far as it will go. Then we stop the car and plunge into the undergrowth. The General's instinct served him well. We find a brick and mortar building with facings of cement that have mostly peeled away, and with earthen ramparts half way up the walls. It's not quite as he remembers it—as a bomb-proof concrete bunker—but this is the ops block, and it's in good shape. Restore the electricity, the water and the furniture, and it could function now.

We drive on through the wood, looking for some remnant of buildings the General remembers—the Roxy Cinema or the Officers' Club, the GI barracks and the Zebra Club ("That was for sergeants," he explains "so called on

left: Ground staff and mechanics gather on the airfield to watch the return of their group, the 91st BG, to Bassingbourn in Cambridgeshire from their raid of June 24 1943 attacking an enemy convoy off Wangerooge Island.

The air was alive with night fighters and bursting shells all along our route. Seventy miles from Essen we saw four machines go down in the space of two minutes. One in the target, one a few hundred yards away on our starboard; the third northwest of Essen and the last behind us as we made our way in. Others could be seen going down all around us. The searchlight cones seemed well occupied, so in we went. Hell! It was like hell in there. Fingers of light were feeling for us; shells bursting very close, bumping and rattling on the fuselage. Even their night fighters were in there. About a thousand yards away I saw one kite cop a packet.

right: A memorial plaque to the men of the 487th Bomb Group in the town square at Lavenham, Suffolk; far right: A bus arrives on the former Lavenham airfield bringing vets and their wives to a reunion of the 487th; bottom: They gather in front of the old control tower for one last look at the base that was their home in 1944.

He burst into flames and started going down. A fighter must have been on his tail— he kept pumping tracer into him as he was going down. After what seemed an eternity we unloaded our bombs and got out of the hottest reception I've yet received from the enemy. Coming home we had to corkscrew nearly all the way. We seemed surrounded by fighters. Don brought us out nicely on track . . . Came at an average of 220 mph. Everyone in the crew admitted on landing that it was the most hair-raising affair they've been on. I'm not afraid to admit I was scared . . . That's 28 behind us and two to go.
–from *Journey Into Night* by Don Charlwood

account of their stripes"). None of these is to be found, but venturing farther on yet another path we come upon a clearing, sparkling in the sunlight, with clear traces of structural foundations. It is the site, says the General, of the communal mess, and upwards of two thousand men, ground staff and aircrew, used to eat their meals here fifty years ago.

Early that evening, we check in at the hotel which the 384th Bomb Group (Heavy) Inc. have chosen for their stay in the UK. Fifty veterans have crossed the Atlantic to be here, and many are accompanied by their wives. If they are jet-lagged, they show no sign of it; they throng the hotel bars and lobbies, and they're having fun. The Group's chairman, Lloyd Whitlow, who piloted a bomber on thirty-five war missions, makes us welcome, as does everybody else, and their friendliness is irresistible.

Everyone has a tale to tell, a memory to share. There are rueful recollections of the English climate, English food and English mud; some are more nostalgic, of girls and gardens, of country folk and country pubs. Some tales are fresh to us, some are familiar (and none the worse for that), and all are light-hearted. There is seldom any mention of the other life they shared at Grafton Underwood. Listening to the conversation, we are not reminded of the biting chill at altitude, of the shriek of slipstream, the twinkling bursts of cannon fire, the deadly barrages of flak, the fall of flaming Fortresses . . .

It is only over dinner, with the help of liquor, that the anecdotes come closer to the bomber war's realities. We hear of how a tail gunner floated down to earth from 20,000 feet, trapped inside the aft end of a shattered Fortress, and landed in a field with no more damage than a headache; of how Nathan Mazer, a Squadron

The Eighth Air Force spent most of its first year of active participation learning first-hand what the British already knew and had tried to impress upon them, that daylight bombing was too costly. The plan to wear down the enemy by bombing both day and night was effective, but as their offensive missions pushed more deeply into enemy territory their fighter escorts—or "little friends," as they were called, had to turn back and head for home before running out of fuel. An auxiliary tank strapped to the belly of the P-47 had extended its protective reach, but still not enough for it to accompany the bombers to farther-flung targets. When left alone to lumber through the skies, the slow-moving B-17s and B-24s became easy pickings for the German fighters. The bombers were jumped from above by Messerschmitt 109 and Focke Wulf 190 single-engined planes and attacked from below by twin-engined Messerschmitt 110s, and the numbers of unescorted heavies downed and aircrew lost during 1943 were appalling.
–from *Donald's Story* by Sandra D. Merrill

I got off the truck and lugged my gear across the pitch-dark hardstand. I could barely make out the outline of the B-17. I must be the first one here, I thought. I opened the nose hatch and shoved my gear into the compartment. I wasn't exactly depressed, but I wasn't in the best spirits either. There really wasn't much to cheer me up. It was cold, damp, dark, and I was going back to a target that scared the pants off me. I decided to go ahead and pre-flight the nose compartment, and grabbed the top of the hatch. I swung my feet through the opening and started to wriggle through. At this point all hell broke loose. A burst of machine-gun fire that sounded like it was right under me broke the absolute quiet of the morning. The B-17 shook like it had come alive. I went limp as a dishrag and dropped to the concrete like a stone. I landed on my tailbone and it hurt like hell, but I was too numb with shock to wonder if I had broken anything. I just laid there, and my brain still hadn't started trying to figure out what had happened. I may have yelled when I fell; I have no idea whether I did or not. But in a few seconds I saw a shadowy form coming toward me from under the

top: A formation of B-17s on a practice mission over England in 1943; right: The American Red Cross providing coffee and sandwiches to air crews after a raid; far right: 8AF enlisted men relaxing in their Nissen hut quarters.

Ordnance Officer, picked up a live incendiary bomb that had fallen from a Fortress and carried it away; of how the group lost seven airplanes attacking Oberpfaffenhofen, on what the General called "that cruel mission" (and he should know—he led it); of how pilot Bill Harvey, flying his last mission, was shot down over France coming home from that same target, and was sheltered by a schoolmarm while the children hid his parachute; of how two French Resistance men who helped him were later betrayed and made to dig their own graves before the soldiers shot them; of how a German officer carefully scrutinized the English map Harvey was carrying, handed it back and waved him on his way; of how he worked with the Maquis until the Allied armies came along . . .

The table service is lamentably slow, but no one seems to mind. Mazer is asked about the wartime food on base. "I don't like to think about it," he replies. "Those powdered eggs were terrible. Finally, the cook chopped green peppers and onions and everything and put them in. He left them twenty-four hours, which killed the odor, and they were almost edible. But they weren't eggs."

Mazer and Harvey shared a billet and, for that last mission, Harvey "borrowed" his roommate's flying jacket. "When I got back from France," he says, "I thought Mazer would be glad to see me, but all he did was grab me by the shoulders and yell, "Where's my goddam jacket, you bastard?"

The General chuckles. "These two guys," he

fuselage. He was bent over in a crouch and I didn't recognize him until he asked if I was OK. It was Koehne, the ball turret gunner. I didn't answer him about being OK or not, but asked, "What the hell happened?" Koehne helped me get to my feet and said, "Oh shit, I really screwed up!" By the time we got to the mechanics' tent a jeep screeched to a stop on the hardstand and an officer jumped out. He was wearing an armband and I guess he was the O.D. He wanted to know what the hell was going on, and I let Koehne explain it. I didn't know myself what had happened, but my mind was beginning to put the pieces together. Koehne was sitting under the airplane behind his ball turret, installing his machine-guns. After he got everything in place he checked the firing solenoids, which was S.O.P. Just push the plunger in with a pencil and if you hear a double click, you know it's working. The only thing he did out of sequence was to hand-charge the gun *before* he checked the solenoid. The gun worked fine. A half a dozen caliber-fifty slugs went ricocheting through the woods. It was impossible to describe the shattering sound a caliber-fifty makes in the stillness of an English morning. My nerves were shot, my butt was sore, and I still had to go to Merseburg. This day was not starting out right at all.
–from *Countdown!* by Fred Koger

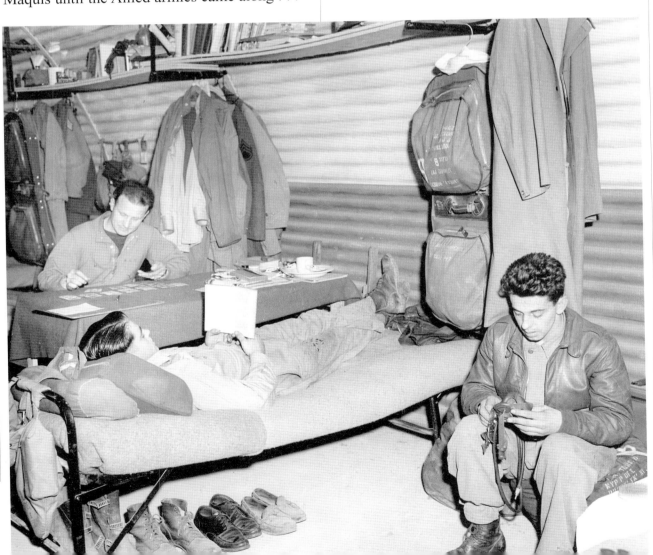

right: The American military cemetery at Madingley near Cambridge, where thousands of WWII fliers are buried; right centre: The wall of casualties and missing soldiers, sailors and airmen; far right: The High street in Lavenham; bottom left: Nissen hut living quarters at the Deopham Green base of the 452nd Bomb Group; bottom right: A wartime runway light fixture minus its glass lens.

He mounted his bike, pedalled down the runway, scattering a formation of plover, turned off at the far end, and followed a narrow concrete road to an outsize Nissen hut which had been the officers' club. Seeing that the door stood ajar, he leaned his bike against the entrance and placed his hand on the rusty doorknob. He had to shove with his shoulder before the door, hanging warped on its creaking hinges, finally scaped inward, sending a hollow reverberation through the empty room. Cobwebs shrouded the windows and a layer of dust powdered the floor. Stripped of its furniture and pictures, the room was lifeless, save for a pair of rats which streaked away from Stovall and disappeared through the hole under the mantelpiece at the far end, near which was a faded square where the radio had stood against the wall. His roving eyes came to a halt on the mantelpiece. Imperceptibly his shoulders straightened and his whole body stiffened. Abruptly he returned to his bicycle, removed his package from the handlebars, untied the cord and lifted out the shiny green Toby. He re-entered the club and strode purposefully to the mantel. With his handkerchief he cleared a spot in the thick dust. And then, with the reverence of a man laying a wreath on the tomb of the Unknown Soldier, he placed the Toby with precision on the clean patch in the center of the mantelpiece, so that the masked robber faced the room.

–from *12 O'Clock High!* by Beirne Lay Jr. and Sy Bartlett

says, "were the only ones in the Group to have airplanes named for them—*The Fighting Hebe* and *Big Dog*.'"

Mazer, we know, is of Hebraic origin, and it emerges that, despite his ground assignment, he flew more combat missions that any other paddlefoot; "Big Dog", it seems, was the Maquis' name for Harvey—we refrain from asking him why.

The evening passes happily, and so does half the night. The morning finds us, somewhat dehydrated but in good heart, on our way to Grafton Underwood for the next part of the program. As we drive along the country lanes, the General remarks upon the colour of the oil seed rape—bright yellow fields contrasting with the greenery—and calls for a halt so he can take a photograph. It may be something in the scenery that turns his thoughts to England and a very English poet: he leans back in his seat and recites Kipling's "Gentleman-rankers" from first to last, while we can only join him in the "Baa, baa, baas".

Passing through the village of Geddington, we come upon an inn, and it calls us like the sirens called Ulysses' sailors. The trouble is that the tavern door is closed. "They'll open in ten minutes," says a passing villager. We fall into conversation, and learn that our informant, now in his early sixties, has lived in the village all his life, and has happy memories of the 384th. "They were very friendly. We used to climb into the aeroplanes, and they didn't mind. There was one parked up the road there, that was painted all colors. We called it 'Spotted Dick'." "That would be our assembly ship," says the General, "the one we used for forming up on." "Aye, that's right. And they gave us gum and candy, and a lovely Christmas party. The Yanks were very good to us kids."

A few steps from the pub there is a ford across a stream—the same stream that flows through Grafton Underwood on its way to join the River Nene. The ford is fine for horses, for vehicles, and perhaps for people wearing Wellington boots, but not, as Mazer remembers, for GIs riding bicycles—especially not GIs who had visited the pub. "I used to sit and watch," he says, "and I'd shout 'Come on, guys, you can make it'. One by one, they'd go down in the water. It really was a laugh."

Having imbibed a restorative potion, we drive on towards the airfield, where the service of

left: Line personnel of the 390th Bomb Group standing around a Red Cross Clubmobile while they consume hot coffee and dough-nuts on their base at Framlingham in October 1943.

War is just one living and dying mass of confusion and delusion and stupidity and brilliance and ineptitude and hysteria and heroism anyway. –from *Mission with LeMay* by General Curtis E. LeMay with MacKinlay Kantor

remembrance is about to start. All other traffic has been halted (fortunately, the milk herd has accustomed local motorists to stoppages). The car parks are manned by Air Training Corps cadets. As we approach the memorial, it seems that half the population of Northamptonshire is there, and most of the Midland's media. The standards of veterans' associations, American and British, are present on parade, the Thrapston Town Band are tuning up their instruments, and two sergeants of the US Air Force, in smart sky-blue uniforms, are standing at attention beside the shining monument.

Quentin Bland, the group's UK liaison man and, in his spare time, the village postmaster, is quietly organizing things.

"A few years back," says Bill Harvey, as we take our seats, "someone had the notion that we ought to march here. It was ridiculous, but that was what we did. One year, it was cold and raining, and we all got wet. The Duke of Buccleugh came along— he owns most of the land around here—and he had a dozen bottles of good Scotch beside him in the station wagon. He said 'I wonder if any of you chaps would care for a snort.' I said 'Yes, sir, Duke, we sure would care for that.' A very nice

above: Nissen huts on a company street at the 384th Bomb Group base, Grafton Underwood as they appeared in 1990; right: The control tower at RAF Woolfox Lodge; far right: The 384th Bomb Group window in the village church at Grafton.

guy, the Duke."

The General launches the proceedings with words as simple and homey as the rural setting. Local dignitaries read the lessons, the band plays and hymns are sung; the standards hang motionless in the quiet air, as still and steady as the sergeants standing guard. Various ministers contribute their benisons, and a tall young USAF chaplain concludes the service with a prayer in verse.

Wreathes of flowers are laid, and the Last Post is sounded—as hauntingly as ever. Then comes a sound that is almost evocative—the strong, vibrant purr of a Merlin engine. A sleek fighter aircraft, in wartime camouflage, streaks across the field. The veterans and air cadets join in a chorus of instant recognition.

top left: The flying eight-ball symbol of the 44th Bomb Group at Shipdam in Norfolk; above: War-time remnants near the flying control tower at RAF Wymeswold in Leicestershire.

"P-51" say the former, "Mustang" cry the latter. They are identifying the finest long-range escort plane of World War II. As it soars away, a sturdy biplane, painted blue and gold, cruises quietly overhead. The air cadets are baffled, not so the older pilots: most of them first soloed in the Stearman PT-17.

The most spectacular salute has been left until last. The very air reverberates as the RAF's Lancaster, escorted (as she rarely was in wartime) by a Spitfire on her starboard wing and a Hurricane to port, sweeps across the crowd; they turn over the village as though tied together, and fly low above us once and twice again. Looking down, the fliers will see a host of upturned faces: what they will not know is that everyone is clapping.

Our sole regret is that *Sally B*, the only surviving UK-based B-17, does not appear on this occasion. We must rely on memory and an inward eye to recreate the airplanes of the 384th, to remind us how they looked and sounded as they climbed over Grafton Underwood, assembled their formations and headed to the east.

Beyond those who died flying for Bomber Command, many more outstanding young men somehow used themselves up in the Second World War, leaving pathetically little energy and imagination to support them through the balance of their lives. Surviving aircrew often feel deeply betrayed by criticism of the strategic offensive. It is disgraceful that they were never awarded their own Campaign Medal after surviving the extraordinary battle they fought for so long against such odds, and in which so many of them died.
–from *Bomber Command* by Max Hastings

Some of the many of memorials to the American and British airmen who flew and fought from fields in England during the Second World War.

The real importance of the air war consisted in the fact that it opened a second front long before the invasion of Europe. That front was the skies over Germany. The fleets of bombers might appear at any time over any large German city or important factory. The unpredictability of the attacks made this front gigantic; every square metre of the territory we controlled was a kind of front line. Defence against air attacks required the production of thousands of anti-aircraft guns, the stockpiling of tremendous quantities of ammunition all over the country, and holding in readiness hundreds of thousands of soldiers, who in addition had to stay in position by their guns, often totally inactive, for months at a time.
—Albert Speer, German Reichs Armaments Minister, from *Spandau: The Secret Diaries*

I am not interested in this plane as a fighter. Does it carry bombs? I order this plane to be built as a bomber!
—Adolf Hitler
on the Me 262 jet fighter, 1944

Picture Credits Photographs by Philip Kaplan are credited: PK. Photographs from the author's collections are credited: AC. Photographs from the United States National Archives and Records Administration are credited: NARA. Photographs from the Library of Congress are credited: LOC. Front endsheet: NARA; back endsheet: AC. Title spread: xxxx. P.10: AC, P.15: PK, PP. 18-19: Both-Mark Brown, USAF, P.21: Courtesy Ray Wild, PP22-23: All-PK, P.24: USAF, P.25: AC, PP.26-27: NARA, P.28, top: NARA, PP.28-29: AC, P.30: PK, P.31: Mark Brown, USAF, PP.32-33: AC, P.34, top, both: PK, P.34, bottom: Mark Brown, USAF, P.35: Toni Frissell, LOC, PP.36-37: NARA, P.38: NARA, P.40-41: R.A.F. Museum, P.43, both: PK, P.44: AC, P.45: NARA, PP.46-47, top, both: PK; bottom: Mark Brown, USAF, PP.48-49: NARA, PP.50-51: PK, PP.52-53, all: NARA, P.54, top, both: PK, P.54, bottom: NARA, P.55: PK, P.57, both: NARA, P.59: NARA, P.60, top left: AC; bottom left: AC; bottom centre: AC; top centre: Toni Frissell, LOC, P.62: PK, P.63: PK, P.65, both: NARA, P.66, both: PK, P.67, all: PK, P. 68, top: Toni Frissell, LOC, PP.68-69, bottom: NARA, PP.70-71: Imperial War Museum, P.72-73: AC, P.73: Courtesy Nick Kosciuk, P.74, all: AC, P.76: AC, P.77: AC, P.78, both: PK, P.79, both: PK, P.80: AC, P.81: AC, P.82, top: Mark Brown, USAF; bottom: PK, P.83, both: PK, PP.84-85: NARA, PP.86-87, both: PK, PP.88-89: NARA, P.90, both: PK, P.91, top: Mark Brown, USAF; bottom: PK, P.92, top: AC; bottom: NARA, PP.94-95: PK, P.96: Toni Frissell, LOC, P.98, all: PK, P.99, all: PK, P.100: NARA, P.101: NARA, P.102: PK, P.103, top, both: PK; bottom: Mark Brown, USAF, PP.106-107: PK, P.108: AC, P.109: AC, P.110: PK, P.111: PK, P.112: Toni Frissell, LOC, P.113: AC, PP.114-115: PK, PP.116-117: AC, P.118, all: PK, PP.120-121: AC, P.123, all: PK, P.124-125: AC, P.126, all: PK, P.127: PK, P.128: AC, P.129: AC, P.130: NARA, P.131: AC, PP.132-133: AC, P.134, top: Mark Brown, USAF; left: Toni Frissell, LOC; centre, both: PK, PP.136-137: AC, P.138: PK, P.139: Mark Brown, USAF, P.140, topleft: Toni Frissell, LOC; top right and bottom: AC, P.142: NARA, P.143, left: Courtesy Roger Armstrong; centre: PK; right: AC, P.144, left: Toni Frissell, LOC; centre top and bottom: AC, P.145, both: AC, P.146, left: AC; centre, all: AC, P.148, left: AC; bottom: PK, centre: Toni Frissell, LOC, P.149, both: Toni Frissell, LOC, PP.150-151: LARA, PP.152-153: AC, PP.154-155, top left: PK; top right: Mark Brown, USAF; bottom: PK, PP.156-157: NARA, PP.158-159: Mark Brown, USAF, P.161, top left: USAF; top right: Courtesy Roger Armstrong; bottom: Mark Brown, USAF, PP.162-163: NARA, P.164, top: AC; bottom: Toni Frissell, LOC, P.165: AC, P.166, top, both: PK; bottom: Courtesy Quentin Bland, P.167: AC, P.168: USAF, PP.170-171: USAF, P.175: PK, PP.176-177: USAF, P.180: AC, P.182: PK, P.186: AC, P.187, top: PK; bottom: AC, P.190, both: PK, P.191, both: PK, P. 192, top left: Mark Brown, USAF; top right: NARA; bottom: AC, P.194, both: PK, P.195: PK, P.196: AC, P.197: USAF, P.198, all: Mark Brown, USAF, P.199: PK, P.200, left: Courtesy Columbia Pictures, PP.200-201: AC, P.202. top: Courtesy Columbia Pictures; bottom left and right: Courtesy Twentieth Century Fox; centre: AC, P.203, both: Courtesy Twentieth Century Fox, P.204: Courtesy Twentieth Century Fox, P.205, all: Courtesy Twentieth Century Fox, PP.206-207, both: Courtesy Twentieth Century Fox, PP.208-209: USAF, PP. 210-211, top: PK; bottom left: AC; bottom right: PK, P.212: NARA, P.214: PK, P.216, top, both: Courtesy John Hurd; bottom: USAF, P.218, top and left: PK; right: AC, P.220: AC, P.221: USAF, P.223, top, all: AC; bottom: PK, P.224, top: NARA, PP.224-225, bottom: NARA, P.225, top: AC, PP.226-227: PK, PP.228-229: USAF, PP.230-231, all: PK, PP.232-233: AC, PP.234-235. all: PK, PP.236-237: USAF, PP.238-239, all: PK, P.240: Toni Frissell, LOC, P.241: USAF, P.242, top: PK; bottom: USAF, P.243: PK, PP.244-245: AC, P.246, top: Mark Brown, USAF; bottom: PK, P.247: PK, PP.248-249: NARA, P.251: AC, PP.252-253: USAF, PP.254-255, all: PK, P.256, bothh: NARA, P.257: USAF, PP.258-259: all: PK, PP.260-261: USAF, PP.262-263, all: PK, PP.264-265: NARA, P.265, right: AC.

Acknowledgments We are grateful to the following people for their generous help in the development of this book: Beth Alston, David Alston, John T. Appleby, Roger W. Armstrong, Alan Ashmore, Jim Barfoot, Eric Barnard, Malcolm Bates, Phyllis Beck, Dana Bell, Mike Benarcik, Jimmy Bennett, Robert Best, Ron Bicker, Larry Bird, Quentin Bland, Charles Bosshardt, Beverly Brannin, Dan Brennan, Mark Brown, Sam Burchell, Richard Bye, Cliff Chatten, Leonard Cheshire, Paul Chryst, Reg Cliffe, Jack Clift, Kate Currie, Jim Dacy, Al Deere, James H. Doolittle, Lawrence Drew, Ira Eakin, Gary Eastman, Jacob T. Elias, Gilly Fielder, W.W. Ford, Alan Forman, Roger A. Freeman, Adolf Galland, Bill Ganz, Stephen Grey, Harold Haft, Roland Hammersley, Bill Harvey, Ian Hawkins, Don Haynes, Allan Healy, John Hersey, Dave Hill, John Hurd, Franc Isla, Richard Johnston, Claire Kaplan, Hargita Kaplan, Joseph Kaplan, Margaret Kaplan, Neal Kaplan, Paul Kemp, Percy Kindred, Edith Kup, William T. Larkins, Curtis LeMay, Robert D. Loomis, David Lustig, Don Maffett, Nathan Mazer, William McCarran, Carroll McColpin, Judy McCutcheon, Richard McCutcheon, Sandra Merrill, Campbell Muirhead, Frank Nelson, Jean Newhouse, Keith Newhouse, John A.Miller, Michael O'Leary, David Oliver, Merle Olmsted, Geoffrey Page, Greg Parlin, David Parry, Alice and John Pawsey, Reg Payne, Max Pinkerton, Gunther Rall, Sidney Rapaport, Walton Rawls, Duane J. Reed, Alan Reeves, Ted Richardson, Peter Rix, Andy Rooney, Dave Shelhamer, Paul Sink, Norman Smart, Dale Smith, Richard Stamp, Bert Stiles, Ken Stone, Lloyd Stovall, Calvin Swaffer, Harry Tickle, Dickie Turley-George, Albert Tyler, David Wade, John Wareing, Tim Wells, Robert White, Lloyd Whitlow, Ray Wild, Ray Wild, Jr., Ruth Wild, Jack Woods, Dennis Wrynn, and Sam Young.

Bibliography

Ambrose, Stephen E., *Wild Blue*, Simon & Schuster, 2001

Armstrong, Roger W., *USA The Hard Way*, Quail House, 1991

Bailey, Ronald, *The Air War in Europe*, Time-Life Books, 1981

Barker, Ralph, *The Thousand Plane Raid*, Chatto & Windus, 1965

Bekker, Cajus, *The Luftwaffe War Diaries*, Doubleday, 1968

Bendiner, Elmer, *The Fall of Fortresses*, Souvenir Press, 1981

Bennett, D.C.T., *Pathfinder*, Frederick Muller, 1958

Bowman, Martin, *Castles In The Air*, Patrick Stephens, 1984

Bowyer, Michael J.F., *The Stirling Bomber*, Faber & Faber, 1980

Brickhill, Paul, *The Dam Busters*, Ballantine, 1951

Caidin, Martin, *Black Thursday*, E.P. Dutton, 1960

Caidin, Martin, *Flying Forts*, Meredith Press, 1968

Campbell, James, *The Bombing of Nuremberg*, Doubleday, 1954

Charlwood, Don, *No Moon Tonight*, Angus & Robertson, 1956

Cheshire, Leonard, *Bomber Pilot*, Hutchinson, 1943

Clark, Ronald, *The Role of the Bomber*, Sidgewick & Jackson, 1977

Comer, John, *Combat Crew*, Leo Cooper, 1988

Cooper, Alan, *The Men Who Breached The Dams*, Airlife, 1993

Crisp, N.J., *Yesterday's Gone*, Viking Penguin, 1983

Crosby, Harry, *A Wing And A Prayer*, HarperCollins, 1993

Cross, Robin, *The Bombers*, Grub Street, 1987

Cumming, Michael, *Pathfinder Cranswick*, William Kimber, 1962

Currie, Jack, *Lancaster Target*, New English Library, 1977

Currie, Jack, *Mosquito Victory*, Goodall Publications, 1983

Currie, Jack, *The Augsburg Raid*, Goodall Publications, 1987

Currier, Donald R., *50 Mission Crush*, Pocket Books, 1992

Deighton, Len, *Bomber*, Harper & Row, 1970

Dunmore, Spencer, *Bomb Run*, Peter Davies Ltd., 1971

Dunmore, Spencer, *Final Approach*, Peter Davies Ltd, 1976

Falconer, Jonathan, *The Bomber Command Handbook 1939-1945*, Sutton, 1998

Farson, Negley, *Bomber's Moon*, Victor Gollancz, 1941

Fitz Gibbon, Constantine, *The Blitz*, Allan Wingate, 1957

Fltcher, Eugene, *Fletcher's Gang*, University of Washington Press, 1988

Frankland, Noble, *The Bombing Offensive Against Germany*, Faber & Faber, 1965

Freeman, Roger A., *The American Airman in Europe*, Cassell, 1991

Freeman, Roger A., *The Mighty Eighth*, Macdonald, 1970

Freeman, Roger A., *Mighty Eighth War Diary*, Jane's, 1981

Freeman, Roger A., *Mighty Eighth War Manual*, Jane's, 1984

Galland, Adolf, *The First And The Last*, Henry Holt, 1954

Garbett, Mike, and Goulding, Brian, *Lancaster At War:3*, Ian Allan Ltd., 1984

Gibson, Guy, *Enemy Coast Ahead*, Michael Joseph, 1946

Godfrey, John, *The Look of Eagles*, Random House, 1958

Halpenny, Bruce, *To Shatter The Sky*, Patrick Stephens, 1984

Harvey, J. Douglas, *Boys, Bombs and Brussels Sprouts*, McClelland and Stewart, 1981

Hastings, Max, *Bomber Command*, Michael Joseph, 1979

Hawkins, Ian, *The Münster Raid*, Aero, 1984

Hersey, John, *The War Lover*, Alfred A.Knopf, 1959

Horwitz, Julius, *Can I Get There by Candlelight*, Bantam, 1965

Hutton, Bud, and Rooney, Andy, *Air Gunner*, Farrar & Rinehart, 1944

Jablonski, Edward, *Flying Fortress*, Doubleday, 1965

Kaplan, Philip, and Smith, Rex Alan, *One Last Look*, Abbeville Press, 1983

Kaplan, Philip, and Currie, Jack, *Round The Clock*, Random House 1993

Koger, fred, *Countdown!*, Algonquin Books, 1990

Lay, Beirne Jr., and Bartlett, Sy, *12 O'Clock High!*, 1948

LeMay, Curtis, with Kantor, MacKinlay, *Mission With LeMay*, Doubleday, 1965

Lewis, Bruce, *Aircrew*, Leo Cooper, 1991

Longmate, Norman, *The Bombers*, Hutchinson, 1983

Lyall, Gavin, *The War In The Air*, William Morrow, 1968

Mason, Francis, *The British Bomber Since 1914*, Putnam, 1994

Mazer, Harry, *The Last Mission*, Dell, 1979

Maurer, Maurer, *Air Force Combat Units of World War II*, Franklin Watts, 1959

Mayhew, Margaret, *The Crew*, Corgi Books, 1997

McBean, John, and Hogben, Arthur, *Bombs Gone*, Patrick Stephens, 1990

McCrary, John and Scherman, David, *First of the Many*, Simon and Schuster, 1944

Merrick, Ken, *By Day & By Night*, Ian Allan, 1989

Merrill, Sandra, *Donald's Story*, Tebidine, 1996

Middlebrook, Martin, *The Battle of Hamburg*, Charles Scribner's Sons, 1981

Middlebrook, Martin, *The Berlin Raids*, Viking, 1988

Middlebrook, Martin, *The Nuremberg Raid*, Penguin, 1973

Middlebrook, Martin, and Everitt, Chris, *The Bomber Command War Diaries*, Viking, 1985

Michie, Allan, *The Air Offensive Against Germany*, Henry Holt, 1943

Morrison, Wilbur, *Fortress Without A Roof*, St Martin's Press, 1982

Morrison, Wilbur, *The Incredible 305th*, E.P. Dutton, 1962

Moyes, Philip, *Bomber Squadrons of the R.A.F. And Their Aircraft*, Macdonald, 1964

Muirhead, John, *Those Who Fall*, Random House, 1986

Nolty, Bernard, and Berger, Carl, *The Men Who Bombed The Reich*, Talisman-Parish Books, 1978

Overy, R.J., *The Air War 1939-1945*, Stein and Day, 1981

Peaslee, Budd, *Heritage of Valor*, J.B. Lippincott, 1964

Penrose, Harald, *Architect of Wings*, Airlife, 1985

Reynolds, Quentin, *A London Diary*, Random House, 1941

Robertson, Bruce, *Lancaster*, Harleyford, 1964

Rust, Ken, *The 9th Air Force in World War II*, Aero, 1967

Saward, Dudley, *'Bomber' Harris*, Cassell, 1984

Shores, Christopher, *Duel For The Sky*, Doubleday, 1985

Sloan, John, *The Route As Briefed*, Argus Press, 1946

Smith, Dale O., *Screaming Eagle*, Algonquin Books, 1990

Steinbeck, John, *Once There Was A War*, Viking, 1958

Stiles, Bert, *Serenade To The Big Bird*, W.W. Norton, 1947

Taylor, Frederick, *Dresden*, Bloomsbury, 2004

Tripp, Miles, *The Eighth Passenger*, William Heinemann, 1969

Vietor, John, *Time Out*, Richard R. Smith, 1951

Verrier, Anthony, *The Bomber Offensive*, B.T. Batsford, 1968

Watry, Charles, and Hall, Duane, *Aerial Gunners*, California Aero Press, 1986

Way, Chris, *Glenn Miller In Britain Then And Now*, After The Battle

Under certain meteorological conditions, and in given circumstances, an air battle of the sort which served to crack open Germany's inner structure takes on a fantastic quality beyond a Wellsian nightmare. Long trails of vapour stream back from each engine nacelle in four-plumed patterns across the five-mile sky. Through those patterns fighters weave their single wakes of vapour. Broadsides of rockets burst crimson and orange in the contrails, while the ground defences set to work building their umbrella of black-puffed flak. In this setting airmen fly and fight, and some die and some live to come back again.

Not unnaturally, the nightmarish quality of such a battle (although not all raids are in such circumstances) is reflected in the conduct of the participants. Too, the incredible speed at which events take place in the air is expressed in the reactions of the individuals: When bomber and fighter rush at each other at a combined speed of, say, six hundred miles an hour, the airmen involved will live or die by their reflexes, not their conscious thought, and that makes for conduct varying in the extreme from the norm. Finally, there is the basic element of this warfare—the unstable, most volatile air itself.
–from *Air Gunner*
by Sgt. Bud Hutton and
Sgt. Andy Rooney